Dictionary of Mathematics Terms

Douglas Downing, Ph.D.

School of Business and Economics
Seattle Pacific University

New York, London, Sydney, Toronto

All inquiries should be addressed to:
Barron's Educational Series, Inc.
250 Wireless Boulevard
Hauppauge, New York 11788

Library of Congress Catalog Card No. 87-12565

International Standard Book No. 0-8120-2641-1

Library of Congress Cataloging-in-Publication Data

Downing, Douglas.
　　Dictionary of mathematics terms.

　　1. Mathematics--Dictionaries. 1. Title.
QA5.D69　　1987　　510′.3′21　　87-12565
ISBN 0-8120-2641-1

PRINTED IN THE UNITED STATES OF AMERICA

123　　977　　987654

CONTENTS

PREFACE

The purpose of this book is to collect in one place reference information that is valuable for students of mathematics and for persons with careers in this field. The book includes topics from algebra, analytic geometry, arithmetic, calculus, computers, geometry, logic, matrices and linear programming, probability and statistics, sets, trigonometry, and vectors. The entries are in alphabetical order, but a list of entries by subject category is included at the front of the book. The appendix includes several useful tables.

Since many of the entries review material covered in high school courses, this book can serve as a background reference for students of calculus or other advanced subjects. Demonstrations of important theorems, such as the Pythagorean theorem and the quadratic formula, are included. Many entries contain background cross references (in boldface) indicating where to find information needed to understand the particular concept. Other entries contain cross references (in italics) that suggest where to look for further information or applications of the topic. A list of symbols at the beginning of the book helps the reader identify unfamiliar symbols.

Douglas Downing, Ph.D.

Seattle, Washington
May 1987

LIST OF SYMBOLS

Algebra

$=$	equals
$\neq$	is not equal
$\approx$	is approximately equal
$>$	is greater than
$\geq$	is greater than or equal to
$<$	is less than
$\leq$	is less than or equal to
$+$	addition
$-$	subtraction
$\times, \cdot$	multiplication
$\div, /$	division
$\sqrt{}$	square root
$\sqrt[n]{}$	nth root
$!$	factorial
$_nC_j, \begin{pmatrix} n \\ j \end{pmatrix}$	number of combinations of n things taken j at a time; also the binomial theorem coefficient
$_nP_j$	number of permutations of n things taken j at a time
$|x|$	absolute value of x
∞	infinity
$\begin{vmatrix} a & b \\ c & d \end{vmatrix}$	determinant of a matrix

Greek Letters

π	pi $(=3.14159\ldots)$
Δ	delta (upper case), represents change in
δ	delta (lower case)
Σ	sigma (upper case), represents summation
σ	sigma (lower case), represents standard deviation
θ	theta (used for angles)
ϕ	phi (used for angles)
μ	mu, represents mean
ϵ	epsilon
χ	chi
ρ	rho (correlation coefficient)
λ	lambda

Calculus

Δx	increment of x
y', $\dfrac{dy}{dx}$	derivative of y with respect to x
y'', $\dfrac{d^2y}{dx^2}$	second derivative of y with respect to x
$\dfrac{\partial y}{\partial x}$	partial derivative of y with respect to x
$\rightarrow$	approaches
lim	limit
e	base of natural logarithms; $e = 2.71828\ldots$
$\int$	integral symbol
$\int f(x)\,dx$	indefinite integral
$\int_a^b f(x)\,dx$	definite integral

Geometry

°	degrees
⌐	perpendicular
$\perp$	perpendicular, as in $\overline{AB} \perp \overline{DC}$
$\angle$	angle
$\triangle$	triangle, as in $\triangle ABC$
$\cong$	congruent
$\sim$	similar
$\parallel$	parallel, as in $\overline{AB} \parallel \overline{CD}$
$\frown$	arc, as in $\overset{\frown}{AB}$
$-$	line segment, as in $\overline{AB}$
$\leftrightarrow$	line, as in $\overleftrightarrow{AB}$
$\rightarrow$	ray, as in $\overrightarrow{AB}$

Vectors

$\|\mathbf{a}\|$	length of vector $\mathbf{a}$
$\mathbf{a} \cdot \mathbf{b}$	dot product
$\mathbf{a} \times \mathbf{b}$	cross product

Set Notation

{ }	braces (indicating membership in a set)
$\cap$	intersection
$\cup$	union
$\varnothing$	empty set

Logic

$\rightarrow$	implication, as in $a \rightarrow b$ (IF a THEN b)
$\sim p$	the negation of a proposition p
$\wedge$	conjunction (AND)
$\vee$	disjunction (OR)
IFF, $\leftrightarrow$	equivalence (IF AND ONLY IF)
$\forall_x$	universal quantifier (means "For all x...")
$\exists_x$	existential quantifier (means "There exists an x...")

GUIDE TO SELECTED TERMS BY CATEGORY

Algebra

absolute value
additive identity
additive inverse
algebra
alternating series
antilogarithm
argument
arithmetic mean
arithmetic progression
arithmetic sequence
arithmetic series
associative property
base
binomial
binomial expansion
binomial theorem
characteristic
closure property
coefficient
common logarithm
commutative property
completing the square
complex fraction
complex number
composite function
conditional equation

conjugate
convergent series
cube
cube root
decreasing function
de Moivre's theorem
dependent variable
difference of two squares
directly proportional
discriminant
distributive property
divergent series
domain
equation
equivalent equations
even function
exponential function
extraneous root
extremes of a proportion
factor
factor theorem
factoring
field
fourth proportional
function
fundamental theorem of algebra
Gauss-Jordan elimination
geometric mean

geometric progression
geometric sequence
geometric series
harmonic sequence
i
identity
identity element
imaginary number
inconsistent equations
increasing function
independent variable
index
inequality
infinite series
interpolation
inverse
inverse function
inversely proportional
joint variation
like terms
linear equation
linear factor
literal
ln
log
logarithm
mantissa
mapping
means of a proportion
modulus
monomial
multinomial
multiplicative identity
multiplicative inverse
odd function
open sentence
operand
operation
placeholder
polynomial
power series
precedence
proportion
quadratic equation

quadratic equation, two
   unknowns
quadratic formula
radical
radicand
range
rank
rational root theorem
rationalizing the denominator
reciprocal
reflexive property
relation
root
scientific notation
sequence
series
sigma notation
simultaneous equations
solution
solution set
solve
square
square root
subscript
substitution property
summation notation
symmetric property of equality
synthetic division
system of equations
system of inequalities
term
transitive property
trinomial
variable
vinculum

Analytic Geometry
abscissa
analytic geometry
asymptote
axis
axis of symmetry
Cartesian coordinates

viii

catenary
closed interval
conic sections
coordinates
cycloid
direction cosines
directrix
eccentricity
ellipse
ellipsoid
foci
focus
graph
hyperbola
intercept
isometry
lattice point
latus rectum
major axis
maxima
minima
number line
open interval
ordered pair
ordinate
origin
parabola
paraboloid
polar coordinates
quadrant
rectangular coordinates
reflection
rotation
semilog graph paper
semimajor axis
semiminor axis
slope
symmetric
translation
x-axis
x-intercept
y-axis
y-intercept

Arithmetic

addition
composite number
counting numbers
cube root
decimal numbers
denominator
difference
digit
dividend
division
divisor
even number
exponent
fraction
fundamental theorem of
    arithmetic
improper fraction
infinity
integers
irrational number
least common denominator
least common multiple
mean
multiplication
natural numbers
negative
number
numeral
numerator
odd number
parenthesis
percent
positive number
power
prime factors
prime number
product
proper fraction
quotient
ratio
rational number
real numbers

remainder
repeating decimal
sign
significant digits
square root
subtraction
sum
terminating decimal
transcendental number
whole numbers
zero

Calculus

acceleration
antiderivative
calculus
centroid
chain rule
continuous
definite integral
delta
derivative
differentiable
differentiation
double integral
e
fundamental theorem of calculus
gradient
hyperbolic functions
implicit differentiation
indefinite integral
infinitesimal
inflection point
integral
integrand
integration
l'Hôpital's rule
limit
Maclaurin series
mean value theorem
natural logarithm
Newton's method
numerical integration

partial derivative
partial fractions
speed
Taylor series
velocity

Computers

algorithm
binary numbers
bit
byte
computer arithmetic
computer function
computer program
constant
exponential notation
fixed point number
floating point number
hexadecimal number
numerical integration
precedence
rounding
truncation
Turing machine

Geometry

acute angle
acute triangle
adjacent angles
alternate interior angles
altitude
angle
apothem
arc
area
base
between
bisect
central angle
centroid
chord
circle
circumcenter

circumcircle
circumference
circumscribed
closed curve
collinear
compass
complementary angles
concave
concurrent lines
cone
congruent
convex
coplanar
corresponding angles
corresponding sides
cube
curve
cylinder
decagon
degree
diagonal
diameter
dihedral angle
dimension
distance
edge
equilateral triangle
Euclidian geometry
exterior angle
face
frustum
geometric construction
geometry
great circle
half plane
heptagon
hexagon
hypotenuse
image
incenter
incircle
inscribed
intercepted arc
isosceles triangle

line
locus
major arc
median
midpoint
minor arc
minute
non-Euclidian geometry
normal
oblique angle
oblique triangle
obtuse angle
obtuse triangle
octagon
orthocenter
parallel
parallelepiped
parallelogram
pentagon
perimeter
perpendicular
pi
plane
polygon
polyhedron
prism
projection
protractor
pyramid
Pythagorean theorem
Pythagorean triple
quadrilateral
radian measure
radius
ray
rectangle
regular polygon
rhombus
right angle
right circular cone
right circular cylinder
right triangle
scalene triangle
secant

null set
set
subset
union
universal set
Venn diagram

Trigonometry

ambiguous case
amplitude
angle of depression
angle of elevation
arccos
arccsc
arcctn
arcsec
arcsin
arctan
circular functions
cofunction
cosecant
cosine
cotangent
coterminal
Hero's formula
inverse trigonometric functions
law of cosines

law of sines
law of tangents
period
periodic
principal values
quadrantal angle
secant
sine
standard position
tangent
terminal side
trigonometric functions of a sum
trigonometry

Vectors

component
cross product
dot product
force
gradient
magnitude
resolution of forces
resultant
scalar
scalar product
vector
velocity

A

ABSCISSA Abscissa means x-coordinate. The abscissa of the point (a, b) in Cartesian coordinates is a.

ABSOLUTE VALUE The absolute value of a real number a is:

$$|a| = \quad a \text{ if } a \geq 0,$$
$$= -a \text{ if } a < 0.$$

Absolute value is symbolized by two vertical lines:

$$|a| = (\text{absolute value of } a).$$

Absolute values are always positive or zero. If all the real numbers are represented on a number line, you can think of the absolute value of a number as being the distance from zero to that number. You can find absolute values by leaving positive numbers alone and ignoring the sign of negative numbers. For example:

$$|17| = 17, \qquad |3.5| = 3.5, \qquad |-105| = 105, \qquad |-4| = 4,$$
$$|4| = 4, \qquad |0| = 0, \qquad |-1| = 1.$$

The absolute value of a complex number $a + bi$ is $\sqrt{a^2 + b^2}$.

ACCELERATION The acceleration of an object measures the rate of change in its velocity. For example, if a car increases its velocity from 0 to 24.6 meters per second (55 miles per hour) in 12 seconds, its acceleration was 2.05 meters per second per second, or 2.05 meters/second^2.

If $x(t)$ represents the position of an object moving in one dimension as a function of time, then the first derivative, dx/dt, represents the velocity of the object, and the second derivative, d^2x/dt^2, represents the acceleration. (See **derivative**.) Newton found that, if F represents the force acting on an object and m represents its mass, the acceleration (a) could be determined from the formula

$$F = ma.$$

ACUTE ANGLE An acute angle is an angle smaller than a 90° angle.

ACUTE TRIANGLE An acute triangle is a triangle wherein each of the three angles is smaller than a 90° angle.

ADDITION   Addition is the operation of combining two numbers to form a sum. For example, $3 + 4 = 7$. Addition satisfies two important properties: the commutative property, which says that

$$a + b = b + a \quad \text{for all } a \text{ and } b;$$

and the associative property, which says that

$$(a + b) + c = a + (b + c) \quad \text{for all } a, b, \text{ and } c.$$

ADDITIVE IDENTITY   The number zero is the additive identity element, because it satisfies the property that the addition of zero does not change a number:

$$a + 0 = a \quad \text{for all } a.$$

ADDITIVE INVERSE   The additive inverse of a number satisfies the property that the sum of a number plus its additive inverse is zero. The additive inverse of a (written as $-a$) is also called the negative of a: $a + (-a) = 0$. For example, -1 is the additive inverse of 1, and 10 is the additive inverse of -10.

ADJACENT ANGLES   Two angles are adjacent if they share the same vertex and have one side in common between them.

ALGEBRA   Algebra is the study of properties of operations carried out on sets of numbers. Algebra is a generalization of arithmetic in which symbols, usually letters, are used to stand for numbers.

   The structure of algebra is based upon *axioms* (or *postulates*), which are statements that are assumed to be true. Some algebraic axioms include the transitive axiom (if $a = b$ and $b = c$, then $a = c$), and the associative axiom of addition: $(a + b) + c = a + (b + c)$. These axioms are then used to prove theorems about the properties of operations on numbers.

   The basic problem in algebra involves solving conditional equations—in other words, finding the values of an unknown that make the equation true. An equation of the general form $ax + b = 0$, where x is unknown and a and b are known, is called a *linear equation*. An equation of the general form $ax^2 + bx + c = 0$ is called a *quadratic equation*. For equations involving higher powers of x, see **polynomial**. For situations involving more than one equation with more than one unknown, see **simultaneous equations**.

ALGORITHM   An algorithm is a sequence of instructions that tell how to solve a particular problem. An algorithm must be specified exactly, so that there can be no doubt about what to do next, and it must have a finite number of steps.

A computer program is an algorithm written in a language that a computer can understand.

ALTERNATE INTERIOR ANGLES   When a transversal cuts two lines, it forms two pairs of alternate interior angles. In the figure, $\angle 1$ and $\angle 2$ are a pair of alternate interior angles, and $\angle 3$ and $\angle 4$ are another pair. A theorem in Euclidian geometry says that, when a transversal cuts two parallel lines, each of any two alternate interior angles will equal the other.

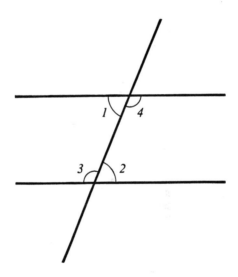

ALTERNATING SERIES   An alternating series is a series in which every term has the opposite sign from the preceding term. For example, $x - x^3/3! + x^5/5! - x^7/7! + x^9/9! - \cdots$ is an alternating series.

ALTERNATIVE HYPOTHESIS   The alternative hypothesis is the hypothesis that states, "The null hypothesis is false." (See **hypothesis testing**.)

ALTITUDE The altitude of a solid is the distance from the plane containing the base to the highest point in the solid. The altitude of a flat figure is the distance from one side, called the base, to the farthest point. In the figure, the dotted lines show the altitude of a triangle, of a parallelogram, and of a cylinder.

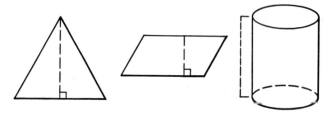

AMBIGUOUS CASE The term "ambiguous case" refers to a situation where you know the lengths of two sides of a triangle and you

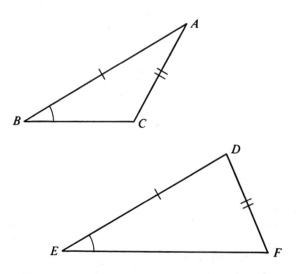

know one of the angles (other than the angle between the two sides of known lengths). If the known angle is less than 90°, it may not be possible to solve for the length of the third side or for the sizes of the other two angles. In the figure, side AB of the upper triangle is the same length as side DE of the lower triangle, side AC is the same length as side DF, and angle B is the same size as angle E. However, the two triangles are quite different.

Given the lengths of two sides of a triangle and the measure of one angle other than the angle between the two given sides, these measures may define two different triangles, or one triangle, or none, depending on the relative sizes of these measures.

AMPLITUDE   The amplitude of a periodic function is one-half the difference between the largest possible value of the function and the smallest possible value. For example, for $y = \sin x$, the largest possible value of y is 1 and the smallest possible value is -1, so the amplitude is 1. In general, the amplitude of the function $y = A \sin x$ is A.

ANALYSIS OF VARIANCE   Analysis of variance (ANOVA) is a procedure used to test the hypothesis that three or more different samples were all selected from populations with the same mean. The method is based on a *test statistic*:

$$F = \frac{nS^{*2}}{S^2},$$

where n is the number of members in each sample, S^{*2} is the variance of the sample averages for all of the groups, and S^2 is the average variance for the groups. If the null hypothesis is true and the population means actually are all the same, this statistic will have an F-distribution with $(m - 1)$ and $m(n - 1)$ degrees of freedom, where m is the number of samples. If the value of the test statistic is too large, the null hypothesis is rejected. (See **hypothesis testing**.) Intuitively, it is clear that a large value of S^{*2} means that the observed sample averages are spread further apart, thereby making the test statistic larger and the null hypothesis less likely to be accepted.

The test described above is called one-way analysis of variance. If there are two possible sources of variations for each observation, it is helpful to perform a test called two-way analysis of variance.

ANALYTIC GEOMETRY   Analytic geometry is the branch of mathematics that uses algebra to help in the study of geometry. It helps you understand algebra by allowing you to draw pictures of algebraic equations, and it helps you understand geometry by allowing you to describe geometric figures by means of algebraic equations.

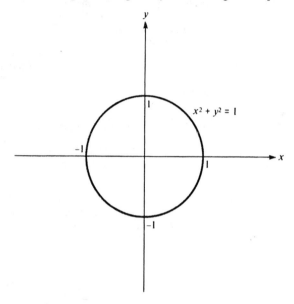

FIGURE 1

Analytic geometry is based on the fact that there is a one-to-one correspondence between the set of real numbers and the set of points on a number line. Any point in a plane can be described by an ordered pair of numbers (x, y). (See **Cartesian coordinates**.) The graph of an equation in two variables is the set of all points in the plane that are represented by an ordered pair of numbers that make the equation true. For example, the graph of the equation $x^2 + y^2 = 1$ (see Figure 1) is a circle with its center at the origin and a radius of 1.

A linear equation is an equation in which both x and y occur to the first power, and there are no terms containing xy. Its graph will be a straight line. (See **linear equation**.) When either x or y (or both) is raised to the second power, some interesting curves can result. (See conic sections; quadratic equation, two unknowns.) When higher powers of the variable are used, it is possible to draw even more interesting curves. (See **polynomial**.)

Graphs can also be used to illustrate the solutions for systems of equations. If you are given two equations in two unknowns, draw the graph of each equation. The places where the two curves intersect will be the solutions to the system of equations. (See **simultaneous equations**.) Figure 2 shows the solution to the system of equations $y = x + 1$, $y = x^2 + 1$.

Although Cartesian, or rectangular, coordinates are the most commonly used, it is sometimes helpful to use another type of coordinates known as *polar coordinates*.

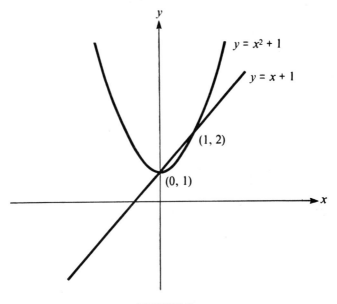

FIGURE 2

AND   The word "AND" is a connective word used in logic. The sentence "p AND q" is true only if both sentence "p" as well as sentence "q" are true. The operation of AND is illustrated by the truth table:

p	q	p AND q
T	T	T
T	F	F
F	T	F
F	F	F

Three symbols are used to represent AND: $\wedge$, &, or $\cdot$. (Different books use different symbols.) An AND sentence is also called a *conjunction*. (See **logic; Boolean algebra.**)

ANGLE An angle is the union of two rays with a common endpoint. If the two rays point in the same direction, then the angle between them is zero. Suppose that ray 1 is kept fixed, and ray 2 is pivoted

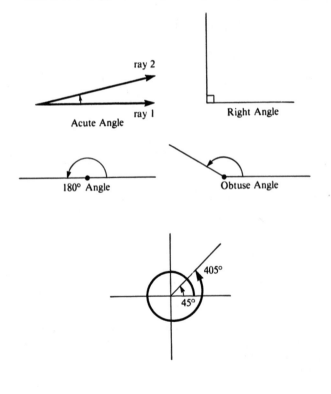

ray 2

ray 1

Acute Angle

Right Angle

180° Angle

Obtuse Angle

405°

45°

counterclockwise about its endpoint. The measure of an angle is a measure of how much ray 2 has been rotated. If ray 2 is rotated a complete turn, so that it again points in the same direction as ray 1, we say that it has been turned 360 *degrees* (written as 360°). A half turn is a 180° angle. A quarter turn, forming a square corner, is a 90° angle, also known as a *right angle* (symbolized by ∟).

An angle smaller than a 90° angle is called an *acute angle*. An angle larger than a 90° angle but smaller than a 180° angle is called an *obtuse angle*.

For some mathematical purposes it is useful to allow for general angles that can be larger than 360°, or even negative. A general angle still measures the amount that ray 2 has been rotated in a counterclockwise direction. A 720° angle is the same as a 360° angle, which in turn is the same as a 0° angle. Likewise, a 405° angle is the same as a 45° angle (since $405 - 360 = 45$) (see figure). A negative angle is simply the amount that ray 2 has been rotated in a clockwise direction. A $-90°$ angle is the same as a 270° angle.

It is often useful to measure angles by means of *radian measure*, instead of degree measure. A circle contains 2π radians, so $360° = 2\pi$. Conversions between radian and degree measure can be made by multiplication:

$$(\text{degree measure}) = \frac{180}{\pi} \times (\text{radian measure}),$$

$$(\text{radian measure}) = \frac{\pi}{180} \times (\text{degree measure}).$$

One radian is about 57°. A right angle has a radian measure of $\pi/2$, and a 180° angle has a radian measure of π.

ANGLE OF DEPRESSION   The angle of depression for an object below your line of sight is the angle whose vertex is at your position, with one side being a horizontal ray in the same direction as the object and the other side being the ray from your eye passing through the object.

ANGLE OF ELEVATION   The angle of elevation for an object above your line of sight is the angle whose vertex is at your position, with one side being a horizontal ray in the same direction as the object and the other side being the ray from your eye passing through the object.

ANTECEDENT The antecedent is the part of a conditional statement such that, if the antecedent is true, then the other part (the *consequent*) must also be true. In other words, the antecedent is the "if" part of a conditional statement. For example, in the statement "If he likes pizza, then he likes cheese," the antecedent is the clause, "he likes pizza."

ANTIDERIVATIVE The antiderivative of a function $f(x)$ is a function $F(x)$ such that $dF(x)/dx = f(x)$. (See **integral**.)

ANTILOGARITHM If $y = \log_a x$, then x is the antilogarithm of y to the base a. (See **logarithm**.)

APOTHEM The apothem of a regular polygon is the distance from the center of the polygon to one of the sides of the polygon.

ARC An arc of a circle is the set of points on the circle that lie in the interior of a particular central angle. Therefore an arc is a part of a circle. The degree measure of an arc is the same as the degree measure of the angle that defines it. If D is the degree measure of an arc, then the length of the arc is $(D/360) \times 2\pi r$.

ARCCOS The arccos function is the inverse cosine function. (See **inverse trigonometric functions**.)

ARCCSC The arccsc function is the inverse cosecant function. (See **inverse trigonometric functions**.)

ARCCTN The arcctn function is the inverse cotangent function. (See **inverse trigonometric functions**.)

ARCSEC The arcsec function is the inverse secant function. (See **inverse trigonometric functions**.)

ARCSIN The arcsin function is the inverse sine function. (See **inverse trigonometric functions**.)

ARCTAN The arctan function is the inverse tangent function. (See **inverse trigonometric functions**.)

AREA   The area of a flat figure measures how much of a plane it fills up. The area of a square of side a is defined as a^2. The area of every other plane figure is defined so as to be consistent with this definition. The area postulate in geometry says that, if two figures are congruent, they have the same area. Area is measured in square units, such as square meters or square miles.

The areas of some common figures are as follows:

rectangle (sides a and b)	ab
parallelogram	(base) (altitude)
triangle	$\frac{1}{2}$(base) (altitude)
circle (radius r)	πr^2
ellipse (semimajor axis a, semiminor axis b)	πab

The area of any polygon can be found by breaking the polygon up into many little triangles. The areas of curved figures can often be found by the process of integration. (See **calculus**.)

ARGUMENT   (1) The argument of a function is the independent variable that is put into the function. In the equation $\sin(\pi/6) = \frac{1}{2}$, the number $\pi/6$ is the argument of the sine function, and the number $\frac{1}{2}$ is the value of the output of the function.

(2) In logic an argument is a sequence of sentences (called *premises*) that lead to a resulting sentence (called the *conclusion*). (See **logic**.)

ARITHMETIC MEAN   The arithmetic mean of a group of n numbers is the sum of the numbers divided by n:

$$(\text{arithmetic mean}) = \frac{a_1 + a_2 + a_3 + \cdots + a_n}{n}.$$

The arithmetic mean is commonly called the average. For example, if your grocery bills for 4 weeks are \$10, \$15, \$12, and \$39, then the average grocery bill is $76/4 = \$19$.

ARITHMETIC PROGRESSION   See **arithmetic sequence**.

ARITHMETIC SEQUENCE   An arithmetic sequence is a sequence of numbers of the form $a, a + b, a + 2b, a + 3b, \ldots, a + (n - 1)b$.

ARITHMETIC SERIES   An arithmetic series is a sum of terms of the form

$$S = a + (a + b) + (a + 2b) + (a + 3b) + \cdots + (a + (n - 1)b).$$

In an arithmetic series the difference between any two successive terms is a constant (in this case b).

The sum of the first n terms in the arithmetic series above is

$$\sum_{i=0}^{n-1} (a + ib) = \frac{n}{2}[2a + (n - 1)b].$$

For example:

$$3 + 5 + 7 + 9 + 11 + 13 = \frac{6}{2}[2(3) + (5)(2)] = 48.$$

ASSOCIATIVE PROPERTY   An operation obeys the associative property if the grouping of the numbers involved does not matter. Formally, the associative property of addition says that

$$(a + b) + c = a + (b + c) \quad \text{for all } a, b, \text{ and } c.$$

The associative property for multiplication says that

$$(a \times b) \times c = a \times (b \times c).$$

For example:

$$(3 + 4) + 5 = 7 + 5 = 12 = 3 + 9 = 3 + (4 + 5),$$
$$(5 \times 6) \times 7 = 30 \times 7 = 210 = 5 \times 42 = 5 \times (6 \times 7).$$

ASYMPTOTE   An asymptote is a straight line that is a close approximation to a particular curve as the curve goes off to infinity in one direction. The curve becomes very, very close to the asymptote line, but never touches it. For example, as x approaches infinity, the curve $y = 2^{-x}$ approaches very close to the line $y = 0$, but it never touches that line (see figure). (This is known as a horizontal asymptote.) As x approaches 3, the curve $y = 1/(x - 3)$ approaches the line $x = 3$.

(This is known as a vertical asymptote.) For another example of an asymptote, see **hyperbola**.

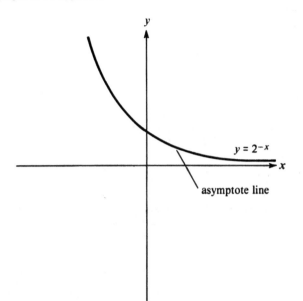

AVERAGE   The average of a group of numbers is the same as the *arithmetic mean*.

AXIOM   An axiom is a statement that is assumed to be true without proof. "Axiom" is a synonym for *postulate*.

AXIS   (1) The x-axis in Cartesian coordinates is the line $y = 0$. The y-axis is the line $x = 0$.

(2) The axis of a figure is a line about which the figure is symmetric. For example, the parabola $y = x^2$ is symmetric about the line $x = 0$.

AXIS OF SYMMETRY   An axis of symmetry is a line that passes through a figure in such a way that the part of the figure on one side of the line is the mirror image of the part of the figure on the other side of the line. (See **reflection**.) For example, an ellipse has two axes of symmetry: the major axis and the minor axis. (See **ellipse**.)

B

BASE (1) In the equation $x = a^y$, a is called the base. In this case the base a is being raised to the power y. The logarithm of x with respect to the base a is the power to which a must be raised to achieve x. (See **logarithm**.)

(2) The base of a positional number system is the number of digits it contains. Our number system is a decimal, or base-10, system; in other words, there are 10 possible digits: 0, 1, 2, 3, 4, 5, 6, 7, 8, 9. For example, the number 123.789 means $1 \times 10^2 + 2 \times 10^1 + 3 \times 10^0 + 7 \times 10^{-1} + 8 \times 10^{-2} + 9 \times 10^{-3}$.

In general, if b is the base of a number system, then the number $d_4 d_3 d_2 d_1 d_0$ means the same as the number

$$d_4 \times b^4 + d_3 \times b^3 + d_2 \times b^2 + d_1 \times b^1 + d_0 \times b^0.$$

Computers commonly use binary (base-2) numbers.

(3) The base of a polygon is one of the sides of the polygon. For an example, see **triangle**. The base of a solid figure is one of the faces. For examples, see **cone, cylinder, prism,** and **pyramid**.

BASIC FEASIBLE SOLUTION Consider a linear programming with m constraints and n total variables (including *slack variables*). (See **linear programming**.) Then a basic feasible solution is a solution that satisfies the constraints of the problem and has exactly $n - m$ variables equal to zero. The basic feasible solutions will be at the corners of the feasible region, and an important theorem of linear programming states that, if there is an optimal solution, it will be a basic feasible solution.

BAYES'S RULE Bayes's rule tells how to find the conditional probability $\Pr(B \mid A)$ (that is, the probability that event B will occur, given that event A has occurred), provided that $\Pr(A \mid B)$ and $\Pr(A \mid B^c)$ are known. (See **conditional probability**.) (B^c represents the event B-complement, which is the event that B will not occur.) Bayes's rule states:

$$\Pr(B \mid A) = \frac{\Pr(A \mid B)\,\Pr(B)}{\Pr(A \mid B)\,\Pr(B) + \Pr(A \mid B^c)\,\Pr(B^c)}.$$

For example, suppose that two dice are rolled. Let A be the event of rolling doubles, and let B be the event where the sum of the numbers on the two dice is greater than or equal to 8. Then

$$\Pr(A) = \frac{6}{36} = \frac{1}{6}; \quad \Pr(B) = \frac{15}{36} = \frac{5}{12}; \quad \Pr(B^c) = \frac{21}{36} = \frac{7}{12}.$$

$\Pr(A \mid B)$ refers to the probability of obtaining doubles if the sum of the two numbers is greater than or equal to 8; this probability is $3/15 = 1/5$. (There are 15 possible outcomes where the sum of the two numbers is greater than or equal to 8, and three of these are doubles: (4, 4), (5, 5), and (6, 6). Also, $\Pr(A \mid B^c) = 3/21 = 1/7$ (the probability of obtaining doubles if the sum on the dice is less than 8). Then we can use Bayes's rule to find the probability that the sum of the two numbers will be greater than or equal to 8, given that doubles were obtained:

$$\Pr(B \mid A) = \frac{1/5 \times 5/12}{1/5 \times 5/12 + 1/7 \times 7/12} = \frac{1/12}{1/12 + 1/12} = \frac{1}{2}.$$

BETWEEN In geometry point B is defined to be between points A and C if $AB + BC = AC$, where AB is the distance from point A to point B, and so on. This formal definition matches our intuitive idea that a point is between two points if it lies on the line connecting these two points and has one of the two points on each side of it.

BICONDITIONAL SENTENCE A biconditional sentence is a compound sentence that says one sentence is true if and only if the sentence is true. Symbolically, this is written as $p \leftrightarrow q$, which means "$p \rightarrow q$" and "$q \rightarrow p$" (see **conditional statement**). For example, "A triangle has three equal sides if and only if it has three equal angles" is a biconditional sentence.

BINARY NUMBERS Binary (base-2) numbers are written in a positional system that uses only two digits: 0 and 1. Each digit of a binary number represents a power of 2. The rightmost digit is the 1's digit, the next digit to the left is the 2's digit, and so on.

Decimal	Binary				
$2^0 = 1$					1
$2^1 = 2$				1	0
$2^2 = 4$			1	0	0
$2^3 = 8$		1	0	0	0
$2^4 = 16$	1	0	0	0	0

For example, the binary number 1 0 1 0 1 represents

$$1 \times 2^4 + 0 \times 2^3 + 1 \times 2^2 + 0 \times 2^1 + 1 \times 2^0$$
$$= 16 + 0 + 4 + 0 + 1$$
$$= 21.$$

The table shows some numbers written in both binary and decimal form.

Decimal	Binary					Decimal	Binary				
0					0	11		1	0	1	1
1					1	12		1	1	0	0
2				1	0	13		1	1	0	1
3				1	1	14		1	1	1	0
4			1	0	0	15		1	1	1	1
5			1	0	1	16	1	0	0	0	0
6			1	1	0	17	1	0	0	0	1
7			1	1	1	18	1	0	0	1	0
8		1	0	0	0	19	1	0	0	1	1
9		1	0	0	1	20	1	0	1	0	0
10		1	0	1	0						

Binary numbers are well suited for use by computers, since many electrical devices have two distinct states: on and off.

BINARY OPERATION   A binary operation is an operation, such as addition, that requires two operands.

BINOMIAL   A binomial is the sum of two terms. For example, $(ax + b)$ is a binomial.

BINOMIAL DISTRIBUTION   A discrete random variable X has the binomial distribution if its *density function* is given by

$$f(i) = \Pr(X = i) = \binom{n}{i} p^i (1-p)^{n-i}.$$

In this formula $\binom{n}{i} = n! / [(n-i)!\ i!]$. (See **binomial theorem; factorial**.)

Suppose that you conduct an experiment n times, with a probability of success of p each time. If X is the number of successes that occurs in those n trials, then X will have the binomial distribution with parameters n and p. For example, roll a set of two dice five times, and let X = the number of sevens that appear. Call it a "success" if a seven appears. Then the probability of success is 1/6, so X has the binomial distribution with parameters $n = 5$ and $p = 1/6$. Therefore:

$$\Pr(X = i) = \frac{5!}{(5-i)!\, i!} \left(\frac{1}{6}\right)^i \left(\frac{5}{6}\right)^{n-i},$$

$$\Pr(X = 0) = .402,$$
$$\Pr(X = 1) = .402,$$
$$\Pr(X = 2) = .161,$$
$$\Pr(X = 3) = .032,$$
$$\Pr(X = 4) = .003,$$
$$\Pr(X = 5) = .0001.$$

Also, if you toss a coin n times, and X is the number of heads that appear, then X has the binomial distribution with $p = \frac{1}{2}$:

$$\Pr(X = i) = \binom{n}{i} 2^{-n}.$$

BINOMIAL EXPANSION   See binomial theorem.

BINOMIAL THEOREM   The binomial theorem tells how to expand the expression $(a + b)^n$.

Some examples of the powers of binomials are as follows:

$$(a + b)^0 = 1,$$
$$(a + b)^1 = a + b,$$
$$(a + b)^2 = a^2 + 2ab + b^2,$$
$$(a + b)^3 = a^3 + 3a^2b + 3ab^2 + b^3,$$
$$(a + b)^4 = a^4 + 4a^3b + 6a^2b^2 + 4ab^3 + b^4,$$
$$(a + b)^5 = a^5 + 5a^4b + 10a^3b^2 + 10a^2b^3 + 5ab^4 + b^5.$$

Some patterns are apparent. The sum of the exponents for a and b is n in every term. The coefficients form an interesting pattern of numbers known as *Pascal's triangle*. This triangle is an array of numbers such that any entry is equal to the sum of the two entries above it.

In general, the binomial theorem states that

$$(a + b)^n = \binom{n}{0} a^n + \binom{n}{1} a^{n-1}b + \binom{n}{2} a^{n-2}b^2$$

$$+ \cdots + \binom{n}{n-1} ab^{n-1} + \binom{n}{n} b^n.$$

The expression $\binom{n}{j}$ is called the binomial coefficient. It is defined to be

$$\binom{n}{j} = \frac{n!}{(n-j)!j!},$$

which is the number of ways of arranging n things, taken j at a time, if you don't care about their order. (See **combinations; factorial**.) For example:

$$\binom{n}{0} = \frac{n!}{n!0!} = 1,$$

$$\binom{n}{1} = \frac{n!}{(n-1)!1!} = n,$$

$$\binom{n}{2} = \frac{n!}{(n-2)!2!} = \frac{n(n-1)}{2},$$

$$\binom{n}{n-1} = \frac{n!}{1!(n-1)!} = n,$$

$$\binom{n}{0} = \frac{n!}{0!n!} = 1.$$

The binomial theorem can be proved by using *mathematical induction*.

BISECT To bisect means to cut something in half. For example, the perpendicular bisector of a line segment $\overline{AB}$ is the line perpendicular to the segment and halfway between A and B.

BIT "Bit" is a shorthand term for "binary digit." There are only two possible binary digits: 0 and 1. (See **binary numbers**.) Bits are represented in computers by devices that can have two states. (See also **byte**.)

BOOLEAN ALGEBRA Boolean algebra is the study of operations carried out on variables that can have only two values: 1 (true) or 0 (false). Boolean algebra was developed by George Boole in the 1850s; it is an important part of the theory of logic (see **logic**) and has become of tremendous importance since the development of computers. Computers consist of electronic circuits (called flip-flops) that can be in either of two states, on or off, called 1 or 0. They are connected by circuits (called gates) that represent the logical operations of NOT, AND, and OR.

Here are some rules from Boolean algebra. In the following statements, p, q, and r represent Boolean variables; $\sim$ represents NOT: and $\leftrightarrow$ represents "is equivalent to." Parentheses are used as they are in arithmetic: an operation inside parentheses is to be done before the operation outside the parentheses.

Double Negation:
$p \leftrightarrow \sim \sim p$

Commutative Principle:
p AND $q \leftrightarrow q$ AND p
p OR $\quad q \leftrightarrow q$ OR p

Associative Principle:
p AND $(q$ AND $r) \leftrightarrow (p$ AND $q)$ AND r
p OR $\quad (q$ OR $r) \quad \leftrightarrow (p$ OR $q) \quad$ OR r

Distribution:
p AND $(q$ OR $r) \leftrightarrow (p$ AND $q)$ OR $(p$ AND $r)$
p OR $(q$ AND $r) \leftrightarrow (p$ OR $q)$ AND $(p$ OR $r)$

De Morgan's Laws:
$\sim p$ AND $\sim q \leftrightarrow \sim (p$ OR $q)$
$\sim p$ OR $\sim q \leftrightarrow \sim (p$ AND $q)$

Truth tables are a valuable tool for studying Boolean expressions. (See **truth table**.) For example, the first distributive property can be demonstrated with a truth table:

p	q	r	q OR r	p AND (q OR r)	p AND q	p AND r	(p AND q) OR (p AND r)
T	T	T	T	T	T	T	T
T	T	F	T	T	T	F	T
T	F	T	T	T	F	T	T
T	F	F	F	F	F	F	F
F	T	T	T	F	F	F	F
F	T	F	T	F	F	F	F
F	F	T	T	F	F	F	F
F	F	F	F	F	F	F	F

The fifth column and the last column are identical, so the sentence "p AND (q OR r)" is equivalent to the sentence "(p AND q) OR (p AND r)."

BYTE A byte is the amount of memory space needed to store one character on a computer, which is normally 8 bits. A computer with 8-bit bytes can distinguish $2^8 = 256$ different characters. The size of a computer's memory is measured in kilobytes, where 1 kilobyte (K) $= 2^{10}$ bytes $= 1024$ bytes.

C

CALCULUS Calculus is divided into two general areas: differential calculus and integral calculus. The basic problem in differential calculus is to find the rate of change of a function. Geometrically, this means finding the slope of the tangent line to a function at a particular point; physically, this means finding the speed of an object if you are given its position function. The slope of the tangent line to the curve $y = f(x)$ at a point $(x, f(x))$ is called the derivative, written as y' or dy/dx, which can be found from this formula:

$$y' = \frac{dy}{dx} = \lim_{\Delta x \to 0} \frac{f(x + \Delta x) - f(x)}{\Delta x}.$$

See **derivative** for a table of the derivatives of different functions. The process of finding the derivative of a function is called *differentiation*.

If y is a function of more than one variable, as in $y = f(x_1, x_2)$, then the partial derivative of y with respect to x_1 is found by taking the derivative of y with respect to x_1 while assuming that x_2 remains constant. (See **partial derivative**.)

The reverse process of differentiation is integration (or anti-differentiation). Integration is represented by the symbol $\int$:

$$y = \int f(x)\, dx = F(x) + C.$$

This expression (called an indefinite integral) means that $F(x)$ is a function such that $dF(x)/dx = f(x)$. C can be any constant number. See **integral** for a brief table of integrals.

A related problem is, What is the area under the curve $y = f(x)$ from $x = a$ to $x = b$? It turns out that this problem can be solved by integration:

$$(\text{area}) = F(b) - F(a),$$

where $F(x)$ is an antiderivative function: $dF(x)/dx = f(x)$. This area can also be written as a definite integral:

$$(\text{area}) = \int_a^b f(x)\, dx = F(b) - F(a).$$

Integrals can also be used to find volume, surface area, and the lengths of curves. In general:

$$\lim_{\Delta x \to 0,\, n \to \infty} \sum_{i=1}^{n} f(x_i)\, \Delta x = \int_a^b f(x)\, dx,$$

if

$$\Delta x = \frac{b - a}{n}, \qquad x_1 = a, \qquad x_n = b.$$

CARTESIAN COORDINATES   A Cartesian coordinate system is a
system whereby points on a plane are identified by an ordered pair
of numbers, representing the distances to two perpendicular axes.
The horizontal axis is usually called the x-axis, and the vertical axis
is usually called the y-axis (see figure). The x-coordinate is always
listed first in the ordered pair (x, y). Cartesian coordinates are also
called rectangular coordinates to distinguish them from polar coordinates. A three-dimensional Cartesian coordinate system can be
constructed by drawing a z-axis perpendicular to the x- and y-axes.
A three-dimensional coordinate system can label any point in space.

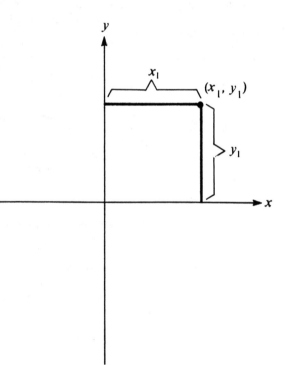

CARTESIAN PRODUCT   The Cartesian product of two sets, A and
B (written $A \times B$), is the set of all possible ordered pairs that have a

member of A as the first entry and a member of B as the second entry. For example, if $A = \{x, y, z\}$ and $B = \{1, 2\}$, then

$$A \times B = \{(x, 1), (x, 2), (y, 1), (y, 2), (z, 1), (z, 2)\}.$$

CATENARY   A catenary is a curve represented by the formula

$$y = \tfrac{1}{2}a(e^{x/a} + e^{-x/a}).$$

The value of e is about 2.7 (see e). The value of a can be adjusted.

The catenary can also be represented by the hyperbolic cosine function

$$y = \cosh x.$$

The curve formed by a flexible rope allowed to hang between two posts will be a catenary. (See figure.)

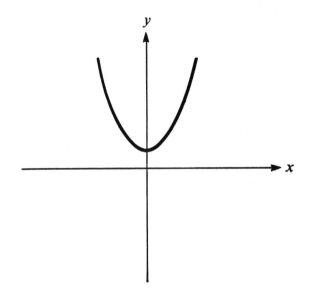

CENTRAL ANGLE   A central angle is an angle that has its vertex at the center of a circle (see figure).

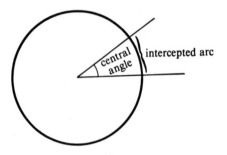

central angle | intercepted arc

CENTRAL LIMIT THEOREM See **normal distribution**.

CENTROID The centroid is the center of mass of an object. It is the point where the object would balance if supported by a single support. For a triangle, the centroid is the point where the three medians intersect. For a one-dimensional object of length L, the centroid can be found by using the integral

$$\frac{\displaystyle\int_0^L x\rho \, dx}{\displaystyle\int_0^L \rho \, dx},$$

where $\rho(x)$ represents the mass per unit length of the object at a particular location x. The centroid for two- or three-dimensional objects can be found with double or triple integrals.

CHAIN RULE The chain rule in calculus tells how to find the derivative of a composite function. If f and g are functions, and if $y = f(g(x))$, then the chain rule states that

$$\frac{dy}{dx} = \frac{df}{dg}\frac{dg}{dx}.$$

For example, suppose that $y = \sqrt{1 + 3x^2}$, and you are required to define these two functions:

$$g(x) = 1 + 3x^2; \qquad f(g) = \sqrt{g}.$$

Then y is a composite function: $y = f(g(x))$, and

$$\frac{df}{dg} = \tfrac{1}{2}g^{-1/2} \qquad \frac{dg}{dx} = 6x$$

$$\frac{dy}{dx} = \tfrac{1}{2}g^{-1/2}6x = 3x(1 + 3x^2)^{-1/2}.$$

Here are other examples (assume that a and b are constants):

$$y = \sin(ax + b) \qquad \frac{dy}{dx} = a\cos(ax + b)$$

$$y = \ln(ax + b) \qquad \frac{dy}{dx} = \frac{a}{ax + b}$$

$$y = e^{ax} \qquad \frac{dy}{dx} = ae^{ax}$$

CHARACTERISTIC   The characteristic is the integer part of a common logarithm. For example, log 115 = 2.0607, where 2 is the characteristic and .0607 is the *mantissa*.

CHEBYSHEV'S THEOREM   Chebyshev's theorem states that, for any group of numbers, the fraction that will be within k standard deviations of the mean will be at least $1 - 1/k^2$. For example, if $k = 2$, the formula gives the value of $1 - \tfrac{1}{4} = \tfrac{3}{4}$. Therefore, for any group of numbers at least 75 percent of them will be within two standard deviations of the mean.

CHI SQUARE   If $X_1, X_2, \ldots, X_n$ are independent and identically distributed standard normal random variables, then the random variable

$$S = X_1^2 + X_2^2 + \cdots + X_n^2$$

will have the distribution chi square with n degrees of freedom. The chi-square distribution with n degrees of freedom is symbolized by χ_n^2, since χ is the Greek letter chi. For the χ_n^2-distribution, $E(X) = n$ and $\text{Var}(X) = 2n$. The χ^2-distribution is used extensively in statistical estimation. It is also used in the definition of the t-distribution.

Table 5 lists some values for the chi-square cumulative distribution function.

CHI-SQUARE TEST The chi-square test provides a method for testing whether a particular probability distribution fits an observed pattern of data, or for testing whether two factors are independent.

The chi-square test statistic is calculated from this formula:

$$\frac{(f_1 - f_1{}^*)^2}{f_1{}^*} + \frac{(f_2 - f_2{}^*)^2}{f_2{}^*} + \cdots,$$

where f_i is the actual frequency of observations, and $f_i{}^*$ is the expected frequency of observations if the null hypothesis is true. If the null hypothesis is true, then the test statistic will have a chi-square distribution. The number of degrees of freedom depends on the number of observations. If the computed value of the test statistic is too large, the null hypothesis is rejected. (See **hypothesis testing**.)

CHORD A chord is a line segment that connects two points on a curve (see figure).

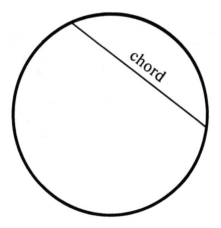

CIRCLE A circle is the set of points in a plane that are all a fixed distance from a given point. The given point is known as the center.

The distance from the center to a point on the circle is called the *radius*. The *circumference* is the distance you would have to walk if you walked all the way around the circle. The *diameter* is the farthest distance across the circle; it is equal to twice the radius.

The analytic equation for a circle with center at (h, k) and radius r is

$$(x - h)^2 + (y - k)^2 = r^2.$$

The circumference of a circle is given by $C = 2\pi r$, where $\pi = 3.14159\ldots$. (See **pi**.) The area of the circle can be found by dividing the circle into n triangular sectors, each with an area approximately equal to $\frac{1}{2}rC/n$ (see figure). To get the total area of the circle, multiply the area of each triangle by n:

$$A = \frac{n\frac{1}{2}rC}{n} = \frac{1}{2}rC = \pi r^2.$$

(To be exact, you have to take the limit as the number of triangles approaches infinity.)

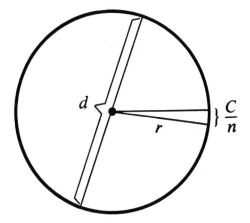

CIRCULAR FUNCTIONS   The circular functions are the same as the trigonometric functions.

CIRCUMCENTER   The circumcenter of a triangle is the center of the circle that can be circumscribed about the triangle. It is at the point where the perpendicular bisectors of the three sides cross. (See **triangle**.)

CIRCUMCIRCLE   The circumcircle for a triangle is the circle that can be circumscribed about the triangle. The three vertices of the triangle are points on the circle.

CIRCUMFERENCE   The circumference of a closed curve (such as a circle) is the total distance around the outer edge of the curve. The circumference of a circle is $2\pi r$, where r is the radius. (See **pi**.) Formally, the circumference of a circle is defined as the limit of the perimeter of a regular inscribed n-sided polygon as the number of sides goes to infinity.

CIRCUMSCRIBED   A circumscribed circle is a circle that passes through all of the vertices of a polygon. For an example, see **triangle**. In general, a figure is circumscribed about another if it surrounds it, touching it at as many points as possible.

CLOSED CURVE   A closed curve is a curve that completely encloses an area (see figure).

Closed Curves   Not-Closed Curves

CLOSED INTERVAL   A closed interval is an interval that contains its endpoints. For example, the interval $0 \leq x \leq 1$ is a closed interval because the two endpoints (0 and 1) are included. For contrast, see **open interval**.

CLOSURE PROPERTY   An arithmetic operation obeys the closure property with respect to a given set of numbers if the result of the operation will always be in that set if the operands (the input numbers) are. For example, the operation of addition is closed with respect to the integers, but the operation of division is not. (If a and b are integers, $a + b$ will always be an integer, but a/b may or may not be.)

| | Set | | | |
Operation	**Natural Numbers**	**Integers**	**Rational Numbers**	**Real Numbers**
addition	closed	closed	closed	closed
subtraction	not closed	closed	closed	closed
division	not closed	not closed	closed	closed
root extraction	not closed	not closed	not closed	not closed

COEFFICIENT   "Coefficient" is a technical term for something that multiplies something else (usually applied to a constant multiplying a variable). In the quadratic equation

$$Ax^2 + Bxy + Cy^2 + Dx + Ey + F = 0,$$

A is the coefficient of x^2, B is the coefficient of xy, and so on.

COEFFICIENT OF DETERMINATION   The coefficient of determination is a value between 0 and 1 that indicates how well the variations in the independent variables in a regression explain the variations in the dependent variable. It is symbolized by r^2. (See **regression; multiple regression**.)

COEFFICIENT OF VARIATION The coefficient of variation for a list of numbers is equal to the standard deviation for those numbers divided by the mean. It indicates how big the dispersion is in comparison to the mean.

COFUNCTION Each trigonometric function has a cofunction. For example, cosine x is the cofunction for sine x, cotangent x is the cofunction for tangent x, and cosecant x is the cofunction for secant x. The cofunction of a trigonometric function $f(\theta)$ is equal to $f(\pi/2 - \theta)$. (Note that $\pi/2 - x$ is the complement of x.)

COLLINEAR A set of points is collinear if they all lie on the same line. (Note that any two points are always collinear.)

COMBINATIONS The term "combinations" refers to the number of possible ways of arranging j objects chosen from a total sample of size n if you don't care about the order in which the objects are arranged. The number of combinations of n things, taken j at a time, is $n!/[(n-j)!j!]$, which is written as $\binom{n}{j}$. (See **factorial; binomial theorem**.) For example, the number of possible poker hands is equal to the number of possible combinations of five objects drawn (without replacement) from a sample of 52 cards. The number of possible hands is therefore:

$$\binom{52}{5} = \frac{52!}{47!5!} = \frac{52 \times 51 \times 50 \times 49 \times 48}{5 \times 4 \times 3 \times 2 \times 1} = 2{,}598{,}960.$$

This formula comes from the fact that there are n ways to choose the first object, $n-1$ ways to choose the second object, and therefore

$$n \times (n-1) \times (n-2) \times \cdots \times (n-j+2) \times (n-j+1)$$

ways of choosing all j objects. This expression is equal to $n!/(n-j)!$. However, this method counts each possible ordering of the objects separately. (See **permutations**.) Many times, as in cards, the order of the objects doesn't matter. For example, the hand 3 of hearts, 4 of hearts, 5 of hearts, 6 of hearts, 7 of hearts is exactly the same as the hand 4 of hearts, 3 of hearts, 5 of hearts, 6 of hearts, 7 of hearts. To find the number of combinations, we need to divide by $j!$, which is the total number of ways of ordering the j objects. That makes the final result $n!/[(n-j)!\,j!]$.

Counting the number of possible combinations for arranging a group of objects is important in probability. Suppose that both you and your dream lover (whom you're desperately hoping to meet) are in a class of 20 people, and five people are to be randomly selected to be on a committee. What is the probability that both you and your dream lover will be on the committee?

The total number of ways of choosing the committee is

$$\binom{20}{5} = 15{,}504.$$

Next, you need to calculate how many possibilities include both of you on the committee. If you've both been selected, then the other three members need to be chosen from the 18 remaining students, and there are

$$\binom{18}{3} = 816$$

ways of doing this. Therefore the probability that you'll both be selected is $816/15{,}504 = .053$. Your chances improve if the size of the committee increases. The table lists the probability of your both being selected if the committee contains s members:

s	Probability
2	.005
3	.016
4	.031
5	.053
6	.079
7	.111
8	.147
9	.189
10	.237
15	.553
18	.804
19	.900
20	1.000

COMMON LOGARITHM   A common logarithm is a logarithm to the base 10. In other words, if $y = \log_{10} x$, then $x = 10^y$. Often $\log_{10} x$ is written as $\log x$. (See **logarithm**.) Here is a table of some common logarithms:

x	$\log x$
1	0
2	0.3010
3	0.4771
4	0.6021
5	0.6990
6	0.7782
7	0.8451
8	0.9031
9	0.9542
10	1.0000
50	1.6990
100	2.0000

COMMUTATIVE PROPERTY   An operation obeys the commutative property if the order of the two numbers involved doesn't matter. The commutative law for addition states that

$$a + b = b + a \quad \text{for all } a \text{ and } b.$$

The commutative law for multiplication states that

$$ab = ba \quad \text{for all } a \text{ and } b.$$

For example, $3 + 6 = 6 + 3 = 9$, and $6 \cdot 7 = 7 \cdot 6 = 42$. Neither subtraction, division, nor exponentiation obeys the commutative property:

$$5 - 3 \neq 3 - 5, \qquad \tfrac{3}{4} \neq \tfrac{4}{3}, \qquad 2^3 \neq 3^2.$$

COMPASS   A compass is a device consisting of two adjustable legs (see figure), used for drawing circles and measuring off equal distance intervals.

COMPLEMENT OF A SET   The complement of a set consists of all the elements of a particular universal set that are not elements of the set. In the Venn diagram (figure), the shaded region is the complement of set *A*.

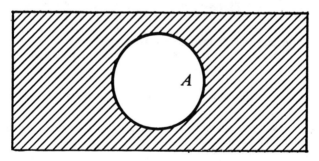

COMPLEMENTARY ANGLES   Two angles are complementary if the sum of their measures is 90°. For example, a 35° angle and a 55° angle are complementary. The two smallest angles in a right triangle are complementary.

COMPLETING THE SQUARE   Completing the square is a method for solving a quadratic equation. (See **quadratic equation**.)

COMPLEX FRACTION   A complex fraction is a fraction in which either the numerator or the denominator or both contain fractions. For example,

$$\frac{2/3}{3/4}$$

is a complex fraction. To simplify the complex fraction, multiply both the numerator and the denominator by the reciprocal of the denominator:

$$\frac{2/3}{3/4} = \frac{2/3 \times 4/3}{3/4 \times 4/3} = \frac{8/9}{12/12} = \frac{8/9}{1} = \frac{8}{9}.$$

COMPLEX NUMBER   A complex number is formed by adding a pure imaginary number to a real number. The general form of a complex number is $a + bi$, where a and b are both real numbers and i is the imaginary unit: $i^2 = -1$. The number a is called the real part of the complex number, and bi is the imaginary part. Two complex numbers are equal to each other only when both their real parts and their imaginary parts are equal to each other.

Complex numbers can be illustrated on a two-dimensional graph, much like a system of Cartesian coordinates. The real axis is the same as the real number line, and the imaginary axis is a line drawn perpendicularly to the real axis.

To add two complex numbers, add the real parts and the imaginary parts separately:

$$(a + bi) + (c + di) = (a + c) + (b + d)i.$$

Two complex numbers can be multiplied in the same way that you multiply two binomials:

$$\begin{aligned}(a + bi)(c + di) &= a(c + di) + bi(c + di) \\ &= ac + adi + bci + bdi^2 \\ &= (ac - bd) + (ad + bc)i.\end{aligned}$$

The absolute value of a complex number $(a + bi)$ is the distance from the point representing that number in the complex plane to the origin, which is equal to $\sqrt{a^2 + b^2}$. The complex conjugate of $a + bi$ is defined to be $a - bi$. The product of any complex number with its conjugate will be a real number, equal to the square of its absolute value:

$$(a + bi)(a - bi) = a^2 - abi + abi - b^2 i^2$$
$$= a^2 + b^2.$$

Complex numbers are also different from real numbers in that you can't put them in order.

COMPONENT In the vector (a, b, c), the numbers a, b, and c are known as the components of the vector. The number a is the first component, or x-component.

COMPOSITE FUNCTION A composite function is a function that consists of two functions arranged in such a way that the output of one function becomes the input of the other function. For example, if $f(u) = \sqrt{u + 3}$, and $g(x) = 5x$, then the composite function $f(g(x))$ s the function $\sqrt{5x + 3}$. To find the derivative of a composite function, see **chain rule**.

COMPOSITE NUMBER A composite number is a whole number that is not a prime number. Therefore, it can be expressed as the product of two whole numbers other than itself and 1.

COMPOUND SENTENCE In logic, a compound sentence is formed by joining two or more simple sentences together with one or more connectives, such as AND, OR, NOT, or IF/THEN. (See **logic**; **Boolean algebra**.)

COMPUTER ARITHMETIC Computers generally represent numbers in binary form. (See **binary numbers**.) The rules for adding binary digits are quite simple:

$$0 + 0 = 0$$
$$0 + 1 = 1$$
$$1 + 0 = 1$$
$$1 + 1 = 0 \quad \text{with a carry of 1 to the next digit}$$

It is possible to connect certain types of logic circuits (AND gates, OR gates, and NOT gates) to perform the addition of two binary numbers.

Two binary numbers can be subtracted by using this formula:

$$a - b = a - (-2^k + 2^k + b)$$
$$= a + (2^k - b) - 2^k,$$

where k is the number of binary digits that the computer stores for each number. The number $2^k - b$, called the 2-complement of the binary number b, can be found easily with logic circuits by reversing each digit of b and then adding 1 to the result. Then the sum $a + (2^k - b)$ can be calculated using the addition circuit. Finally, it is necessary to subtract 2^k. This subtraction can be done easily by dropping the digit in the column for 2^k.

A multiplication table for binary digits is much simpler than a multiplication table for decimal digits:

$$0 \times 0 = 0$$
$$0 \times 1 = 0$$
$$1 \times 0 = 0$$
$$1 \times 1 = 1$$

Two binary numbers can be multiplied by working through one of the numbers one digit at a time. If that digit is 0, then proceed to the next digit; if it is 1, then add the other number to the result (shifted the appropriate number of places) before proceeding to the next digit.

Division is the most complicated arithmetic operation for computers. It can be performed by repeated subtraction.

COMPUTER FUNCTION A function in a computer program acts the same as a mathematical function: it gives a unique result for a given value of the input (or inputs). For example, in the BASIC programming language functions can be defined with the DEF command:

$$\text{DEF } F(X) = X \wedge 2 + 3*X + 5$$

This statement defines the function $f(x) = x^2 + 3x + 5$. The function can now be used in expressions. For example,

PRINT F(2)

will cause the value $f(2) = 15$ to be printed;

$$A = 10 + F(3)$$

will cause A to take the value $10 + f(3) = 10 + 23 = 33$.

COMPUTER PROGRAM   A computer program is a set of instructions for a computer to follow. Computer programs may be written in a computer programming language, such as BASIC or Pascal, or in assembly language, which more closely resembles the internal machine language. (See also **algorithm**.)

CONCAVE   A set of points is concave if it is possible to draw a line segment that connects two points that are in the set, but includes also some points that are not in the set. (See Figure 1.) Note that a concave figure looks as though it has "caved" in. For contrast, see **convex**.

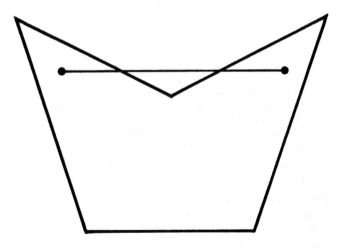

FIGURE 1

A curve (other than a straight line) has two sides: a concave side and a convex side. In Figure 2, curve *A* is oriented so that its concave side is down; curve *B* is oriented so that its concave side is up.

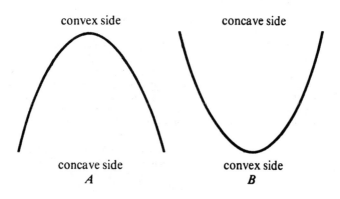

concave side
A

convex side
B

FIGURE 2

CONCLUSION   The conclusion is the sentence in an argument that follows as a result of the premises. (See **logic**.)

In a conditional statement the conclusion is the "then" part of the statement. It is the part that is true if the hypothesis (the "if" part) is true. For example, in the statement "If he likes pizza, then he likes cheese," the conclusion is the clause "he likes cheese." The conclusion of a conditional statement is also called the *consequent*.

CONCURRENT LINES   Two lines are concurrent if they pass through the same set of points.

CONDITIONAL EQUATION   A conditional equation is an equation that is true only for some values of the unknowns contained in the equation. For contrast, see **identity**.

CONDITIONAL PROBABILITY   The conditional probability that event *A* will occur, given that event *B* has occurred, is

$$\Pr(A \mid B) = \frac{\Pr(A \cap B)}{\Pr(B)}.$$

For example, what is the probability that you will turn up three heads in three coin flips, given that the first flip results in heads? The total set of possible outcomes is

{HHH, HHT, HTH, HTT, THH, THT, TTH, TTT},

where T stands for tails and H stands for heads. If A is the event that three heads appear, then $A = \{HHH\}$. If B is the event that the first coin is heads, then $B = \{HHH, HHT, HTH, HTT\}$. Then

$$(A \cup B) = \{HHH\},$$

so

$$\Pr(A \cup B) = 1/8 \quad \text{and} \quad \Pr(B) = 1/2.$$

Therefore the conditional probability that A will occur, given that B has occurred (written as $\Pr(A \mid B)$), is $(1/8)/(1/2) = 1/4$.

CONDITIONAL STATEMENT A conditional statement is a statement of this form: "If a is true, then b is true." Symbolically, this is written as $a \rightarrow b$ ("a implies b"). For example, the statement "If a triangle has three equal sides, then it has three equal angles" is true, but the statement "If a quadrilateral has four equal sides, then it has four equal angles" is false.

CONE A cone (see figure) is formed by the union of all line segments that connect a given point (called the vertex) and the points on a closed curve that is not in the same plane as the vertex. If the closed curve is a circle, then the cone is called a circular cone. The region enclosed by the circle is called the base. The distance from the plane

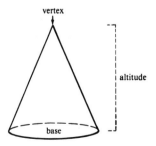

containing the base to the vertex is called the altitude. The volume of the cone is equal to $\frac{1}{3}$ (base area)(altitude). Each line segment from the vertex to the circle is called an element of the cone.

The term "cone" also refers to the figure formed by all possible lines that pass through both the vertex point and a given circle. This type of cone goes off to infinity in two directions. (See **conic section**.)

An ice cream cone is an example of a cone. Mount St. Helens was close to being a cone before May 18, 1980.

CONFIDENCE INTERVAL   A confidence interval is an interval based on observations of a sample so constructed that there is a specified probability that the interval contains the unknown true value of a population parameter. It is common to calculate confidence intervals that have a 95 percent probability of containing the true value.

For example, suppose that you are trying to estimate the mean weight of loaves of bread produced at a bakery. It would be too expensive to weigh every single loaf, but you can estimate the mean by selecting and weighing a random sample of loaves. Suppose that the weights of the entire population of loaves have a normal distribution with a mean mu (μ), whose value is unknown, and a standard deviation sigma (σ), whose value is known. Suppose also that you have selected a sample of n loaves and have found that the average weight of this sample is $\bar{x}$. (The bar over the x stands for "average.") Because of the properties of the normal distribution, $\bar{x}$ will have a normal distribution with mean μ and standard deviation $\sigma/\sqrt{n}$.

Now define Z as follows:

$$Z = \frac{\sqrt{n}(\bar{x} - \mu)}{\sigma};$$

Z will have a standard normal distribution (that is, a normal distribution with mean 0 and standard deviation 1). There is a 95 percent chance that a standard normal random variable will be between -1.96 and 1.96:

$$\Pr(-1.96 < Z < 1.96) = .95.$$

Therefore:

$$\Pr\left(-1.96 < \frac{\sqrt{n}(\bar{x} - \mu)}{\sigma} < 1.96\right) = .95,$$

which can be rewritten as

$$\Pr\left(\bar{x} - \frac{1.96\sigma}{\sqrt{n}} < \mu < \bar{x} + \frac{1.96\sigma}{\sqrt{n}}\right) = .95.$$

The last equation tells you how to calculate the confidence interval. There is a 95 percent chance that the interval from $\bar{x} - 1.96\sigma/\sqrt{n}$ to $\bar{x} + 1.96\sigma/\sqrt{n}$ will contain the true value of the mean, μ.

However, in many practical situations you will not know the true value of the population standard deviation, σ, and therefore cannot use the preceding method. Instead, after selecting your random sample of size n, you will need to calculate both the sample average, $\bar{x}$, and the sample standard deviation, s:

$$s = \sqrt{\frac{(x_1 - \bar{x})^2 + (x_2 - \bar{x})^2 + \cdots + (x_n - \bar{x})^2}{n - 1}}.$$

The confidence interval calculation is based on the fact that the quantity $T = \sqrt{n}(\bar{x} - \mu)/s$ will have a t-distribution with $n - 1$ degrees of freedom (see **t-distribution**). Note that the quantity T is the same as the quantity Z used above, except that the known value of the sample standard deviation s has been substituted for the population standard deviation, σ, which is now unknown.

Now you need to look in a t-distribution table for a value (a) such that $\Pr(-a < T < a) = .95$, where T has a t-distribution with the appropriate degrees of freedom. See Table 7 at the back of the book. Then the 95 percent confidence interval for the unknown value of μ is from

$$\bar{x} - \frac{as}{\sqrt{n}} \quad \text{to} \quad \bar{x} + \frac{as}{\sqrt{n}}.$$

For example, suppose you are investigating the mean commuting time along a particular route into the city. You have recorded the commuting times for 7 days:

39, 43, 29, 52, 35, 38, 39

and would like to calculate a 95 percent confidence interval for the mean commuting time. Calculate the sample average, $\bar{x} = 39.286$. Then calculate the sample standard deviation $s = 7.088$. Look in Table 7 for a t-distribution with $7 - 1 = 6$ degrees of freedom to find the value of $a = 2.447$. Then the 95 percent confidence interval is

$$39.286 \pm 2.447 \times \frac{7.088}{\sqrt{7}},$$

which is from 32.730 to 45.841.

CONGRUENT   Two polygons are congruent if they have exactly the same shape and exactly the same size. In other words, if you pick one of the polygons up and put it on top of the other, the two would match exactly. Each side of one polygon is exactly the same length as one side of the congruent polygon. These two sides with the same length are called corresponding sides. Also, each angle on one polygon has a corresponding angle on the other polygon. All of the pairs of corresponding angles are equal. See **triangle** for some examples of ways to prove that two triangles are congruent.

CONIC SECTIONS   The four curves *circles*, *ellipses*, *parabolas*, and *hyperbolas* (see Figure 1) are called conic sections because they can be formed by the intersection of a plane with a right circular cone. If the plane is perpendicular to the axis of the cone, the intersection will be a circle. If the plane is slightly tilted, the result will be an ellipse. If the plane is parallel to one element of the cone, the result will be a parabola. If the plane intersects both parts of the cone, the result will be a hyperbola. (Note that a hyperbola has two branches.)
      There is another definition of conic sections that makes it possible to define parabolas, ellipses, and hyperbolas by one equation. A conic section can be defined as a set of points such that the distance from a fixed point divided by the distance from a fixed line is a constant. The fixed point is called the *focus*, the fixed line is called the *directrix*, and the constant ratio is called the *eccentricity* of the conic section, or *e*. When *e* = 1 this definition exactly matches the defini-

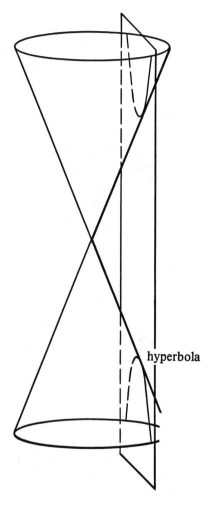

hyperbola

FIGURE 1

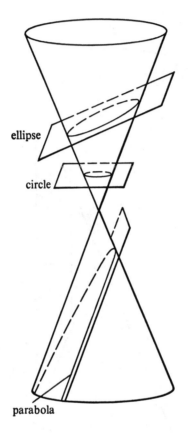

ellipse

circle

parabola

FIGURE 1

tion of a parabola. If $e \neq 1$, you can find the equation for a conic section with the line $x = 0$ as the directrix and the point $(0, p)$ as the focus (see Figure 2):

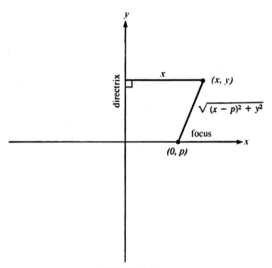

FIGURE 2

$$\frac{\sqrt{(x-p)^2+y^2}}{x}=e.$$

Simplifying:

$$x^2(1-e^2)-2px+y^2+p^2=0,$$
$$x^2-\frac{2px}{1-e^2}+\frac{y^2}{1-e^2}+\frac{p^2}{1-e^2}=0.$$

Completing the square for x:

$$x^2-\frac{2px}{1-e^2}+\frac{p^2}{(1-e^2)^2}-\frac{p^2}{(1-e^2)^2}+\frac{y^2}{1-e^2}+\frac{p^2}{1-e^2}=0,$$
$$\left[x-\left(\frac{p}{1-e^2}\right)\right]^2+\frac{y^2}{1-e^2}=\frac{e^2p^2}{(1-e^2)^2}.$$

This equation can be rewritten as

$$\frac{(x-h)^2}{a^2} + \frac{y^2}{B} = 1,$$

where

$$h = \frac{p}{1-e^2}, \qquad a^2 = \frac{e^2p^2}{(1-e^2)^2}, \qquad \text{and} \qquad B = \frac{e^2p^2}{1-e^2}.$$

If $e < 1$, then B is positive, and this is the standard equation of an ellipse. If $e > 1$, then B is negative, and this is the standard equation of a hyperbola.

CONJUGATE The conjugate of a complex number is formed by reversing the sign of the imaginary part. The conjugate of $a + bi$ is $a - bi$. (See **complex number**.) The conjugate of a complex number A is written as $\bar{A}$. One important property is that $A \cdot \bar{A}$ will always be a real nonnegative number:

$$(a + bi)(a - bi) = a^2 - abi + abi - b^2i^2 = a^2 + b^2.$$

Another property is that $A = \bar{A}$ if and only if A is a real number.

If a complex number $a + bi$ occurs in the denominator of a fraction, it often helps to multiply both the numerator and the denominator of the fraction by $a - bi$:

$$\frac{3+2i}{4+6i} = \frac{(3+2i)}{(4+6)}\frac{(4-6i)}{(4-6i)} = \frac{12-18i+8i-12i^2}{16-24i+24i-36i^2}$$
$$= \frac{6}{13} - \frac{5}{26}i.$$

CONJUNCTION A conjunction is an AND statement of this form: "A and B." It is true only if both A and B are true. For example, the statement "Two points determine a line and three noncollinear points determine a plane" is true, but the statement "Triangles have three sides and pentagons have four sides" is false.

CONSEQUENT The consequent is the part of a conditional statement that is true if the other part (the *antecedent*) is true. The consequent is the "then" part of a conditional statement. For example, in the statement "If he likes pizza, then he likes cheese," the consequent is the clause, "he likes cheese." The consequent is also called the *conclusion* of a conditional statement.

CONSISTENT ESTIMATOR   A consistent estimator is an estimator that tends to converge toward the true value of the parameter it is trying to estimate as the sample size becomes larger. (**See statistical inference.**)

CONSTANT   A constant represents a quantity that does not change. It can be expressed either as a literal (that is, a numeral) or as a letter (or other variable name) whose value is taken to be a constant.

CONTINUOUS   A continuous function is one that you can graph without lifting your pencil from the paper (see figure). Most functions that have practical applications are continuous, but it is easy to think of examples of discontinuous functions. The formal definition of "continuous" is: The graph of $y = f(x)$ is continuous at a point a if (1) $f(a)$ exists; (2) $\lim_{x \to a} f(x)$ exists; and (3) $\lim_{x \to a} = f(a)$.

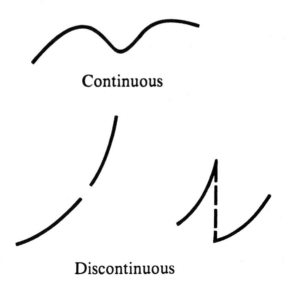

Continuous

Discontinuous

CONTINUOUS RANDOM VARIABLE A continuous random variable is a random variable that can take on any real-number value within a certain range. It is characterized by a density function curve such that the area under the curve between two numbers represents the probability that the random variable will be between those two numbers. The normal, chi-square, t-, and F-distributions are all examples of continuous random variable distributions. (See **random variable**).

For contrast, see **discrete random variable**.

CONTRADICTION A contradiction is a statement that is necessarily false because of its logical structure, regardless of the facts. For example, the statement "p AND $\sim p$" is false, regardless of what p represents. The negation of a contradiction is called a *tautology*.

CONTRAPOSITIVE The contrapositive of the statement $A \rightarrow B$ is the statement (not B) $\rightarrow$ (not A). The contrapositive is equivalent to the original statement. If the original statement is true, the contrapositive is true; if the original statement is false, the contrapositive is false. For example, the statement "If x is a rational number, then x is a real number" has the contrapositive "If x is not a real number, then it is not a rational number."

CONVERGENT SERIES A convergent series is an infinite series that has a finite sum. For example:

$$\sum_{i=0}^{\infty} x^i = 1 + x + x^2 + x^3 + \cdots$$
$$= \frac{1}{1-x} \quad \text{if } -1 < x < 1.$$

The value of the series is infinity if $|x| \geq 1$. In this case the series is convergent if $|x| < 1$; otherwise it is called a divergent series.

CONVERSE The converse of an IF-THEN statement is formed by interchanging the "if" part and the "then" part:

statement: $a \rightarrow b$ \qquad converse: $b \rightarrow a$.

The converse of a true statement may be true, or it may be false. For example:

Statement (true)

"If a triangle is a right triangle, then the square of the length of the longest side is equal to the sums of the squares of the lengths of the other two sides."

Converse (true)

"If the square of the longest side of a triangle is equal to the sums of the squares of the other two sides, then the triangle is a right triangle."

Statement (true)

"If you're in medical school now, then you had high grades in college."

Converse (false)

"If you had high grades in college, then you're in medical school now."

CONVEX A set of points is convex if, for any two points in the set, all the points on the line segment joining them are also in the set (see figure). For contrast, see **concave**.

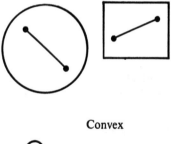

Convex

Not Convex

COORDINATES The coordinates of a point are a set of numbers that identify the location of that point. For example:

($x = 1$, $y = 2$) are Cartesian coordinates for a point in two-dimensional space.

($r = 3$, $\theta = 45°$) are polar coordinates for a point in two-dimensional space.

($x = 4$, $y = 5$, $z = 6$) are Cartesian coordinates for a point in three-dimensional space.

(latitude = $51°$ north, longitude = $0°$) are the terrestrial coordinates of the city of London.

(declination = $-5°25'$, right ascension = 5 hours 33 minutes) are the celestial coordinates of the Great Nebula in Orion.

COPLANAR A set of points is coplanar if they all lie in the same plane. Any three points are always coplanar. The vertices of a triangle are coplanar, but not the vertices of a pyramid. Two lines are coplanar if they lie in the same plane, that is, if they either intersect or are parallel.

COROLLARY A corollary is a statement that can be proved easily once a major theorem has been proved.

CORRELATION COEFFICIENT The correlation coefficient between two random variables X and Y is defined to be:

$$(\text{correlation coefficient}) = \rho(X, Y) = \frac{\text{Cov}(X, Y)}{\sigma_X \sigma_Y}.$$

Cov(X, Y) is the covariance between X and Y; σ_X is the standard deviation of X, and σ_Y is the standard deviation of Y. The correlation coefficient is always between -1 and 1.

The correlation coefficient tells whether or not there is a linear relationship between X and Y. If $X = aY + b$, where a and b are constants and $a > 0$, then $\rho(X, Y) = 1$. If $a < 0$, then $\rho(X, Y) = -1$. If X and Y are almost, but not quite, linearly related, then $\rho(X, Y)$ will be close to 1. If X and Y are completely independent, then $\rho(X, Y) = 0$.

Observations of two variables can be used to estimate the correlation between them. For example, the correlation between the youth unemployment rate and the overall unemployment rate in a recent year was .921, suggesting that these two variables are positively related. On the other hand, the correlation between population and January precipitation for a sample of 21 large cities was −.146, which is fairly small. You would not expect to find a significant correlation between population and precipitation.

CORRESPONDING ANGLES (1) When a transversal cuts two lines, it forms four pairs of corresponding angles. In the figure, angle 1 and angle 2 are a pair of corresponding angles. Angle 3 and angle 4 are another pair. A postulate of Euclidian geometry says that, if a transversal cuts two parallel lines, then the pairs of corresponding angles that are formed will be equal.

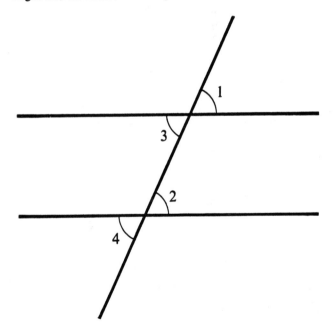

(2) When two polygons are congruent, or similar, each angle on one polygon is equal to a corresponding angle on the other polygon.

CORRESPONDING SIDES When two polygons are congruent, each side on one polygon is equal to a corresponding side on the other polygon. When two polygons are similar, the ratio of the length of a side on the big polygon to the length of its corresponding side on the little polygon is the same for all the sides.

COSECANT The cosecant of θ is defined to be

$$\csc \theta = \frac{1}{\sin \theta}.$$

(See **trigonometry**.)

COSINE The cosine of an angle θ in a right triangle is defined to be

$$\cos \theta = \frac{(\text{adjacent side})}{(\text{hypotenuse})}.$$

The name comes from the fact that the cosine function is the cofunction for the sine function, because $\cos(\pi/2 - \theta) = \sin \theta$. The graph of the cosine function is periodic with an amplitude of 1 and a period of 2π. (See **trigonometry**.)

Some special values of the cosine function are as follows: $\cos 0 = 1$, $\cos(\pi/6) = \sqrt{3}/2$, $\cos(\pi/4) = 1/\sqrt{2}$, and $\cos(\pi/2) = 0$. In general, $\cos \theta$ can be found from the infinite series

$$\cos \theta = 1 - \frac{\theta^2}{2!} + \frac{\theta^4}{4!} - \frac{\theta^6}{6!} + \frac{\theta^8}{8!} - \cdots.$$

COTANGENT The cotangent of θ is defined to be

$$\text{ctn } \theta = \frac{1}{\tan \theta}.$$

(See **trigonometry**.)

COTERMINAL Two angles are coterminal if they have the same terminal side when placed in standard position. (See **terminal side**.) For example, a 45° angle is coterminal with a 405° angle.

COUNTING NUMBERS The counting numbers are the same as the natural numbers: 1, 2, 3, 4, 5, 6, 7, ... They're the numbers you use to count something.

COVARIANCE The covariance of two random variables X and Y is a measure of how much X and Y move together. The definition is

$$\text{Cov}(X, Y) = E[(X - E(X))(Y - E(Y))].$$

If X and Y are completely independent, then $\text{Cov}(X, Y) = 0$. If Y is large at the same time that X is large, then $\text{Cov}(X, Y)$ will be large. (See **correlation coefficient**.) The covariance can also be found from this expression:

$$\text{Cov}(X, Y) = E(XY) - E(X)E(Y).$$

CRAMER'S RULE Cramer's rule is a method for solving a set of simultaneous linear equations using determinants. For the 3×3 system:

$$a_1x + a_2y + a_3z = k_1,$$
$$b_1x + b_2y + b_3z = k_2,$$
$$c_1x + c_2y + c_3z = k_3.$$

The rule states:

$$x = \frac{\begin{vmatrix} k_1 & a_2 & a_3 \\ k_2 & b_2 & b_3 \\ k_3 & c_2 & c_3 \end{vmatrix}}{\begin{vmatrix} a_1 & a_2 & a_3 \\ b_1 & b_2 & b_3 \\ c_1 & c_2 & c_3 \end{vmatrix}},$$

$$y = \frac{\begin{vmatrix} a_1 & k_1 & a_1 \\ b_1 & k_2 & b_3 \\ c_1 & k_3 & c_3 \end{vmatrix}}{\begin{vmatrix} a_1 & a_2 & a_3 \\ b_1 & b_2 & b_3 \\ c_1 & c_2 & c_3 \end{vmatrix}}.$$

$$z = \frac{\begin{vmatrix} a_1 & a_2 & k_1 \\ b_1 & b_2 & k_2 \\ c_1 & c_2 & k_3 \end{vmatrix}}{\begin{vmatrix} a_1 & a_2 & a_3 \\ b_1 & b_2 & b_3 \\ c_1 & c_2 & c_3 \end{vmatrix}}.$$

The determinant of a matrix is written with vertical lines outside the matrix. (See **determinant**.)

To use Cramer's rule, first calculate the determinant of the whole matrix of coefficients. This determinant appears in the denominator of the solution for each variable. To calculate the numerator of the solution for x, set up the same matrix but make one substitution: cross out the column that contains the coefficients of x, and replace that column with the column of constants from the other side of the equal sign.

To use the rule to solve a system of n equations in n unknowns, you will have to calculate $(n + 1)$ determinants of dimension $n \times n$. This procedure could get tedious, but it is the kind of calculation that is well suited to be performed by a computer.

For an example of the method, we can find the solution of the three-equation system

$$5x + y - 4z = -1,$$
$$3x - 6y + 2z = -5,$$
$$9x - y - 2z = 13.$$

The determinant in the denominator is

$$\begin{vmatrix} 5 & 1 & -4 \\ 3 & -6 & 2 \\ 9 & -1 & -2 \end{vmatrix} = -110.$$

The three determinants in the numerators are

$$\begin{vmatrix} -1 & 1 & -4 \\ -5 & -6 & 2 \\ 13 & -1 & -2 \end{vmatrix} = -330, \qquad \begin{vmatrix} 5 & -1 & -4 \\ 3 & -5 & 2 \\ 9 & 13 & -2 \end{vmatrix} = -440,$$

$$\begin{vmatrix} 5 & 1 & -1 \\ 3 & -6 & -5 \\ 9 & -1 & 13 \end{vmatrix} = -550.$$

Then:

$$x = \frac{-330}{-110} = 3, \qquad y = \frac{-440}{-110} = 4, \qquad \text{and} \qquad z = \frac{-550}{-110} = 5.$$

CRITICAL REGION   If the calculated value of a test statistic falls within the critical region, then the null hypothesis is rejected. (See **hypothesis testing**.)

CROSS PRODUCT   The cross product of two three-dimensional vectors

$$\mathbf{a} = (a_1, a_2, a_3) \qquad \text{and} \qquad \mathbf{b} = (b_1, b_2, b_3)$$

is

$$\mathbf{a} \times \mathbf{b} = ((a_2 b_3 - a_3 b_2), (a_3 b_1 - a_1 b_3), (a_1 b_2 - a_2 b_1)).$$

$\mathbf{a} \times \mathbf{b}$ (read: **a** cross **b**) is a vector with the following properties:

$$\|\mathbf{a} \times \mathbf{b}\| = \|\mathbf{a}\| \cdot \|\mathbf{b}\| \cdot \sin \theta_{ab},$$

where θ_{ab} is the angle between **a** and **b**.

$\mathbf{a} \times \mathbf{b}$ is perpendicular to both **a** and **b**.

The direction of $\mathbf{a} \times \mathbf{b}$ is determined by the right-hand rule: Put your right hand so that your fingers point in the direction from **a** to **b**. Then your thumb points in the direction of $\mathbf{a} \times \mathbf{b}$.

$\mathbf{a} \times \mathbf{b} = 0$ if **a** and **b** are parallel (i.e., if $\theta_{ab} = 0$).

$\|\mathbf{a} \times \mathbf{b}\| = \|\mathbf{a}\| \cdot \|\mathbf{b}\|$ if **a** and **b** are perpendicular.

The cross product is not commutative, since $\mathbf{a} \times \mathbf{b} = -\mathbf{b} \times \mathbf{a}$. For example:

$$(1, 0, 0) \times (0, 1, 0) = (0, 0, 1),$$
$$(1, 1, 1) \times (2, 2, 2) = (0, 0, 0),$$
$$(5, 1, 1) \times (10, 2, 2) = (0, 0, 0).$$

The cross product is important in physics. The angular momentum vector **L** is defined by the cross product: $\mathbf{L} = \mathbf{r} \times \mathbf{p}$, where **p** is the linear momentum vector and **r** is the position vector.

CUBE   (1) A cube is a solid with six congruent square faces. A cube can be thought of as a right prism with square bases and four square lateral faces. (See **prism**.) Dice are cubes and many ice cubes are cubes. The volume of a cube with an edge equal to a is a^3, which is read as a cubed. The surface area of a cube is $6a^2$.

(2) The cube of a number is that number raised to the third power. For example, the cube of 2 is 8, since $2^3 = 8$.

CUBE ROOT   The cube root of a number is the number that, when multiplied together three times, gives that number. For example, 4 is the cube root of 64, since $4 \times 4 \times 4 = 64$. The cube root of x is symbolized by $\sqrt[3]{x}$ or $x^{1/3}$.

CUMULATIVE DISTRIBUTION FUNCTION   A cumulative distribution function gives the probability that a random variable will be less than or equal to a specific value. (See **random variable.**)

CURVE   A curve can be thought of as the path traced out by a point if it is allowed to move around space. A straight line is one example of a curve. A curve can have either infinite length, such as a parabola, or finite length, such as the ones shown in the figure. If a curve completely encloses a region of a plane, it is called a closed curve. If a closed curve does not cross over itself, then it is a simple closed curve. A circle and an ellipse are both examples of simple closed curves.

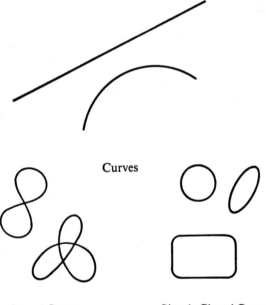

Curves

Closed Curves   Simple Closed Curves

CYCLOID   If a wheel rolls along a flat surface, a point on the wheel traces out a multiarch curve known as a cycloid (see figure). The cycloid can be defined by the parametric equations

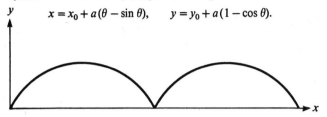

$$x = x_0 + a(\theta - \sin \theta), \qquad y = y_0 + a(1 - \cos \theta).$$

One important use of the cycloid is based on the fact that, if a ball is to roll from uphill point A to downhill point B, it will reach B the fastest along a cycloid-shaped ramp.

CYLINDER   A circular cylinder is formed by the union of all line segments that connect corresponding points on two congruent circles lying in parallel planes. The two circular regions are the bases. The segment connecting the centers of the two circles is called the axis. If the axis is perpendicular to the planes containing the circles, then the cylinder is called a right circular cylinder. The distance between the two planes is called the altitude of the cylinder. The volume of a cylinder is the product of the base area times the altitude. A soup can is one example of a cylindrical object (see figure).

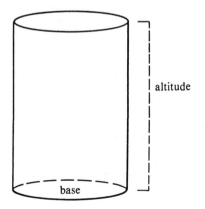

D

DECAGON A decagon is a polygon with 10 sides. A regular decagon has 10 equal sides and 10 angles, each of measure $144°$. (See figure.)

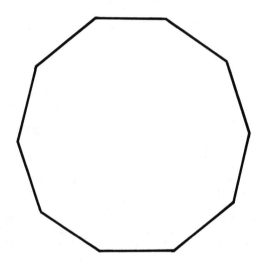

DECIMAL NUMBERS The common way of representing numbers is by a decimal, or base-10, number system, wherein each digit represents a multiple of a power of 10. The position of a digit tells what power of 10 it is to be multiplied by. For example:

$$32{,}456 = 3 \times 10^4 + 2 \times 10^3 + 4 \times 10^2 + 5 \times 10^1 + 6 \times 10^0.$$

We are so used to thinking of decimal numbers that we usually think of the decimal representation of the number as being the number itself. It is possible, though, to use other bases for number systems. Computers often use base-2 numbers, and the ancient Babylonians used base-60 numbers.

A decimal fraction is a number in which the digits to the right of the decimal point are to be multiplied by 10 raised to a negative power:

$$32.364 = 3 \times 10^1 + 2 \times 10^0 + 3 \times 10^{-1} + 6 \times 10^{-2} + 4 \times 10^{-3}.$$

DECREASING FUNCTION   A function $f(x)$ is a decreasing function if $f(a) < f(b)$ when $a > b$.

DEDUCTION   A deduction is a conclusion arrived at by reasoning.

DEFINITE INTEGRAL   If $f(x)$ represents a function of x that is always nonnegative, then the definite integral of $f(x)$ between a and b represents the area under the curve $y = f(x)$, above the x-axis, to the right of the line $x = a$, and to the left of the line $x = b$. (See figure.) The definite integral is represented by the expression

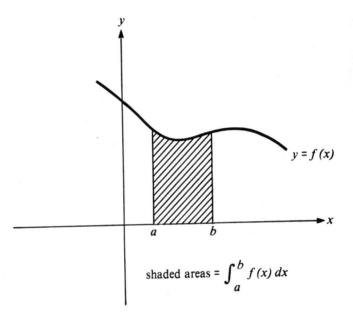

$$\text{shaded areas} = \int_a^b f(x)\, dx$$

The value of the definite integral can be found from the formula

$$F(b) - F(a),$$

where F is an antiderivative function for f [that is, $dF/dx = f(x)$.]

If $f(x)$ is negative everywhere between a and b, then the value of the definite integral will be the negative of the area above the curve $y = f(x)$, below the x-axis, and between $x = a$ and $x = b$.

Definite integrals can also be used to find volumes, surface areas, centers of mass, and other quantities.

For contrast, see **indefinite integral**.

DEGREE (1) A degree is a unit of measure for angles. One degree is equal to 1/360 of a full rotation. The symbol for degree is a little raised circle: °. A full circle measures 360°. A half turn measures 180°. A quarter turn (a right angle) measures 90°.

Angles can also be measured with *radian measure*, which is necessary when trigonometric functions are used in calculus: $360° = 2\pi$ radians.

(2) The degree of a polynomial is the highest power of the variable that appears in the polynomial. (See **polynomial**.)

DELTA The Greek capital letter delta, which has the shape of a triangle: Δ, is used to represent "change in." For example, the expression Δx represents "the change in x." (See **calculus**.)

DE MOIVRE'S THEOREM De Moivre's theorem tells how to find the exponential of an imaginary number:

$$e^{i\theta} = \cos\theta + i\sin\theta.$$

(Note that θ is measured in radians.)

For example:

$$e^0 = \cos 0 + i\sin 0 = 1,$$

$$e^{i\pi/2} = \cos\left(\frac{\pi}{2}\right) + i\sin\left(\frac{\pi}{2}\right) = i,$$

$$e^{i\pi} = \cos\pi + i\sin\pi = -1.$$

To see why the theorem is reasonable, consider $(e^{ix})^2$. This expression should equal e^{2ix}, according to the laws of exponents. We can assume that the theorem is true and show that it is consistent with the law of exponents:

$$(e^{ix})^2 = e^{i2x}$$

$$(\cos x + i\sin x)^2 = \cos^2 x + 2i\sin x\cos x - \sin^2 x$$

$$= \cos 2x + i\sin 2x.$$

The theorem can also be shown by looking at the series expansion of e^{ix}:

$$e^{ix} = 1 + ix - \frac{x^2}{2!} - \frac{ix^3}{3!} + \frac{x^4}{4!} + \cdots$$

$$= \left(1 - \frac{x^2}{2!} + \frac{x^4}{4!} - \frac{x^6}{6!} + \cdots\right)$$

$$+ i\left(x - \frac{x^3}{3!} + \frac{x^5}{5!} - \frac{x^7}{7!} + \cdots\right).$$

The two series in parentheses are the series expansions for cos x and sin x, so

$$e^{ix} = \cos x + i \sin x.$$

This theorem plays an important part in the solution of some differential equations.

DE MORGAN'S LAWS   De Morgan's laws determine how the connectives AND, OR, and NOT interact in symbolic logic:

$\sim p$ AND $\sim q$ is equivalent to $\sim(p$ OR $q)$;

$\sim p$ OR $\sim q$ is equivalent to $\sim(p$ AND $q)$.

In these expressions, p and q represent any sentences that have truth values (in other words, are either true or false). For example, the sentence

"He is not an officer and a gentleman"

is equivalent to the sentence

"He is not an officer or else he is not a gentleman."

For a proof, see **truth table**.

DENOMINATOR   The denominator is the bottom part of a fraction. In the fraction $\frac{2}{3}$, 3 is the denominator and 2 is the *numerator*. (To

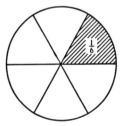

keep the terms straight, you might remember that "denominator" starts with "d," the same as "down.") If a fraction measures an amount of pie, the denominator tells how many equal slices the pie has been cut into (see figure). The numerator tells you how many slices you have.

DENSITY FUNCTION   See **random variable**.

DEPENDENT VARIABLE   The dependent variable stands for any of the set of output numbers of a function. In the equation $y = f(x)$, y is the dependent variable and x is the independent variable. The value of y depends on the value of x. You are free to choose any value of x that you wish (so long as it is in the domain of the function), but once you have chosen x the value of y is determined by the function. (See **function**.)

DERIVATIVE   The derivative of a function is the rate of change of that function. On the graph of the curve $y = f(x)$, the derivative at the point x is equal to the slope of the tangent line at the point $(x, f(x))$. If the function represents the position of an object as a function of time, then the derivative represents the speed of the object. Derivatives can be calculated from this expression:

function: $y = f(x)$,

derivative: $y' = f'(x) = \dfrac{dy}{dx} = \lim\limits_{\Delta x \to 0} \dfrac{f(x + \Delta x) - f(x)}{\Delta x}$.

Several rules are available that tell how to find the derivatives of different functions (c and n are constants):

$y = c$ $y' = 0$

$y = cx$ $y' = c$

*Sum Rule

$y = f(x) + g(x)$ $y' = f'(x) + g'(x)$

*Product Rule

$y = f(x) \times g(x)$ $y' = f(x)\,g'(x) + f'(x)\,g(x)$

*Power Rule

$y = x^n$ $y' = nx^{n-1}$

*Chain Rule

$$y = g(f(x)) \qquad y' = (dg/df)(df/dx) = dg/dx$$

*Trigonometric Functions

$y = \sin x$	$y' = \cos x$
$y = \cos x$	$y' = -\sin x$
$y = \tan x$	$y' = \sec^2 x$
$y = \operatorname{ctn} x$	$y' = -\csc^2 x$
$y = \sec x$	$y' = \sec x \tan x$
$y = \csc x$	$y' = -\csc x \operatorname{ctn} x$
$y = \arcsin x$	$y' = (1 - x^2)^{-1/2}$
$y = \arctan x$	$y' = (1 + x^2)^{-1}$

*Exponential Functions

$$y = a^x \qquad y' = (\ln a)a^x$$

*Natural Logarithm Functions

$$y = \ln x \qquad y' = 1/x$$

If y is a function of more than one independent variable, **see partial derivative.**

The derivative of the derivative is called the second derivative, written as $y''(x)$ or d^2y/dx^2. When the first derivative is positive, the curve is sloping upward. When the second derivative is positive, the curve is oriented so that it is concave upward.

DESCRIPTIVE STATISTICS   Descriptive statistics is the study of ways to summarize data. For example, the mean, median, and standard deviation are descriptive statistics that summarize some of the properties of a list of numbers. For contrast, see **statistical inference**.

DETERMINANT   The determinant of a 2×2 matrix is

$$\begin{vmatrix} a & b \\ c & d \end{vmatrix} = ad - cb.$$

The determinant of a 3×3 matrix can be found from

$$\begin{vmatrix} a_1 & a_2 & a_3 \\ b_1 & b_2 & b_3 \\ c_1 & c_2 & c_3 \end{vmatrix} = a_1 \begin{vmatrix} b_2 & b_3 \\ c_2 & c_3 \end{vmatrix} - a_2 \begin{vmatrix} b_1 & b_3 \\ c_1 & c_3 \end{vmatrix} + a_3 \begin{vmatrix} b_1 & b_2 \\ c_1 & c_2 \end{vmatrix}.$$

The 3×3 determinant consists of three terms. Each term contains an element of the top row multiplied by its *minor*. The minor of an element of a matrix can be found in this way: First, cross out all the elements in its row. Then cross out all the elements in its column. Then take the determinant of the 2×2 matrix consisting of all the elements that are left. The diagram shows how to find the minor of the element a_2:

$$\begin{vmatrix} a_1 & a_2 & a_3 \\ b_1 & b_2 & b_3 \\ c_1 & c_2 & c_3 \end{vmatrix}$$

There is one complication, though. The signs must alternate. The first term has a positive sign, the second term has a negative sign, and so on. For example:

$$\begin{vmatrix} 2 & 3 & 6 \\ 3 & 4 & 5 \\ 1 & 1 & 2 \end{vmatrix} = 2 \begin{vmatrix} 4 & 5 \\ 1 & 2 \end{vmatrix} - 3 \begin{vmatrix} 3 & 5 \\ 1 & 2 \end{vmatrix} + 6 \begin{vmatrix} 3 & 4 \\ 1 & 1 \end{vmatrix}$$

$$= 2(8 - 5) - 3(6 - 5) + 6(3 - 4)$$

$$= 6 - 3 - 6 = -3.$$

To find the determinant, you don't have to expand along the first row. If there is any row or column that contains many zeros, it is usually easiest to expand along that row (or column). For example:

$$\begin{vmatrix} 1 & 1 & 0 \\ 4 & 6 & 0 \\ 2 & 5 & 3 \end{vmatrix} = 0 \begin{vmatrix} 4 & 6 \\ 2 & 5 \end{vmatrix} - 0 \begin{vmatrix} 1 & 1 \\ 2 & 5 \end{vmatrix} + 3 \begin{vmatrix} 1 & 1 \\ 4 & 6 \end{vmatrix} = 3(6 - 4) = 6.$$

In this case we expanded along the last column.

The determinant of a 3×3 matrix can also be found from the formula

$$\begin{vmatrix} a_1 & a_2 & a_3 \\ b_1 & b_2 & b_3 \\ c_1 & c_2 & c_3 \end{vmatrix} = a_1 b_2 c_3 + c_1 a_2 b_3 + b_1 c_2 a_3$$

$$- c_1 b_2 a_3 - a_1 c_2 b_3 - b_1 a_2 c_3.$$

There is no simple formula for determinants larger than 3×3, but the same method of expansion along a column or row may be used. One useful fact is that the value of the determinant will remain unchanged if you add a multiple of one row (or column) to another row (or column). By careful use of this trick, you can usually create a row consisting mostly of zeros, thus making it easier to evaluate the determinant. Even so, evaluation of large determinants is best left to a computer.

The determinant of a matrix is a number that determines some important properties of the matrix. If the determinant is zero, then the matrix cannot be inverted. (See **inverse matrix**.) Some properties of determinants are as follows:

$$\det(\mathbf{AB}) = \det \mathbf{A} \det \mathbf{B},$$

$$\det \mathbf{I} = 1 \qquad (\mathbf{I} \text{ is the identity matrix}),$$

$$\det \mathbf{A}^{-1} = \frac{1}{\det \mathbf{A}}.$$

Determinants can be used to solve simultaneous linear equation systems. (See **Cramer's rule**.)

DIAGONAL   A diagonal is a line segment connecting two nonadjacent vertices of a polygon. For example, a rectangle has two diagonals, each connecting a pair of opposite corners.

DIAMETER   The diameter of a circle is the length of a line segment joining two points on the circle and passing through the center. The term "diameter" can also mean the segment. The diameter is equal to twice the radius, and $d = c/\pi$, where c is the circumference. The diameter is the longest possible distance across the circle. Our Milky Way galaxy is shaped like a disk with a bulge in the middle. The diameter of the circle that makes up the outer edge of the disk is about 100,000 light-years. The diameter of a sphere is the length of a line segment joining two points on the sphere and passing through the center. The sun is a sphere with a diameter of 865,000 miles.

DIFFERENCE   The difference between two numbers is the result obtained by subtracting them. In the equation $5 - 3 = 2$, the number 2 is the difference. If two points are located along a number line, then the absolute value of their difference will be the distance between them. For example, Bridgeport is at mile 28 of the Connecticut Turnpike, and Stamford is at mile 7. The distance between them is the difference: $28 - 7 = 21$ miles.

DIFFERENCE OF TWO SQUARES   An expression is a difference of two squares if it is of the form $a^2 - b^2$. This expression can be factored as follows:

$$a^2 - b^2 = (a - b)(a + b).$$

DIFFERENTIABLE   A function is differentiable if its derivative exists. (See **calculus; derivative**.) This means that the graph of the function is smooth, with no kinks or cusps.

DIFFERENTIATION   Differentiation is the process of finding a derivative. See **derivative**.

DIGIT   The digits are the 10 symbols 0, 1, 2, 3, 4, 5, 6, 7, 8, 9. For example, 1462 is a four-digit number, and the number 3.46 contains two digits to the right of the decimal point. There are 10 digits in the commonly used decimal system. In the binary system only two digits are used (see **binary numbers**).

DIHEDRAL ANGLE   A dihedral angle is the figure formed by two intersecting planes.

DIMENSION   The dimension of a space is the number of coordinates needed to identify a location in that space. For example, a line is one dimensional; a plane is two dimensional; and the space we live in is three dimensional.

DIRECTION COSINES   The direction cosines of a line are the cosines of the angles that the line makes with the three coordinate axes.

DIRECTLY PROPORTIONAL   If y and x are related by an equation of the form $y = kx$, where k is a constant, then y is said to be directly proportional to x.

DIRECTRIX   A directrix is a line that helps to define a geometric figure. In particular, a directrix line is used in the definition of conic sections.

DISCRETE   A quantity is discrete if it comes in fixed lumps. For example, the number of people in a city is discrete, because there is no such thing as a fractional person. Measurements of time and distance, however, are not discrete. Measurements of the energy levels of electrons in quantum mechanics are discrete, because there are only a few possible values for the energy.

DISCRETE RANDOM VARIABLE   A discrete random variable is a random variable for which a list of all possible values can be made. The density function lists the probability that the variable will take on each of the possible values. The binomial distribution is an example of a discrete random variable distribution. (See **random variable**).

For contrast, see **continuous random variable**.

DISCRIMINANT   The discriminant (D) of a quadratic equation $ax^2 + bx + c = 0$ is $D = b^2 - 4ac$. The discriminant allows you to determine the characteristics of the solution for x. If D is a positive perfect square, then x will have two rational values. If $D = 0$, then x will have one rational solution. If D is positive but is not a perfect square, then x will have two irrational solutions. If D is negative, then x will have two complex solutions. (See **quadratic equation**.)

DISJOINT   Two sets are disjoint if they have no elements in common, that is, if their intersection is the empty set. The set of triangles and the set of quadrilaterals are disjoint.

DISJUNCTION   A disjunction is an OR statement of the form: "A or B." It is true if either A or B is true.

DISTANCE   The distance postulate states that for every two points in space there exists a unique positive number that can be called the distance between these two points. The distance between point A and point B is often written as AB. If $A = (a_1, a_2)$ and $B = (b_1, b_2)$, then the distance between them can be found from the distance formula (which is based on the Pythagorean theorem):

$$AB = \sqrt{(a_1 - b_1)^2 + (a_2 - b_2)^2}.$$

DISTRIBUTIVE PROPERTY   The distributive property says that $a(b + c) = ab + ac$, for all a, b, and c. For example:

$$3(4 + 5) = 3 \cdot 4 + 3 \cdot 5,$$
$$3 \cdot 9 = 12 + 15,$$
$$27 = 27.$$

DIVERGENT SERIES   A divergent series is an infinite series with no finite sum. A series that does have a finite sum is called a convergent series.

DIVIDEND   In the equation $a \div b = c$, a is called the dividend.

DIVISION   Division is the opposite operation of multiplication. If
$a \times b = c$, then $c \div b = a$. For example, $6 \times 8 = 48$, and $48 \div 6 = 8$.
The symbol " $\div$ " is used to represent division in arithmetic. In algebra most divisions are written as fractions: $a \div b = a/b$. For compu-
tational purposes, a/b is symbolized by $a\overline{)b}$.

DIVISOR   In the equation $a \div b = c$, b is called the divisor.

DOMAIN   The domain of a function is the set of all possible values
for the argument (the input number) of the function. (See **function**.)

DOT PRODUCT   The dot product of two n-dimensional vectors
(written as $\mathbf{a} \cdot \mathbf{b}$) is defined to be:

$$\mathbf{a} = (a_1, a_2, a_3, \ldots, a_n),$$

$$\mathbf{b} = (b_1, b_2, b_3, \ldots, b_n),$$

$$\mathbf{a} \cdot \mathbf{b} = (a_1b_1 + a_2b_2 + a_3b_3 + \cdots + a_nb_n).$$

(See **vector**.)
 To find a dot product, you multiply all the corresponding com-
ponents of each vector and then add together all of these products.
In two-dimensional space this becomes:

$$\mathbf{v_1} = (x_1, y_1),$$

$$\mathbf{v_2} = (x_2, y_2),$$

$$\mathbf{v_1} \cdot \mathbf{v_2} = (x_1x_2 + y_1y_2).$$

 Note that the dot product is a number, or scalar, rather than a
vector. The dot product is also called the *scalar product*. Another
form for the dot product can be found by defining the length of each
vector:

$$r_1 = \sqrt{x_1^2 + y_1^2}, \qquad r_2 = \sqrt{x_2^2 + y_2^2}.$$

Then:

$$\mathbf{v_1} \cdot \mathbf{v_2} = r_1r_2 \left(\frac{x_1x_2}{r_1r_2} + \frac{y_1y_2}{r_1r_2} \right).$$

 Let θ_1 be the angle between vector 1 and the x-axis, θ_2 be the
angle between vector 2 and the x-axis, and $\theta = \theta_1 - \theta_2$ be the angle
between the two vectors. Then:

$$\frac{x_1}{r_1} = \cos \theta_1, \qquad \frac{x_2}{r_2} = \cos \theta_2,$$

$$\frac{y_1}{r_1} = \sin \theta_1, \qquad \frac{y_2}{r_2} = \sin \theta_2.$$

We can rewrite the dot product formula:

$$\mathbf{v_1} \cdot \mathbf{v_2} = r_1 r_2 (\cos \theta_1 \cos \theta_2 + \sin \theta_1 \sin \theta_2).$$

Using the formula for the cosine of the difference between two angles gives

$$\mathbf{v_1} \cdot \mathbf{v_2} = r_1 r_2 \cos \theta.$$

The last formula says that the dot product can be found by multiplying the magnitude of the two vectors and the cosine of the angle between them. This means that the dot product is already good for two things:

1. Two nonzero vectors will be perpendicular if and only if their dot product is zero. (A zero dot product means that $\cos \theta = 0$, meaning $\theta = 90°$.)
2. The dot product $\mathbf{a} \cdot \mathbf{b}$ can be used to find the *projection* of vector $\mathbf{a}$ on vector $\mathbf{b}$:

$$\text{projection of } \mathbf{a} \text{ on } \mathbf{b} = \mathbf{P} = \frac{\mathbf{a} \cdot \mathbf{b}}{\mathbf{b} \cdot \mathbf{b}} \mathbf{b}.$$

Note that the quantity $\mathbf{a} \cdot \mathbf{b}/\mathbf{b} \cdot \mathbf{b}$ is a scalar, so the projection vector is formed by multiplying a scalar times the vector $\mathbf{b}$ (see figure).

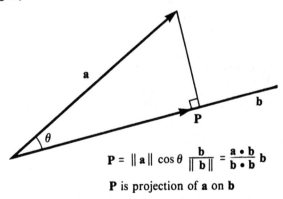

$$\mathbf{P} = \|\mathbf{a}\| \cos \theta \, \frac{\mathbf{b}}{\|\mathbf{b}\|} = \frac{\mathbf{a} \cdot \mathbf{b}}{\mathbf{b} \cdot \mathbf{b}} \mathbf{b}$$

P is projection of **a** on **b**

Here is an example of how the dot product can be used to find the angle between two vectors. The cosine of the angle between the vectors $(1, 1)$ and $(2, 4)$ will be given by

$$\cos \theta = \frac{1 \cdot 2 + 1 \cdot 4}{\sqrt{2} \times \sqrt{20}} = 0.95,$$

$$\theta = \arccos 0.95 = 18°.$$

DOUBLE INTEGRAL The double integral of a two-variable function $f(x, y)$ represents the volume under the curve in a specific region. For example, consider a sphere of radius r with center at the origin. The equation of this sphere is

$$x^2 + y^2 + z^2 = r^2.$$

The equation

$$z = f(x, y) = \sqrt{r^2 - x^2 - y^2}$$

defines a surface, which is the top half of the sphere. The volume below this surface and above the plane $z = 0$ is given by the double integral

$$\int_{-r}^{r} \int_{-\sqrt{r^2 - x^2}}^{\sqrt{r^2 - x^2}} \sqrt{r^2 - x^2 - y^2} \, dy \, dx.$$

To evaluate the double integral it is necessary to determine the limits of integration. In this case the values for y will be from $-\sqrt{r^2 - x^2}$ to $\sqrt{r^2 - x^2}$, and the limits for x will be from $-r$ to r.

Evaluate the inner integral (involving y) first, using the trigonometric substitution $y = \sin \theta$. While evaluating the inner integral, treat x as a constant:

$$\int_{-\sqrt{r^2 - x^2}}^{\sqrt{r^2 - x^2}} \sqrt{r^2 - x^2 - y^2} \, dy = \frac{\pi}{2}(r^2 - x^2).$$

Now evaluate the outer integral involving x:

$$\int_{-r}^{r} \frac{\pi}{2}(r^2 - x^2) \, dx = \tfrac{2}{3}\pi r^3.$$

DYADIC OPERATION A dyadic operation is an operation that requires two operands. For example, addition is a dyadic operation. The logical operation AND is dyadic, but the logical operation NOT is not dyadic.

E

---

e The letter *e* is used to represent a fundamental irrational number with the decimal approximation $e = 2.7182818\ldots$. The letter *e* is the base of the natural logarithm function. (See **calculus; logarithm**.) The area under the curve $y = 1/x$ from $x = 1$ to $x = e$ is equal to 1. The value of *e* can be found from this series:

$$e = 2 + \frac{1}{2!} + \frac{1}{3!} + \frac{1}{4!} + \frac{1}{5!} + \cdots.$$

The value of *e* can also be found from the expression

$$e = \lim_{w \to 0} (1 + w)^{1/w}.$$

ECCENTRICITY The eccentricity of a conic section is a number that indicates the shape of the conic section. The eccentricity (*e*) is the distance to the focal point divided by the distance to the directrix line. (This ratio will be a constant, according to the definition of a conic section. See **conic section**.) If $e = 1$, then the conic section is a parabola; if $e > 1$, it is a hyperbola; and if $e < 1$, it is an ellipse.

The eccentricity of an ellipse measures how far the ellipse differs from being a circle. You can think of a circle as being normal (eccentricity = 0), with the ellipses becoming more and more eccentric as they become flatter. The eccentricity of the ellipse $x^2/a^2 + y^2/b^2 = 1$ is equal to

$$e = \frac{\sqrt{a^2 - b^2}}{a}.$$

EDGE The edge of a polyhedron is a line segment where two faces intersect. For example, a cube has 12 edges.

ELEMENT An element of a set is a member of the set.

ELLIPSE   An ellipse is the set of all points in a plane such that the sum of the distances to two fixed points is a constant. Ellipses look like flattened circles (see Figure 1). The two fixed points are known as the *foci*. The longest distance across the ellipse is known as the *major axis*. (Half of this distance is known as the *semimajor axis*.) The shortest distance across is the *minor axis*.

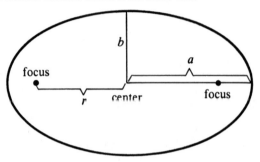

FIGURE 1

The center of the ellipse is the midpoint of the segment that joins the two foci. The equation of an ellipse with center at the origin is

$$\frac{x^2}{a^2} + \frac{y^2}{b^2} = 1,$$

where a is the length of the semimajor axis, and b is the length of the semiminor axis. The equation of an ellipse with center at point (h, k) is

$$\frac{(x - h)^2}{a^2} + \frac{(y - k)^2}{b^2} = 1.$$

(In each of these cases the ellipse is oriented so that the foci are along the x-axis. To learn how to find the equation of an ellipse with a different orientation, see **rotation**.)

The area of an ellipse is $A = \pi ab$.

The shape of an ellipse can be characterized by a number that measures the degree of flattening, known as the *eccentricity*. The eccentricity (e) is

$$e = \frac{\sqrt{a^2 - b^2}}{a} = \frac{r}{a},$$

where *r* is defined in Figure 1. When $e = 0$, there is no flattening and the ellipse is the same as a circle. As *e* becomes larger, the ellipse becomes flatter and flatter (see Figure 2).

An ellipse can also be defined as the set of points such that the distance to a fixed point divided by the distance to a fixed line is a constant that is less than 1. The constant is the eccentricity of the ellipse. (See **conic sections.**)

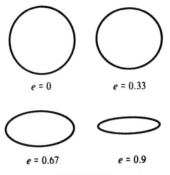

$e = 0$ $e = 0.33$

$e = 0.67$ $e = 0.9$

FIGURE 2

One reason why ellipses are important is that the path of an orbiting planet is an ellipse, with the sun at one focus. The orbit of the earth is an ellipse that is almost a perfect circle. Its eccentricity is only 0.017.

ELLIPSOID An ellipsoid is a solid of revolution formed by rotating an ellipse about one of its axes. If the ellipse has semimajor axis *a* and semiminor axis *b*, then the ellipsoid formed by rotating the ellipse about its major axis will have the volume $\frac{4}{3}\pi a^2 b$.

EMPTY SET An empty set is a set that contains no elements. For example, the set of all people over 100 feet tall is an example of an empty set. It is symbolized by $\varnothing$.

EQUATION An equation is a statement that says that two mathematical expressions have the same value. The symbol "$=$" means "equals," as in $4 \times 5 = 20$. If all the items in an equation are numbers, then the equation is an arithmetic equation and it is either true or false. For example, $10 + 25 = 35$ is true, but $2 + 2 = 5$ is false. If the equation contains a letter that represents an unknown number,

EQUATION 74

then there will usually be some values of the unknown that make the equation true. For example, the equation $5 + 3 = x$ is true if x has the value 8; otherwise it is false. An equation in one unknown is said to be solved when it is written in the form $x = $ (expression), where (expression) depends only on numbers or on letters that stand for known quantities.

When solving an equation, the basic rule is: Whatever you do to one side of the equation, make sure you do exactly the same thing to the other side. For example, the equation $10x + 5 = 6x + 2$ can be solved by subtracting $6x + 2$ from both sides:

$$10x + 5 - (6x + 2) = 0,$$
$$4x + 3 = 0.$$

Subtract 3 from both sides:

$$4x = -3.$$

Divide both sides by 4:

$$x = -\frac{3}{4}.$$

However, you cannot divide both sides of an equation by zero, since division by zero is meaningless. It also does no good to multiply both sides by zero. Squaring both sides of an equation, or multiplying both sides by an expression that might equal zero, can sometimes introduce an extraneous root: a root that is a solution of the new equation but is not a solution of the original equation. For example, you might solve the equation $\sqrt{x^2 - 2x + 1} = 2x - 5$ by squaring both sides:

$$x^2 - 2x + 1 = 4x^2 - 20x + 25,$$
$$3x^2 - 18x + 24 = 0,$$
$$x^2 - 6x + 8 = 0,$$
$$(x - 4)(x - 2) = 0.$$

In this case $x = 4$ does satisfy the original equation, but $x = 2$ does not. This means that $x = 2$ is an extraneous root.

An equation that can be put in the general form $ax + b = 0$, where x is unknown and a and b are known, is called a *linear equation*. Any one unknown equation can be written in this form provided that it contains no terms with x^2, $1/x$, or any term with x raised to any power other than 1. An equation that contains terms involving x^2 and x is called a *quadratic equation*, and can be written in the form $ax^2 + bx + c = 0$. For equations involving higher powers of x, see **polynomial**.

When an equation contains two unknowns, there will in general be many possible pairs of the unknowns that make the equation true. For example, $2x + y = 20$ will be satisfied by $x = 0$, $y = 20$; $x = 5$, $y = 10$; $x = 10$, $y = 0$; and many other pairs of values. In a case like this, you can often solve for one unknown as a function of the other, and you can draw a picture of the relationship between the unknowns. Also, you can find a unique solution for the two unknowns if you have two equations that must be true simultaneously. (See **simultaneous equations**.)

Another kind of equation is an equation that is true for all values of the unknown. This type of equation is called an *identity*. For example, $y^3 = y \times y \times y$ is true for every possible value of y. Usually it is possible to tell from the context the difference between a regular (or conditional) equation and an identity, but sometimes a symbol with three lines ("$\equiv$") is used to indicate an identity:

$$\sin^2 x + \cos^2 x \equiv 1.$$

The above equation is true for every possible value of x.

EQUILATERAL TRIANGLE   An equilateral triangle is a triangle with three equal sides. All three of the angles in an equilateral triangle are 60° angles. The area of an equilateral triangle of side s is $s^2\sqrt{3}/4$.

EQUIVALENT   Two logic sentences are equivalent if they will always have the same truth value. For example, the sentence "$p \rightarrow q$" ("IF p THEN q") is equivalent to the sentence "$\sim q \rightarrow \sim p$."

EQUIVALENT EQUATIONS   Two equations are equivalent if their solutions are the same. For example, the equation $x + y = 10$ is equivalent to the equation $2x + 2y = 20$.

ESTIMATOR   An estimator is a quantity, based on observations of a sample, whose value is taken as an indicator of the value of an unknown population parameter. For example, the sample average $\bar{x}$ is often used as an estimator of the unknown population mean μ. (See **statistical inference**.)

EUCLIDIAN GEOMETRY   Euclidian geometry is the geometry based on the postulates of Euclid, who lived in Alexandria in 300 B.C. Euclidian geometry in three-dimensional space corresponds to our intuitive ideas of what space is like.

EULER'S CIRCLES   Euler's circles are a diagrammatic way of representing the relationships between classes of objects. If one set is entirely contained within another set, it is represented by a circle located inside the circle representing the other set. If two sets do not intersect, they are represented by two nonintersecting circles. If two sets contain some members in common, they are represented by two intersecting circles; the intersection position represents the common members of both sets.

EVEN FUNCTION   The function $f(x)$ is an even function if it satisfies the property that $f(x) = f(-x)$. For example, $f(x) = \cos x$ and $g(x) = x^2$ are both even functions.

EVEN NUMBER   An even number is a natural number that is divisible evenly by 2. For example, 2, 4, 6, 8, 10, 12, and 14 are all even numbers. Any number whose last digit is 0, 2, 4, 6, or 8 is even.

EXISTENTIAL QUANTIFIER   A backwards letter E, "∃," is used to represent the expression "There exists at least one. . . ," and is called the existential quantifier. For example, the sentence "There exists at least one x such that $x^2 = x$" can be written with symbols:

$$(1) \qquad \exists_x\,(x^2 = x).$$

For another example, let P_x represent the sentence "x is a politician," and H_x represent the sentence "x is honest." Then the expression

$$(2) \qquad \exists_x\,[(P_x) \text{ AND } (H_x)]$$

represents the sentence "There exists at least one x such that x is both a politician and x is honest." In more informal terms, the sentence could be written as "Some politicians are honest."

You must be careful when you determine the negation for a sentence that uses the existential quantifier. The negation of sentence (2) is not the sentence "Some politicians are not honest," which could be written as

$$(3) \qquad \exists_x\,[(P_x) \text{ AND } (\sim H_x)].$$

Instead, the negation of sentence (2) is the sentence "No politicians are honest," which can be written symbolically as

$$(4) \qquad \sim(\exists_x)\,[(P_x) \text{ AND } (H_x)].$$

Sentence (4) could also be written as

(5) $\forall_x [(P_x) \rightarrow (\sim H_x)].$

(See **universal quantifier**.)

EXPECTATION   The expectation of a discrete random variable X with a density function $f(x_i)$ is

$$E(X) = \sum_i x_i f(x_i),$$

where the summation is taken over all possible values for X. The expectation is the average value that you would expect to see if you conducted an experiment to measure X. For example, if you flip a coin five times and X is the number of heads that appears, then $E(X) = 2.5$. This is what you would expect: the number of heads should be about half of the number of total flips. (Note that $E(X)$ itself does not have to be a possible value of X.)

The expectation of a continuous random variable with density function $f(x)$ is

$$E(X) = \int_{-\infty}^{\infty} x f(x)\, dx.$$

Some properties of expectations are as follows:

$E(A + B) = E(A) + E(B),$

$E(AB) = E(A)E(B) + \text{Cov}(A, B)$

   ($\text{Cov}(A, B)$ is the *covariance* of A and B),

$E(cX) = cE(X)$ (if c is a constant).

The expectation of a random variable is also called the mean of the distribution of the random variable. If the value of the summation (or the integral) used in the definition is infinite for a particular distribution, then it is said that the mean of the distribution does not exist.

EXPONENT   An exponent is a number that indicates the operation of repeated multiplication. Exponents are written as little numbers raised above the main line. For example:

$3^2 = 3 \cdot 3 = 9, \quad 2^4 = 2 \cdot 2 \cdot 2 \cdot 2 = 16, \quad 10^3 = 10 \cdot 10 \cdot 10 = 1000.$

The exponent number is also called the *power* that the base is being raised to. The second power of x (x^2) is called x squared, and the third power of x (x^3) is called x cubed.

Exponents obey these properties:

1. Addition property: $x^a x^b = x^{a+b}$
   For example: $4^3 \cdot 4^5 = (4 \cdot 4 \cdot 4)(4 \cdot 4 \cdot 4 \cdot 4 \cdot 4) = 4^8$.
2. Subtraction property: $x^a/x^b = x^{a-b}$
   For example: $2^6/2^2 = 2 \cdot 2 \cdot 2 \cdot 2 \cdot 2 \cdot 2/2 \cdot 2 = 2 \cdot 2 \cdot 2 \cdot 2 = 2^4$.
3. Multiplication property: $(x^a)^b = x^{ab}$
   For example: $(3^2)^3 = 3^2 \cdot 3^2 \cdot 3^2 = (3 \cdot 3) \cdot (3 \cdot 3) \cdot (3 \cdot 3) = 3^6$.

So far it makes sense to use only exponents that are positive integers. There are definitions that we can make, however, that will allow us to use negative exponents or fractional exponents.

For negative exponents, we define:

$$x^{-a} = \frac{1}{x^a}.$$

For example, $x^{-1} = 1/x$, $2^{-5} = 1/2^5 = 1/32$. This definition is consistent with the subtraction property:

$$3^{-2} = \frac{3^4}{3^6} = \frac{3 \cdot 3 \cdot 3 \cdot 3}{3 \cdot 3 \cdot 3 \cdot 3 \cdot 3 \cdot 3} = \frac{1}{3 \cdot 3} = \frac{1}{3^2}.$$

If the exponent is zero, we define:

$$x^0 = 1 \quad \text{for all } x \quad (x \neq 0).$$

This definition seems peculiar at first, but we must have $x^0 = 1$ if the addition property of exponents is to be satisfied:

$$3^4 = 3^{4+0} = 3^4 \cdot 3^0 = (3 \cdot 3 \cdot 3 \cdot 3) \cdot (3^0).$$

To find the value of a fractional exponent, we define a fractional exponent to be the same as taking a root. For example, $x^{1/2} = \sqrt{x}$.
By the multiplication property: $(x^{1/2})^2 = x^{2/2} = x^1$.
In general: $x^{1/a} = \sqrt[a]{x}$ and $x^{a/b} = (\sqrt[b]{x})^a$. (See **root**.)

EXPONENTIAL FUNCTION An exponential function is a function of the form $f(x) = a^x$, where a is a constant known as the base. The most common exponential function is $f(x) = e^x$ (see **e**), which has the interesting property that its derivative is equal to itself. Exponential functions can be used as approximations for the rate of population growth or the growth of compound interest. The inverse function of an exponential function is the logarithm function.

EXPONENTIAL NOTATION Exponential notation provides a way of expressing very big and very small numbers on computers. A number in exponential notation is written as the product of a number from 1 to 10 and a power of 10. The letter E is used to indicate what power of 10 is needed. For example, 3.8 E 5 means 3.8×10^5. Exponential notation is the same as *scientific notation*.

EXTERIOR ANGLE   An exterior angle of a polygon is an angle formed by one side of the polygon and the line that is the extension of an adjacent side.

   When a line crosses two other lines, the four angles formed that are outside the two lines are called exterior angles. (See figure.)

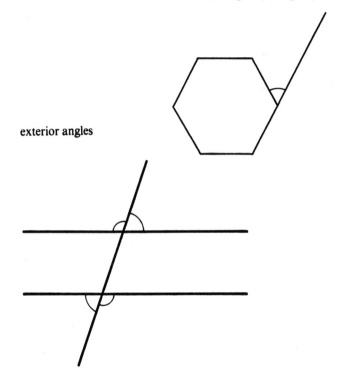

exterior angles

EXTRANEOUS ROOT   See equation.

EXTREMES OF A PROPORTION   In the proportion $a/b = c/d$, a and d are called the extremes of the proportion.

F

F-DISTRIBUTION   The *F*-distribution is a continuous random variable distribution that is frequently used in statistical inference. (For an example, see **analysis of variance**.) There are many different *F*-distributions. Each one is identified by specifying two quantities, called the degree of freedom for the numerator (listed first) and the degree of freedom for the denominator. Table 8 at the back of the book lists some values. For example, there is a 95 percent chance that an *F*-distribution with 5 and 20 degrees of freedom will be less than 2.71.

If *X* is a random variable with a chi-square distribution with *m* degrees of freedom, and *Y* has a chi-square distribution with *n* degrees of freedom that is independent of *X*, then this random variable:

$$\frac{X/m}{Y/n}$$

will have an *F*-distribution with *m* and *n* degrees of freedom.

FACE   A polyhedron consists of several sections of planes, each of which is called a face. For example, dice and all other cubes have six faces. A triangular pyramid has four faces, and a square-based pyramid has five faces.

FACTOR   (1) A factor is one of two or more expressions that are multiplied together. The factors of a number are its integral divisors.
(2) To factor an expression means to express it as a product of several factors. For example, the expression $x^2 - 2x - 15$ can be factored into the following product: $(x + 3)(x - 5)$. (See **factoring**.)

FACTORIAL   The factorial of a positive integer is the product of all the integers from 1 up to the integer in question. The exclamation point ("!") is used to designate factorial. For example,

$1! = 1, \quad 2! = 2 \times 1 = 2, \quad 3! = 3 \times 2 \times 1 = 6, \quad 4! = 4 \times 3 \times 2 \times 1 = 24,$

$5! = 5 \times 4 \times 3 \times 2 \times 1 = 120, \qquad n! = n(n-1)(n-2)\ldots 3 \times 2 \times 1.$

By convention, the factorial of zero is defined to be 1: $0! = 1$. Factorials become very big very fast. Thus 69! (read: "sixty-nine factorial") is equal to 1.7×10^{98}. Factorials are used extensively in probability. (See **probability; permutations; combinations.**) There are $52! = 8.1 \times 10^{67}$ ways of shuffling a deck of cards. There are 52 choices for the top card. For each choice of the top card there are 51 choices for the second card. For each of these combinations there are 50 choices for the third card, and so on. Factorials are also used in the *binomial theorem*.

FACTORING Factoring is the process of splitting a complicated expression into the product of two or more simpler expressions, called factors. For example, $x^2 - 5x + 6$ can be split into two factors:

$$x^2 - 5x + 6 = (x - 3)(x - 2).$$

Factoring is a useful technique for solving polynomial equations and for simplifying complicated fractions. Some general tricks for factoring are:

1. If all the terms have a common factor, then that factor can be pulled out:

$$ax^3 + bx^2 + cx = x(ax^2 + bx + c).$$

2. The expression $x^2 + bx + c$ can be factored if you can find two numbers m and n that multiply to give c and add to give b:

$$(x + m)(x + n) = x^2 + (m + n)x + mn.$$

3. The difference of two squares can always be factored:

$$a^2 - b^2 = (a - b)(a + b).$$

4. The difference of two cubes can be factored:

$$(x^3 - a^3) = (x - a)(x^2 + ax + a^2).$$

5. The sum of two cubes can be factored:

$$(x^3 + a^3) = (x + a)(x^2 - ax + a^2).$$

FACTOR THEOREM Suppose that $P(x)$ represents a polynomial in x. The factor theorem says that, if $P(r) = 0$, then $(x - r)$ is one of the factors of $P(x)$.

FALSE "False" is one of the two truth values attached to sentences in logic. It corresponds to what we normally suppose: "false" means "not true." (See **logic; Boolean algebra.**)

FEASIBLE SOLUTION   A feasible solution is a set of values for the choice variables in a linear programming problem that satisfies the constraints of the problem. (See **linear programming**.)

FIELD   A field is a set of at least two elements for which two operations (called *addition* and *multiplication*) are defined, which satisfy the closure, associative, commutative, and distributive properties.

FINITE   Something is finite if it doesn't take forever to count or measure it. The opposite of finite is infinite, which means limitless. There is an infinite number of natural numbers. There is a finite (but very large) number of grains of sand on Palm Beach or of stars in the Milky Way galaxy.

FIXED POINT NUMBER   A fixed point number is a number stored in a computer in which the number of digits to the right of the decimal point is constant. For example, an amount of money in U.S. currency can be represented by a fixed point number with two digits to the right of the decimal point.

For contrast, see **floating point number.**

FLOATING POINT NUMBER   A floating point number is a number stored in a computer in which the number of digits to the right of the decimal point is allowed to vary. A floating point number is represented by a base and an exponent. For example, in the floating point number 4.65 E 4, 4.65 is the base and 4 is the exponent. (See **exponential notation**.)

For contrast, see **fixed point number.**

FOCI   "Foci" is the plural of *focus.*

FOCUS   (1) A parabola is the set of points that are the same distance from a fixed point (the focus) and a fixed line (the directrix). The focus, or focal point, is important because starlight striking a parabolically shaped telescope mirror will be reflected back to the focus.

(2) An ellipse is the set of points such that the sum of the distances to two fixed points is a constant. The two points are called foci (plural of "focus"). Planetary orbits are shaped like ellipses, with the sun at one focus.

FORCE   A force in physics acts to cause an object to move, or else restrains its motion. For example, gravity is a force. A force is a vector quantity because it has both magnitude and direction. (See **resolution of forces; acceleration**.)

FOURTH PROPORTIONAL If you are given three numbers, a, b, and c, their fourth proportional is the number, d, that will complete the proportion involving those numbers, $a/b = c/d$, that is, $d = bc/a$.

FRACTION A fraction a/b is defined by the equation

$$\frac{a}{b} \times b = a.$$

The fractional number a/b is the same as the answer to the division problem $a \div b$. The top of the fraction (a) is called the *numerator*, and the bottom of the fraction (b) is called the *denominator*. Suppose that the fraction measures the amount of pie that you have. Then the denominator tells you how many equal slices the pie has been cut into, and the numerator tells you how many slices you have. The fraction $\frac{1}{8}$ says that the pie has been cut into eight pieces, and you have only one of them. If you have $\frac{8}{8}$, then you have eight pieces, or the whole pie. In general, $a/a = 1$ for all a (except $a = 0$). If $a > b$ in the fraction a/b, then you have more than a whole pie and the value of the fraction is greater than 1. A fraction greater than 1 is sometimes called an improper fraction. An improper fraction can always be written as the sum of an integer and a proper fraction. For example, $\frac{10}{3} = \frac{9}{3} + \frac{1}{3} = 3 + \frac{1}{3} = 3\frac{1}{3}$.

The fraction a/b becomes larger if a becomes larger, but it becomes smaller if b becomes larger. For example, $\frac{5}{11} < \frac{6}{11}$, and $\frac{5}{11} > \frac{5}{12}$.

The value of the fraction is unchanged if both the top and the bottom are multiplied by the same number: $a/b = ac/bc$. For example, $\frac{4}{5} = (3 \times 4)/(3 \times 5) = \frac{12}{15}$.

A decimal fraction, such as $\frac{1}{4} = 0.25$, is a fraction in which the part to the right of the decimal point is assumed to be the numerator of a fraction that has some power of 10 in the denominator. (See **decimal numbers**.) Decimal fractions are easier to add and compare than ordinary fractions.

A fraction is said to be in simplest form if there are no common factors between the numerator and the denominator. For example, $\frac{2}{3}$ is in simplest form because 2 and 3 have no common factors. However, $\frac{24}{30}$ is not in simplest form. To put it in simplest form, multiply both the top and the bottom by $\frac{1}{6}$:

$$\frac{\frac{1}{6} \times 24}{\frac{1}{6} \times 30} = \frac{4}{5}.$$

FRUSTUM A frustum is a portion of a cone or a pyramid bounded by two parallel planes. (See figure.)

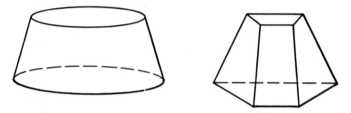

Frustum of Cone   Frustum of Pyramid

FUNCTION A function is a rule that turns each member of one set into a member of another set. The most common functions are functions that turn one number into another number.

For example, the function $f(x) = 3x^2 + 5$ turns 1 into 8, 2 into 17, 3 into 32, and so on.

The input number to the function is called the *independent variable*, or argument. The set of all possible values for the independent variable is called the *domain*. The output number is called the *dependent variable*. The set of all possible values for the dependent variable is called the *range*.

Here are some common functions with their ranges and domains (assuming that we are considering only real numbers):

Function	Domain	Range
$y = f(x) = 3x$	all real numbers	all real numbers
$y = f(x) = x^2$	all real numbers	all nonnegative real numbers
$y = f(x) = \sin x$	all real numbers	$-1 \leq y \leq 1$
$y = f(x) = e^x$	all real numbers	$y > 0$
$y = f(x) = 1/x$	$x \neq 0$	$y \neq 0$
$y = f(x) = \ln x$	$x > 0$	all real numbers
$y = f(x) = \sqrt{x}$	$x \geq 0$	$y \geq 0$

An important property of functions is that for each value of the independent variable there is one and only one value of the dependent variable. For example, the equation of a circle $(x^2 + y^2 = r^2)$ does not define y as a function of x, since for every value of x there are two values of y ($\sqrt{r^2 - x^2}$ and $-\sqrt{r^2 - x^2}$).

An *inverse function* does exactly the opposite of the original function. If you put x into the original function and get out y, then, if you put y into the inverse function, you will get out x. The range of the inverse function is the same as the domain of the original function, and vice versa. For example, the logarithm function is the inverse of the exponential function, and the arcsin function is the inverse of the sine function.

FUNDAMENTAL THEOREM OF ALGEBRA The fundamental theorem of algebra says that an nth-degree polynomial equation has exactly n roots, provided that you include complex roots and you realize that a root may occur more than once. (See **polynomial**.)

FUNDAMENTAL THEOREM OF ARITHMETIC The fundamental theorem of arithmetic says that any natural number can be expressed as a unique product of prime numbers. (See **prime factors**.)

FUNDAMENTAL THEOREM OF CALCULUS The fundamental theorem of calculus says that

$$\lim_{n \to \infty, \Delta x \to 0} \sum_{i=1}^{n} f(x_i)\, \Delta x = F(b) - F(a),$$

where $x_1 = a$, $x_n = b$, $\Delta x = (b - a)/n$, and $dF(x)/dx = f(x)$. The theorem tells how to find the area under a curve by taking an *integral*. (See **calculus**.)

G

GAUSS-JORDAN ELIMINATION Gauss-Jordan elimination is a method for solving a system of linear equations. The method involves transforming the system so that the last equation contains only one variable, the next-to-last equation contains only two variables, and so on. The system is easy to solve when it is in that form. For example, to solve this system:

$$2x - 3y + z = 5$$
$$6x + y - 5z = 51$$
$$4x + 14y - 8z = 100$$

eliminate the term with x from the last two equations. To do this, subtract twice the first equation from the last equation to obtain a new last equation, and subtract three times the first equation from the second equation to obtain a new second equation. The system then looks like this:

$$2x - 3y + z = 5$$
$$10y - 8z = 36$$
$$20y - 10z = 90$$

Now, to eliminate the term with y from the last equation, subtract twice the second equation from the last equation. Here is the new system:

$$2x - 3y + z = 5$$
$$10y - 8z = 36$$
$$6z = 18$$

Solve the last equation for z (solution: $z = 3$). Then insert this value for z into the second equation to solve for y (solution: $y = 6$). Finally, insert the values for z and y into the first equation to solve for x (solution: $x = 10$).

GEOMETRIC CONSTRUCTION Geometric construction is the process of drawing geometric figures using only two instruments: a straightedge and a compass.

GEOMETRIC MEAN The geometric mean of a group of n numbers $(a_1, a_2, a_3, \ldots, a_n)$ is equal to $(a_1 \times a_2 \times a_3 \times \cdots \times a_n)^{1/n}$. For example, the geometric mean of 4 and 9 is $\sqrt{4 \times 9} = 6$.

GEOMETRIC PROGRESSION See **geometric sequence**.

GEOMETRIC SEQUENCE   A geometric sequence is a sequence of numbers of the form $a, ar, ar^2, ar^3, \ldots, ar^{n-1}$. The ratio between any two consecutive terms is a constant.

GEOMETRIC SERIES   A geometric series is a sum of terms of this form:

$$S = a + ar + ar^2 + ar^3 + ar^4 + \cdots + ar^{n-1}.$$

In a geometric series the ratio of any two terms is a constant (in this case r). The sum of the first n terms of the geometric series above is

$$\sum_{i=0}^{n-1} ar^i = \frac{a(1-r^n)}{1-r}.$$

For example:

$$2 + 4 + 8 + 16 + 32 + 64 = \frac{(2)(1-2^6)}{1-2} = 126.$$

If n approaches infinity, then the summation will also go to infinity if $|r| > 1$. However, if $-1 < r < 1$, then r^n approaches zero, so the expression for the sum of the terms becomes

$$\sum_{i=0}^{\infty} ar^i = \frac{a}{1-r}.$$

For example:

$$1 + \tfrac{1}{2} + \tfrac{1}{4} + \tfrac{1}{8} + \tfrac{1}{16} + \tfrac{1}{32} + \cdots = \frac{1}{1-\frac{1}{2}} = 2.$$

GEOMETRY   Geometry is the study of shape and size. Normal geometry is based on the work of Euclid, who lived in 300 B.C. Euclidian geometry has a rigorously developed logical structure. Three basic undefined terms are *point*, *line*, and *plane*. A point is like a tiny dot: it has zero height, zero width, and zero thickness. A line goes off straight in both directions. A plane is a flat surface, like a tabletop, extending off to infinity. We cannot see any of these idealized objects, but we can imagine them and draw pictures to represent them. Euclid developed some basic postulates, which include "Two distinct points are contained in one and only one line" and "Three distinct points not on the same line are contained in one and only one plane."

The geometry of flat figures is called plane geometry, because a flat figure is contained in a plane. The geometry of figures in three-dimensional space is called solid geometry.

Other types of geometries (called non-Euclidian geometries) have been developed, which make different assumptions about the nature of parallel lines. Although these geometries do not match our intuitive concept of what space is like, they have been useful in developing general relativity theory.

GRADIENT The gradient of a multivariable function is a vector consisting of the partial derivatives of that function. If $f(x, y, z)$ is a function of three variables, then the gradient of f, written as ∇f, is the vector $(\partial f/\partial x, \partial f/\partial y, \partial f/\partial z)$. For example, if

$$f(x, y, z) = x^a y^b z^c,$$

then the gradient is the vector

$$(ax^{a-1}y^b z^c, bx^a y^{b-1} z^c, cx^a y^b z^{c-1}).$$

If the gradient is evaluated at a particular point (x_1, y_1, z_1), then the gradient points in the direction of the greatest increase of the function f, starting at the point (x_1, y_1, z_1). If the gradient is equal to the zero vector at a particular point, then that point is a local maximum or minimum.

GRAPH The graph of an equation is the set of points that make the equation true. By drawing a picture of the graph it is possible to visualize an algebraic equation. For example, the set of points that make the equation $x^2 + y^2 = r^2$ true is a circle.

GREAT CIRCLE A great circle is a circle that is formed by the intersection of a sphere and a plane passing through the center. (See **sphere**.)

GROUPED DATA The term "grouped data" refers to a way of arranging data whereby, instead of each individual value being listed, a table is made that shows how many values fall within certain categories. For example, if you have data listing the incomes for 50 million different families, you are not likely to want to look at a list of all 50 million different values. Instead, you would like a table showing how many families had incomes from $15,000 to $16,000, how many had incomes from $16,000 to $17,000, and so on.

H

HALF PLANE A half plane is the set of all points in a plane that lie on one side of a line.

HARMONIC SEQUENCE A sequence of numbers is a harmonic sequence if the reciprocals of the terms form an arithmetic sequence. The general form of a harmonic sequence is

$$\frac{1}{a}, \quad \frac{1}{a+d}, \quad \frac{1}{a+2d}, \quad \frac{1}{a+3d}, \quad \cdots, \quad \frac{1}{a+(n-1)d}.$$

HEPTAGON A heptagon is a polygon with seven sides.

HERO'S FORMULA Hero's formula tells how to find the area of a triangle if you know the length of its sides. Let a, b, and c be the lengths of the sides, and let $s = (a + b + c)/2$. Then the area of the triangle is given by the formula

$$\sqrt{s(s-a)(s-b)(s-c)}.$$

HEXADECIMAL NUMBER A hexadecimal number is a number written in base 16. A hexadecimal system consists of 16 possible digits. The digits from 0 to 9 are the same as they are in the decimal system. The letter A is used to represent 10; B = 11; C = 12; D = 13; E = 14; and F = 15. For example, the number A4C2 in hexadecimal means

$$10 \times 16^3 + 4 \times 16^2 + 12 \times 16^1 + 2 \times 16^0 = 42,178.$$

HEXAGON A hexagon is a six-sided polygon. The sum of the angles in a hexagon is 720°. Regular hexagons have six equal sides and six equal angles of 120°.

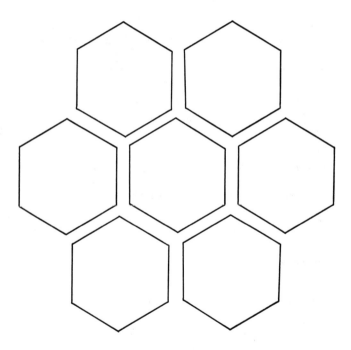

Honeycombs are shaped like hexagons, for a good reason. With a fixed perimeter, the area of a polygon increases as the number of sides increases. If you have a fixed amount of fencing, you will have more area if you build a square rather than a triangle. A pentagon would be even better, and a circle would be best of all. There is one disadvantage to adding more sides, though. If a polygon has too many sides, you can't pack several of those polygons together without wasting a lot of space. You can't pack circles tightly, or even octagons. You can pack hexagons, though. Hexagons make a nice compromise: they have more area for a fixed perimeter than any other polygon that can be packed together tightly with others of the same type (see figure).

HISTOGRAM A histogram is a bar diagram that illustrates the frequency distribution for a set of data. Each bar is drawn so that its area is proportional to the number of items in the interval it represents.

HYPERBOLA A hyperbola is the set of all points such that the difference between the distances to two fixed points is a constant. A hyperbola has two branches that are mirror images of each other.

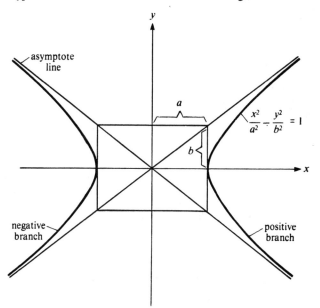

Each branch looks like a misshaped parabola. The general equation for a hyperbola with center at the origin is

$$\frac{x^2}{a^2} - \frac{y^2}{b^2} = 1.$$

The meaning of a and b is shown in the figure. The two diagonal lines are called *asymptotes*. As x gets larger and larger, the positive branch of the curve will come closer and closer to the asymptote line, but it will never actually touch it.

HYPERBOLIC FUNCTIONS The hyperbolic functions are a set of functions defined as follows:

hyperbolic cosine: $\cosh x = \frac{1}{2}(e^x + e^{-x})$

hyperbolic sine: $\sinh x = \frac{1}{2}(e^x - e^{-x})$

hyperbolic tangent: $\tanh x = \dfrac{\sinh x}{\cosh x}$

For an example of an application, see **catenary**.

HYPERGEOMETRIC DISTRIBUTION The hypergeometric distribution is a discrete random variable distribution that applies when you are selecting a sample without replacement from a population. Suppose that the population contains M "desirable" objects and $N - M$ "undesirable" objects. Select n objects from the population at random without replacement (in other words, once an object has been selected, you will not return it to the population and therefore it cannot be selected again). Let X be the number of desirable objects in your sample. Then X is a discrete random variable with the hypergeometric distribution. Its density function is given by this formula:

$$\Pr(X = i) = \frac{\dbinom{M}{i} \times \dbinom{N-M}{n-1}}{\dbinom{N}{n}}$$

The symbols

$$\binom{M}{i}, \binom{N-M}{n-i}, \text{ and } \binom{N}{n}$$

are all examples of the binomial coefficient. (See **binomial theorem**.) The expected value of X is equal to nM/N, and its variance is

$$n\left(\frac{M}{N}\right)\left(1 - \frac{M}{N}\right)\left(\frac{N-n}{N-1}\right).$$

HYPOTENUSE The hypotenuse is the side in a right triangle that is opposite the right angle. It is the longest of the three sides in the triangle. (See **Pythagorean theorem**.)

HYPOTHESIS A hypothesis is a proposition that is being investigated; it has yet to be proved. (See **hypothesis testing**.)

Hypothesis is also used to mean the antecedent of a conditional statement. (See **antecedent**.)

HYPOTHESIS TESTING A situation often arises where a researcher needs to test a hypothesis about the nature of the world. Frequently it is necessary to use a statistical technique known as hypothesis testing for this purpose.

The hypothesis that is being tested is termed the *null hypothesis*. (The other possible hypothesis, which says "The null hypothesis is wrong," is called the *alternative hypothesis*.) Here are some examples of null hypotheses:

"There is no significant difference in effectiveness between Brand X cold medicine and Brand Z medicine."

"On average, the favorite colors for Democrats are the same as the favorite colors for Republicans."

"The average reading ability of fourth graders who watch less than 10 hours of television per week is above that of fourth graders who watch more than 10 hours of television."

The term "null hypothesis" is used because the hypothesis that is being tested is often of the form "There is no relation between two quantities," as in the first example above. However, the term "null hypothesis" is used also in other cases, whether or not it is a "no-effect" type of hypothesis.

In many practical situations it is not possible to determine with certainty whether the null hypothesis is true or false. The best that can be done is to collect evidence and then decide whether the null hypothesis should be accepted or rejected. There is always a possibility that the researcher will choose incorrectly, since the truth is not known conclusively. A situation where the null hypothesis has been rejected, but it is actually true, is referred to as a *type 1 error*. The opposite type of error, called a *type 2 error*, occurs when the null hypothesis has been accepted, but it is actually false.

A good testing procedure is designed so that the chance of committing either of these errors is small. However, it often works out that a test procedure with a smaller probability of leading to a type 1 error will also have a larger probability of resulting in a type 2 error. Therefore, no single testing procedure is guaranteed to be best. It is customary in statistics to design a testing procedure such that the probability of a type 1 error is less than a specified value (often 5 percent or 1 percent). The probability of committing a type 1 error is called the *level of significance* of the test. Therefore, if it is said that a test has been conducted at the 5 percent level of significance, this means that the test has been designed so that there is a 5 percent chance of a type 1 error.

The normal procedure in hypothesis testing is to calculate a quantity called a *test statistic*, whose value depends on the values that are observed in the sample. The test statistic is designed so that, *if* the null hypothesis is true, then the test-statistic value will be a random variable that comes from a known distribution, such as the standard normal distribution or a *t*-distribution. After the value of the test statistic has been calculated, that value is compared with the values that would be expected from the known distribution. If the observed test-statistic value might plausibly have come from the indicated distribution, then the null hypothesis is accepted. However, if it is unlikely that the observed value could have resulted from that distribution, then the null hypothesis is rejected.

Suppose that we are conducting a test based on a test statistic Z, which will have a standard normal distribution if the null hypothesis is true. There is a 95 percent chance that the value of a random variable with a standard normal distribution will be between 1.96 and -1.96. Therefore, we will design the test so that the null hypothesis will be accepted if the calculated value of Z falls between -1.96 and 1.96, since these are plausible values. However, if the value of Z is less than -1.96 or greater than 1.96, we will reject the hypothesis because the value of a random variable with a standard normal distribution is unlikely to fall outside the -1.96 to 1.96 range. The range of values for the test statistic where the null hypothesis is rejected is known as the *critical region*. In this case the critical region consists of two parts. (The two regions at the end of the distribution are called the tails of the distribution.) Notice that there still is a 5 percent chance of committing a type 1 error. If the null hypothesis is true, then Z will have a standard normal distribution, and there is a 5 percent chance that the value of Z will be greater than 1.96 or less than -1.96.

Here is an example of a hypothesis-testing problem involving coins. Suppose that we wish to test whether a particular coin is fair (that is, equally likely to turn up heads or tails). Our null hypothesis is "The probability of heads is .5." The alternative hypothesis is "The probability of heads is not .5." To conduct our test, we will flip the coin 10,000 times. Let X be the number of heads that occurs; X is a random variable. If the null hypothesis is true, then X has a normal distribution with mean 5000 and standard deviation 50. We define a new random variable Z as follows: $Z = (X - 5000)/50$. Now Z will have a standard normal distribution. If the calculated value of Z is between -1.96 and 1.96, we will accept the null hypothesis that the coin is fair; otherwise we will reject the hypothesis. For example, if we observe 5063 heads, then $X = 5063$, $Z = 1.26$, and we will accept the null hypothesis. On the other hand, if we observe 5104 heads, then $X = 5104$, $Z = 2.08$, and we will reject the null hypothesis because the observed value of Z falls in the critical region.

For other examples of hypothesis testing, see **chi-square test** and **analysis of variance**.

I

i   The symbol i is the basic unit for imaginary numbers, and is defined by the equation $i^2 = -1$. (See **imaginary number**.)

IDENTITY   An identity is an equation that is true for every possible value of the unknowns. For example, the equation $4x = x + x + x + x$ is an identity, but $2x + 2 = 4$ is not. (See **equation**.) For contrast, see **conditional equation**.

IDENTITY ELEMENT   If "$\circ$" stands for an operation (such as addition), then the identity element (called I) for the operation "$\circ$" is the number such that $I \circ a = a$, for all a. For example, zero is the identity element for addition, because $0 + a = a$, for all a. One is the identity element for multiplication, because $1 \times a = a$, for all a.

IDENTITY MATRIX An identity matrix is a square matrix with ones along the diagonal and zeros everywhere else. For example:

$$\begin{pmatrix} 1 & 0 \\ 0 & 1 \end{pmatrix},$$

(2 × 2 identity)

$$\begin{pmatrix} 1 & 0 & 0 \\ 0 & 1 & 0 \\ 0 & 0 & 1 \end{pmatrix},$$

(3 × 3 identity)

$$\begin{pmatrix} 1 & 0 & 0 & 0 \\ 0 & 1 & 0 & 0 \\ 0 & 0 & 1 & 0 \\ 0 & 0 & 0 & 1 \end{pmatrix}$$

(4 × 4 identity)

The letter I is used to represent an identity matrix. An identity matrix satisfies the property that $IA = A$, for any matrix for which IA exists.

For example:

$$\begin{pmatrix} 1 & 0 & 0 \\ 0 & 1 & 0 \\ 0 & 0 & 1 \end{pmatrix}\begin{pmatrix} a_1 & a_2 & a_3 \\ b_1 & b_2 & b_3 \\ c_1 & c_2 & c_3 \end{pmatrix} = \begin{pmatrix} a_1 + 0 \cdot b_1 + 0 \cdot c_1 & a_2 & a_3 \\ 0 \cdot a_1 + b_1 + 0 \cdot c_1 & b_2 & b_3 \\ 0 \cdot a_1 + 0 \cdot b_1 + c_1 & c_2 & c_3 \end{pmatrix}$$

If two matrices satisfy $AB = I$, then B is called the inverse matrix for A. (See inverse matrix.)

IF The word "IF" in logic is used in conditional statements of the form "IF p, THEN q." (See conditional statement.)

IMAGE The image of a point is the point that results after the original point has been subjected to a transformation. For an example of a transformation, see reflection.

IMAGINARY NUMBER An imaginary number is a number of the form ni, where n is a real number that is being multiplied by the imaginary unit i, and i is defined by the equation $i^2 = -1$. Since the product of any two real numbers that have the same sign will be positive (or zero), there clearly is no way that you can find any real number that, when multiplied by itself, will give you a negative number. Imaginary numbers are needed to describe certain equations in some branches of physics, such as quantum mechanics. However, any measurable quantity, such as energy, momentum, or length, will always be represented by a real number.

The square root of any negative number can be expressed as a pure imaginary number:

$$\sqrt{(-10)} = \sqrt{(-1)(+10)} = \sqrt{-1}\sqrt{10} = i\sqrt{10}.$$

An interesting cyclic property occurs when i is raised to powers:

$$i^0 = 1, \quad i^1 = i, \quad i^2 = -1, \quad i^3 = -i, \quad i^4 = 1,$$

$$i^5 = i, \quad i^6 = -1, \ldots.$$

A *complex number* is formed by the addition of a pure imaginary number and a real number. The general form of a complex number is $a + bi$, where a and b are both real numbers.

IMPLICATION An implication is a statement of this form; "$A \rightarrow B$" ("A implies B"). (See **conditional statement**.)

IMPLICIT DIFFERENTIATION Implicit differentiation provides a method for finding derivatives if the relationship between two variables is not expressed as an explicit function. For example, consider the equation $x^2 + y^2 = r^2$, which describes a circle of radius r centered at the origin. This equation defines a relationship between x and y, but it does not express that relationship as an explicit function. To find the derivative dy/dx, take the derivatives of both sides of the equation with respect to x:

$$\frac{d}{dx}(x^2 + y^2) = \frac{d(r^2)}{dx},$$

$$\frac{dx^2}{dx} + \frac{dy^2}{dx} = \frac{dr^2}{dx}.$$

Assume that r is a constant; then dr^2/dx is zero. Use the chain rule to find the two derivatives on the left:

$$2x\frac{dx}{dx} + 2y\frac{dy}{dx} = 0.$$

Since dx/dx is equal to 1:

$$2x + 2y\frac{dy}{dx} = 0.$$

Now solve for dy/dx:

$$\frac{dy}{dx} = -\frac{x}{y}.$$

For another example, suppose that $y = a^x$. Take the logarithms of both sides:

$$\ln y = \ln a^x,$$

$$\ln y = x \ln a.$$

Now y is no longer written as an explicit function of x, but you can again use implicit differentiation:

$$\frac{d}{dx}(\ln y) = \frac{d}{dx}(x \ln a).$$

Assume that a is a constant:

$$\frac{d}{dx}(\ln y) = \ln a.$$

Use the chain rule on the left-hand side:

$$\frac{1}{y}\frac{dy}{dx} = \ln a,$$

and then solve for dy/dx:

$$\frac{dy}{dx} = y \ln a = a^x \ln a.$$

IMPROPER FRACTION An improper fraction is a fraction with a numerator that is greater than the denominator, for example, $\frac{7}{4}$. An improper fraction can be written as the sum of a whole number and a proper fraction. For example, $\frac{7}{4} = 1 + \frac{3}{4} = 1\frac{3}{4}$. For contrast, see **proper fraction**.

INCENTER The incenter of a triangle is the center of the circle inscribed inside the triangle. It is the intersection of the three angle bisectors of the triangle. (See **incircle**.)

INCIRCLE The incircle of a triangle is the circle that can be inscribed within the triangle. (See figure.)

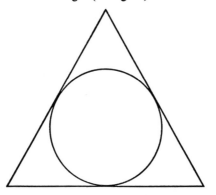

INCONSISTENT EQUATIONS Two equations are inconsistent if they contradict each other and therefore cannot be solved simultaneously. For example, $2x = 4$ and $3x = 9$ are inconsistent.

INCREASING FUNCTION   A function $f(x)$ is an increasing function if $f(a) > f(b)$ when $a > b$.

INCREMENT   In mathematics, the word "increment" means "change in." An increment in a variable x is usually symbolized as Δx.

INDEFINITE INTEGRAL   The indefinite integral of a function f is equal to $F(x) + C$, where F is an antiderivative function for f [that is, $dF/dx = f(x)$] and C can be any constant. The indefinite integral is symbolized as follows:

$$\int f(x)\, dx.$$

C is called the arbitrary constant of integration. Since the derivative of a constant is equal to zero, it is possible to add any constant to a function without changing its derivative. That is the reason why this type of integral is called an indefinite integral.

For example, suppose that a car is driven at a constant speed of 55 miles per hour. Then its position at time t will be given by the indefinite integral

$$\int 55\, dt = 55t + C.$$

Because of the arbitrary constant, we do not know the exact value of the position. We know that the car has been traveling 55 miles per hour, but we cannot figure out its position unless we also know where it started from. If the car started at milepost 25 at time zero, we can solve for the value of the arbitrary constant in this case, and then we will know that the position of the car at time t is given by the function

$$55t + 25.$$

In general, it is possible to solve for the arbitrary constant of integration if we are given an initial condition.

For contrast, see **definite integral**.

INDEPENDENT EVENTS   Two events are independent if they do not affect each other. For example, the probability that a new baby will be a girl is not affected by the fact that a previous baby was a girl. Therefore, these two events are independent. If A and B are two independent events, the conditional probability that A will occur, given that B has occurred, is just the same as the (unconditional) probability that A will occur:

$$\Pr(A \mid B) = \Pr(A).$$

(See **conditional probability**.)

Also, if A and B are independent, the probability that both A and B will occur is equal to the probability of A times the probability of B:

$$\Pr(A \text{ and } B) = \Pr(A) \times \Pr(B).$$

For example, suppose that the probability that the primary navigation system on a spacecraft will fail is .01, suppose that the probability that the backup navigation system will fail is .05, and suppose that these two events are independent. In other words, the probability that the backup system will fail is not affected by whether or not the primary system has failed. Then the probability that both systems will fail is $.01 \times .05 = .0005$. Therefore, the probability that both systems will fail is much smaller than the probability that either of the individual systems will fail. This result would not be true, however, if these two events were not independent. If the probability that the backup system will fail rises if the primary system has failed, then the spacecraft could be in trouble.

INDEPENDENT VARIABLE The independent variable stands for any of the set of input numbers to a function. In the equation $y = f(x)$, x is the independent variable and y is the dependent variable. (See **function**.)

INDEX The index of a radical is the little number that tells what root is to be taken. For example, in the expression $\sqrt[3]{64} = 4$, the number 3 is the index of the radical. It means to take the cube root of 64. If no index is specified, then the square root is assumed:

$$\sqrt{36} = \sqrt[2]{36} = 6.$$

INDIRECT PROOF The method of indirect proof begins by assuming that a theorem is false, and then proceeds to show that a contradiction results. In that case the theorem must be true.

INDUCTION Induction is the process of reasoning from a particular circumstance to a general conclusion. (See **mathematical induction**.)

INEQUALITY An inequality is a statement of this form: "x is less than y," written as $x < y$, or "x is greater than y," written as $x > y$. The arrow in the inequality sign always points to the smaller number. Inequalities containing numbers will either be true (such as

10 > 7), or be false (such as 4 < 3). Inequalities containing variables (such as $x < 3$) will usually be true for some values of the variable.

The symbol " $\leq$ " means "is less than or equal to," and the symbol " $\geq$ " means "is greater than or equal to."

A true inequality will still be true if you add or subtract the same quantity from both sides of the inequality. The inequality will still be true if both sides are multiplied by the same positive number, but if you multiply by a negative number you must reverse the inequality:

$$4 > 3, \qquad\qquad 4 > 3;$$
$$2 \times 4 > 2 \times 3, \qquad -2 \times 4 < -2 \times 3;$$
$$8 > 6, \qquad\qquad -8 < -6.$$

INFINITE SERIES An infinite series is the sum of an infinite number of terms. In some cases the series may have a finite sum. (See **geometric series.**)

INFINITESIMAL An infinitesimal is a variable quantity that approaches very close to zero. In calculus Δx is usually used to represent an infinitesimal. Infinitesimals play an important role in the study of limits, particularly in calculus.

INFINITY The symbol " ∞ " (infinity) represents a limitless quantity. It would take you forever to count an infinite number of objects. There is an infinite number of numbers. As x goes to zero, the quantity $1/x$ goes to infinity. (However, that does not mean that there is a number called ∞ such that $1/0 = \infty$.) The opposite of "infinite" is *finite*.

INFLECTION POINT An inflection point on a curve is a point such that the curve is oriented concave-upward on one side of the point and concave-downward on the other side of the point. (See figure.) If the curve represents the function $y = f(x)$, then the second derivative d^2y/dx^2 is equal to zero at the inflection point.

point of
inflection

INSCRIBED (1) An inscribed polygon is a polygon placed inside a circle so that each vertex of the polygon touches the circle. For an example, see **pi**.

(2) An inscribed circle of a polygon is a circle located inside a polygon, with each side of the polygon being tangent to the circle. For an example, see **incircle**.

INTEGERS The set of integers contains zero, the natural numbers, and the negatives of all the natural numbers:

$$\ldots, -6, -5, -4, -3, -2, -1, 0, 1, 2, 3, 4, 5, 6, \ldots.$$

An integer is a real number that does not include a fractional part. The natural numbers are also called the positive integers, and the integers smaller than zero are called the negative integers.

INTEGRAL The indefinite integral of a function $f(x)$ is a function $F(x) + C$ such that the derivative of $F(x)$ is equal to $f(x)$, and C is an arbitrary constant. The indefinite integral is written with the integral sign:

$$\int f(x)\, dx = F(x) + C.$$

(See **calculus: derivative**.)

The process of finding an integral (called integration) is the reverse process of finding a derivative. Here is a table of integrals of some functions:

*Perfect Integral Rule

$$\int dx = x + C$$

*Sum Rule

$$\int [f(x) + g(x)]\, dx = \int f(x)\, dx + \int g(x)\, dx$$

*Product Rule

$$\int af(x)\, dx = a \int f(x)\, dx \quad \text{(if } a \text{ is a constant)}$$

*Power Rule

$$\int x^n\, dx = \frac{1}{n+1} x^{n+1} + C \quad \text{(if } n \neq -1)$$

$$\int x^{-1}\, dx = \ln |x| + C$$

*Trigonometric Integrals

$\int \sin x \, dx = -\cos x + C$

$\int \cos x \, dx = \sin x + C$

$\int \tan x \, dx = \ln |\sec x| + C$

$\int \sec x \, dx = \ln |\sec x + \tan x| + C$

$\int \sqrt{1 - x^2} \, dx = \frac{1}{2} \arcsin x + \frac{1}{2} x \sqrt{1 - x^2}$

*Integration by Parts

$\int u \, dv = uv - \int v \, du$

To solve for the arbitrary constant of integration, you need to know an initial condition. For example, if you know that $dy/dx = 2x$, then that means that $y = x^2 + C$. There are many curves that satisfy that equation. However, if you know that the point $(0, 5)$ lies on the curve you're looking for, then you know that $C = 5$, so the final answer for y is $y = x^2 + 5$.

The definite integral of a function $f(x)$ is the area under the curve $y = f(x)$ from $x = a$ to $x = b$, which is equal to $F(b) - F(a)$. The definite integral is written with an integral sign and two limits of integration, a and b:

$$\int_a^b f(x) \, dx = F(b) - F(a).$$

For example, the area under the sine function from $x = 0$ to $x = \pi$ is given by $\int_0^\pi \sin x \, dx$. In this case we know that the antiderivative function is $-\cos x$, so

$$\int_0^\pi \sin x \, dx = -\cos \pi + \cos 0 = -(-1) + 1 = 2.$$

INTEGRAND The integrand is a function that is to be integrated. In the expression $\int f(x) \, dx$, the function $f(x)$ is the integrand. (See **integral**.)

INTEGRATION Integration is the process of finding an integral. (See **integral**.)

INTERCEPT The y-intercept of a curve is the value of y where it crosses the y-axis, and the x-intercept is the value of x where the curve crosses the x-axis. For the line $y = mx + b$, the y-intercept is b and the x-intercept is $-b/m$.

INTERCEPTED ARC   The intercepted arc is the arc of a circle that a particular angle cuts across.

INTERPOLATION   Interpolation provides a means of estimating the value of a function for a particular number if you know the value of the function for two other numbers above and below the number in question. For example, $\sin 26° = 0.4384$ and $\sin 27° = 0.4540$. It seems reasonable to suppose that $\sin(26\frac{2}{3}°)$ will be approximately two thirds of the way between 0.4384 and 0.4540, or 0.4488. This approximation is close to the true value as long as the two numbers you are interpolating between are close to each other.

The general formula for interpolation when $a < c < b$ is

$$f(c) = f(a) + \frac{c-a}{b-a}[f(b) - f(a)].$$

INTERSECTION   The intersection of two sets is the set of all elements contained in both sets. For example, the intersection of the sets $\{1, 2, 3, 4, 5, 6\}$ and $\{2, 4, 6, 8, 10, 12\}$ is the set $\{2, 4, 6\}$. William Howard Taft is the only member of the intersection between the set of Presidents of the United States and the set of Chief Justices of the United States. The set of squares is the intersection between the set of rhombuses and the set of rectangles. The intersection of set A and set B is symbolized by $A \cap B$.

INVERSE   If "$\circ$" represents an operation (such as addition), and I represents the identity element of that operation, then the inverse of a number x is the number y such that $x \circ y = I$. For example, the additive inverse of a number x is $-x$ (also called the *negative* of x) because $x + (-x) = 0$. The multiplicative inverse of x is $1/x$ (also called the *reciprocal* of x) because $(x) \times (1/x) = 1$.

INVERSE FUNCTION   An inverse function is a function that does exactly the opposite of the original function. If the function g is the inverse of the function f, and if $y = f(x)$, then $x = g(y)$. The domain (i.e., the set of possible values for the independent variable) of the function f is the same as the range (the set of possible values of the dependent variable) of the *function f* inverse. For example, the logarithm function is the inverse of the exponential function. If $y = e^x$, then $x = \ln y$. (See **function**.)

INVERSELY PROPORTIONAL   If y and x are related by the equation $y = k/x$, where k is a constant, then y is said to be inversely proportional to x.

INVERSE MATRIX   The inverse of a square matrix **A** is the matrix that, when multiplied by **A**, gives the identity matrix. A inverse is written as $\mathbf{A}^{-1}$:

$$\mathbf{A}\mathbf{A}^{-1} = \mathbf{I}.$$

(See **matrix; matrix multiplication**.)

$\mathbf{A}^{-1}$ exists if det $\mathbf{A} \neq 0$. (See **determinant**.)

The inverse of a 2×2 matrix can be found from the formula

$$\begin{pmatrix} a & b \\ c & d \end{pmatrix}^{-1} = \begin{pmatrix} \dfrac{d}{ad - bc} & \dfrac{b}{bc - ad} \\ \dfrac{c}{bc - ad} & \dfrac{a}{ad - bc} \end{pmatrix}.$$

In general, the inverse of a matrix can be found from

$$\text{element } (i, j) \text{ in } \mathbf{A}^{-1} = \frac{a_{ij}^{\text{cofactor}}}{\det \mathbf{A}},$$

where

$$a_{ij}^{\text{cofactor}} = (-1)^{i+j} \times \det(a_{ij}^{\text{minor}}),$$

and a_{ij}^{minor} is the matrix formed by crossing out row i and column j in matrix **A**. (See **minor**.)

INVERSE TRIGONOMETRIC FUNCTIONS   The inverse trigonometric functions (see figure) are the inverse functions for the trigonometric functions. For example, the inverse of the sine function is written as arcsin a or $\sin^{-1} a$, and it satisfies:

$$\text{If } a = \sin b, \text{ then } b = \arcsin a.$$

For example, $\sin(\pi/4) = 1/\sqrt{2}$, so $\arcsin(1/\sqrt{2}) = \pi/4$.

In general, the inverse trigonometric functions are not really functions, because there are many values of b for which $\sin b = a$. For example, $\sin(\pi/2) = 1$, $\sin(5\pi/2) = 1$, $\sin(9\pi/2) = 1$, $\sin(13\pi/2) = 1$, so

$$\arcsin(1) = \frac{\pi}{2}, \quad \text{or } \frac{5\pi}{2}, \quad \text{or } \frac{9\pi}{2}, \quad \text{or } \frac{13\pi}{2}.$$

Usually, the expression Arcsin a refers to the number between $-\pi/2$ and $\pi/2$ that satisfies $\sin b = a$. The values between $-\pi/2$ and $\pi/2$ are called the principal values of the arcsin function. The table lists the domain and the range of the principal values for the inverse trigonometric functions.

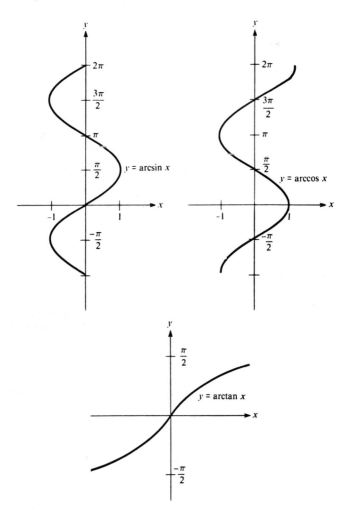

Function	Inverse Function	Domain	Range (principal values)
$x = \sin y$	$y = \text{Arcsin } x$	$-1 \le x \le 1$	$-\pi/2 \le y \le \pi/2$
$x = \cos y$	$y = \text{Arccos } x$	$-1 \le x \le 1$	$0 \le y \le \pi$
$x = \tan y$	$y = \text{Arctan } x$	all real numbers	$-\pi/2 \le y \le \pi/2$
$x = \text{ctn } y$	$y = \text{Arcctn } x$	all real numbers	$0 \le y \le \pi$
$x = \sec y$	$y = \text{Arcsec } x$	$|x| > 1$	$0 < y < \pi$
$x = \csc y$	$y = \text{Arccsc } x$	$|x| > 1$	$-\pi/2 \le y \le \pi/2$

For example, if you need to walk in a straight line toward a point 4 miles north and 3 miles east, then you need to walk at an angle arctan $\frac{4}{3}$ = 53.1 degrees north of east.

IRRATIONAL NUMBER An irrational number is a real number that is not a rational number (i.e., it cannot be expressed as the ratio of two integers). Irrational numbers can be represented by decimal fractions in which the digits go on forever without ever repeating a pattern. Some of the most common irrational numbers are square roots, such as $\sqrt{3} = 1.732050808\ldots$ or $\sqrt{10} = 3.16227766\ldots$. Also, most values of trigonometric functions are irrational, such as $\sin(10°) = 0.173648177\ldots$.

To show that $\sqrt{2}$ is not a rational number, we need to show that there are no two integers such that their ratio is $\sqrt{2}$. Suppose that there were two such integers (call them a and b) with no common factors. Then $2 = a^2/b^2$, or $a^2 = 2b^2$. Therefore a^2 is even (meaning that it is divisible by 2). If a^2 is even, then a itself must be even. This means that a can be expressed as $a = 2c$, where c is some other integer. Then $a^2 = 4c^2 = 2b^2$, or $b^2 = 2c^2$. This means that b^2 is even, so b must be even. This means that we have reached a contradiction, since we originally assumed that a and b had no common factors. Since we reach a contradiction if we assume that $\sqrt{2}$ is rational, it must be irrational. We can easily find a distance that is $\sqrt{2}$ units long, though. If we draw a right triangle with two sides each one unit long, then the third side will have length $\sqrt{2}$. (See **Pythagorean theorem**.) The radical $\sqrt{2}$ can be approximated by the decimal fraction $\sqrt{2} = 1.414213562\ldots$.

ISOMETRY An isometry is a way of transforming a figure that does not change the distances between any two points on the figure. For example, a translation or a rotation is an isometry. However, if a figure was transformed by making it twice as big, then the transformation would not be an isometry.

ISOSCELES TRIANGLE An isosceles triangle is a triangle with two equal sides.

J

JOINT VARIATION   If $z = kxy$, where k is a constant, then z is said to vary jointly with x and y.

L

LATTICE POINT   A point (a, b) in a plane is called a lattice point if a and b are both integers. For example, $(0, 0)$, $(1, 2)$, $(8, 9)$, and $(4, 20)$ are all lattice points, but $(0.5, 3)$ is not.

LATUS RECTUM   The latus rectum of a parabola (see figure) is the chord through the focus perpendicular to the axis of symmetry. The latus rectum of an ellipse is one of the chords through a focus that is perpendicular to the major axis.

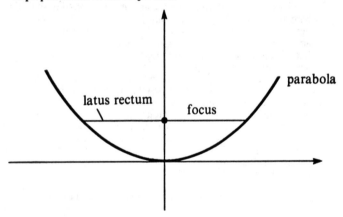

LAW OF COSINES   The law of cosines (see figure) allows us to calculate the third side of a triangle if we know the other two sides and the angle between them:

$$c^2 = a^2 + b^2 - 2ab \cos C.$$

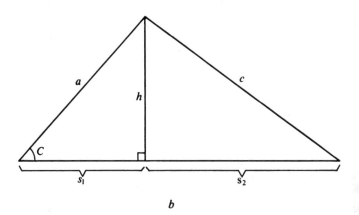

Calling the altitude of the triangle h, we know from the *Pythagorean theorem* that $h^2 + s_2{}^2 = c^2$. Solving for h and s_2 gives

$$h = a \sin C,$$
$$s_2 = b - s_1,$$
$$s_1 = a \cos C,$$
$$s_2 = b - a \cos C,$$
$$c^2 = a^2 \sin^2 C + b^2 - 2ab \cos C + a^2 \cos^2 C.$$

Using the fact that $\sin^2 C + \cos^2 C = 1$, we obtain

$$c^2 = a^2 + b^2 - 2ab \cos C.$$

The final equation is the law of cosines. It is a generalization of the Pythagorean theorem. For $C = 90° = \pi/2$, we have a right triangle with c as the hypotenuse, so the law of cosines reduces to the regular Pythagorean theorem.

For example, to calculate the third side of an isosceles triangle with two sides that are 10 units long adjacent to a 100° angle, we use this formula:

$$c^2 = 10^2 + 10^2 - 2 \times 10 \times 10 \times \cos 100°,$$
$$c = 15.3.$$

LAW OF LARGE NUMBERS   The law of large numbers states that, if a random variable is observed many times, the average of these observations will tend toward the expected value (mean) of that random variable. For example, if you roll a die many times and calculate the average value for all of the rolls, you will find that the average value will tend to approach 3.5.

LAW OF SINES   The law of sines expresses a relationship involving the sides and angles of a triangle:

$$\frac{a}{\sin A} = \frac{b}{\sin B} = \frac{c}{\sin C}.$$

In each case a small letter refers to the length of a side, and a capital letter designates the angle opposite that side (see figure). The law can be demonstrated by calling h the altitude of the triangle.

$$\frac{h}{b} = \sin A,$$

$$\frac{h}{a} = \sin B,$$

$$b \sin A = a \sin B,$$

$$\frac{b}{\sin B} = \frac{a}{\sin A}.$$

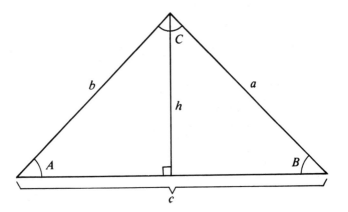

LAW OF TANGENTS   If a, b, and c are the lengths of the sides of a triangle, and A, B, and C are the angles opposite these three sides, respectively, then the law of tangents states that the following relations will be true:

$$\frac{a-b}{a+b} = \frac{\tan\left[\frac{1}{2}(A-B)\right]}{\tan\left[\frac{1}{2}(A+B)\right]},$$

$$\frac{b-c}{b+c} = \frac{\tan\left[\frac{1}{2}(B-C)\right]}{\tan\left[\frac{1}{2}(B+C)\right]},$$

$$\frac{c-a}{c+a} = \frac{\tan\left[\frac{1}{2}(C-A)\right]}{\tan\left[\frac{1}{2}(C+A)\right]}.$$

LEAST COMMON DENOMINATOR   The least common denominator of two fractions a/b and c/d is the smallest integer that contains both b and d as a factor. For example, the least common denominator of the fractions $\frac{3}{4}$ and $\frac{5}{6}$ is 12, since 12 is the smallest integer that has both 4 and 6 as a factor.

The best way to add two fractions is to turn them both into equivalent fractions whose denominator is the least common denominator:

$$\frac{3}{4} = \frac{3}{4} \times \frac{3}{3} = \frac{9}{12},$$

$$\frac{5}{6} = \frac{5}{6} \times \frac{2}{2} = \frac{10}{12},$$

$$\frac{3}{4} + \frac{5}{6} = \frac{9}{12} + \frac{10}{12} = \frac{19}{12}.$$

LEAST COMMON MULTIPLE   The least common multiple of two natural numbers is the smallest natural number that has both of them as a factor. For example, 6 is the least common multiple of 2 and 3, and 30 is the least common multiple of 10 and 6.

LEAST SQUARES ESTIMATOR   See **regression; multiple regression.**

LEMMA   A lemma is a theorem that is proved mainly as an aid in proving another theorem.

LEVEL OF SIGNIFICANCE   The level of significance for a hypothesis-testing procedure is the probability of committing a type 1 error. (See **hypothesis testing**).

L'HÔPITAL'S RULE   L'Hôpital's rule tells how to find the limit of the ratio of two functions. Let y represent the ratio between two functions, $f(x)$ and $g(x)$:

$$y = \frac{f(x)}{g(x)}.$$

Then l'Hôpital's rule states that

$$\lim_{x \to a} y = \frac{\displaystyle\lim_{x \to a} f'(x)}{\displaystyle\lim_{x \to a} g'(x)},$$

where $f'(x)$ and $g'(x)$ represent the derivatives of these functions with respect to x.

For example, suppose that

$$y = \frac{2x^2 + 18x - 44}{2x - 4}$$

and we need to find $\lim_{x \to 2} y$. We cannot find this limit directly, because inserting the value $x = 2$ in the expression for y gives the expression $0/0$. However, by setting $f(x) = 2x^2 + 18x - 44$, we can find $f'(x) = 4x + 18$, $\lim_{x \to 2} f'(x) = 26$, $g(x) = 2x - 4$, $g'(x) = 2$.

Therefore,

$$\lim_{x \to 2} y = \frac{26}{2} = 13.$$

For another example, suppose that

$$y = \frac{Pr(1 + r)^n}{(1 + r)^n - 1},$$

and assume that n and P are constant. To find $\lim_{r \to 0} y$, we must use l'Hôpital's rule. We let

$$f(r) = Pr(1 + r)^n; \quad f'(r) = Prn(1 + r)^{n-1} + P(1 + r)^n;$$

$$\lim_{r \to 0} f'(r) = P;$$

$$g(r) = (1 + r)^n - 1; \quad g'(r) = n(1 + r)^{n-1}; \quad \lim_{r \to 0} g'(r) = n.$$

Therefore

$$\lim_{r \to 0} y = \frac{P}{n}.$$

This formula represents the monthly payment for a home mortgage, where r is the monthly interest rate, n is the number of months to repay the loan, and P is the principal amount (the amount that is borrowed). The result says that, if the interest rate is zero, the monthly payment is simply equal to the principal amount divided by the number of months.

LIKE TERMS   Two terms are like terms if all parts of both terms except for the numerical coefficients are the same. For example, the terms $3a^2b^3c^4$ and $-6.5a^2b^3c^4$ are like terms. If two like terms are added, they can be combined into one term. For example, the sum of the two terms above is $-3.5a^2b^3c^4$.

LIMIT   The limit of a function is the value that the dependent variable approaches as the independent variable approaches some fixed value. The expression "The limit of $f(x)$ as x approaches a" is written as

$$\lim_{x \to a} f(x) \qquad \text{or} \qquad \text{limit}_{x \to a} f(x).$$

For example:

$$\lim_{x \to 2} x^2 = 4, \qquad \lim_{x \to \pi/2} \sin x = 1, \qquad \lim_{x \to 1} x^2 + 3x + 1 = 5.$$

In each of these cases the limit is not very interesting, because we can easily find $f(2)$, $f(\pi/2)$, or $f(1)$. However, there are cases where $\lim_{x \to a} f(x)$ exists, but $f(a)$ does not. For example,

$$f(x) = \frac{(x-1)(x+2)}{x-1}$$

is undefined if $x = 1$. However, the closer that x comes to 1, the closer $f(x)$ approaches 3. For example, $f(1.0001) = 3.0001$. All of calculus is based on this type of limit. (See **derivative**.)

The formal definition of limit is: The limit of $f(x)$ as x approaches a exists and is equal to B if, for any positive number ε, there exists a positive number δ such that, if $|x - a| < \varepsilon$, then $|f(x) - B| < \delta$.

LINE   A line is a straight set of points that extends off to infinity in two directions. The term "line" is one of the basic undefined terms in Euclidian geometry, so it is not possible to give a rigorous definition of line. You will have to use your intuition as to what it means for a line to be straight. According to a postulate, any two distinct points determine one and only one line. A line has infinite length, but zero width and zero thickness.

LINEAR EQUATION A linear equation with unknown x is an equation that can be written in the form $ax + b = 0$. For example, $2x - 10 = 2$ can be written as $2x - 12 = 0$, so this is a linear equation with the solution $x = 6$.

LINEAR FACTOR A linear factor is a factor that includes only the first power of an unknown. For example, in the expression $y = (x - 2)(x^2 + 3x + 4)$, the factor $(x - 2)$ is a linear factor, but the factor $(x^2 + 3x + 4)$ is a quadratic factor.

LINEAR PROGRAMMING A linear programming problem is a problem for which you need to choose the optimal set of values for some variables subject to some constraints. The goal is to maximize or minimize a function called the *objective function*. In a linear programming problem, the objective function and the constraints must all be linear functions; that is, they cannot involve variables raised to any power (other than 1), and they cannot involve two variables being multiplied together.

Some examples of problems to which linear programming can be applied include finding the least-cost method for producing a given product, or finding the maximum possible revenue that can be earned from a production facility with several capacity limitations.

Here is an example:

$$\text{Maximize } 6x + 8y$$
subject to

$$y \le 10$$
$$x + y \le 15$$
$$2x + y \le 25$$
$$x \ge 0$$
$$y \ge 0$$

There are two choice variables: x and y. The objective function is $6x + 8y$, and there are three constraints (not counting the two nonnegativity constraints $x \ge 0$ and $y \ge 0$).

It is customary to rewrite the constraints so that they contain equals signs instead of inequality signs. In order to do this some new variables, called *slack variables*, are added. One slack variable is added for each constraint. Here is how the problem given above looks when three slack variables (s_1, s_2, and s_3) are included:

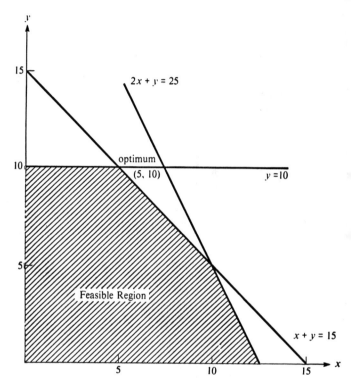

Maximize $6x + 8y$
subject to
$$y + s_1 = 10$$
$$x + y + s_2 = 15$$
$$2x + y + s_3 = 25$$
$$x \geq 0, \ y \geq 0, \ s_1 \geq 0, \ s_2 \geq 0, \ s_3 \geq 0$$

Each slack variable represents the excess capacity associated with the corresponding constraint.

The feasible region consists of all points that satisfy the constraints. (See figure.) A theorem of linear programming states that the optimal solution will lie at one of the corner points of the feasible region. In this case the optimal solution is at the point $x = 5$, $y = 10$.

A linear programming problem with two choice variables can be solved by drawing a graph of the feasible region, as was done above. If there are more than two variables, however, it is not possible to draw a graph, and the problem must then be solved by an algebraic procedure, such as the *simplex method*.

LITERAL A literal number is a number expressed as a numeral, not as a variable. For example, in the equation

$$x = 2.4y$$

2.4 is a literal number.

ln See **natural logarithm.**

LOCUS The term "locus" is a technical way of saying "set of points." For example, a circle can be defined as being "the locus of points that are a fixed distance from a given point." The plural of "locus" is "loci."

LOG The function $y = \log x$ is an abbreviation for the logarithm function to the base 10. (See **logarithm.**)

LOGARITHM A logarithm is an inverse of an exponential. The equation $y = a^x$ can be written as $x = \log_a y$, which means "x is the logarithm to the base a of y." Any positive number (except 1) can be used as the base for a logarithm function. The two most useful bases are 10 and e. Logarithms to the base 10 are called *common logarithms*. They are very convenient to use, since we use a base-10 number system. For example:

$$\log_{10} 1 = 0 \quad \text{(because)} \quad 10^0 = 1,$$
$$\log_{10} 10 = 1,$$
$$\log_{10} 100 = 2,$$
$$\log_{10} 1000 = 3.$$

Table 1 lists some values of the common logarithm function.

If no base is specified in the expression $\log x$, then base 10 is usually meant: $\log x = \log_{10} x$.

Logarithms to any base satisfy:

$$\log ab = \log a + \log b,$$

$$\log (a/b) = \log a - \log b,$$

$$\log a^n = n \log a.$$

These properties follow directly from the properties of exponents.

Logarithms are convenient if we have to measure very large quantities and very small quantities at the same time. For example, the stellar magnitude system for measuring the brightness of stars is based on a logarithmic scale.

Logarithms to the base e (called *natural logarithms*) are important in calculus. The natural logarithm (written as $\ln x$) can be defined by the integral

$$\ln x = \int_1^x t^{-1} \, dt.$$

(See **calculus; integral**.) The base e is an irrational number that can be approximated by $e = 2.718. \ldots$

LOGIC Logic is the study of sound reasoning. The study of logic focuses on the study of *arguments*. An argument is a sequence of sentences (called *premises*) that lead to a resulting sentence (called the *conclusion*). An argument is a valid argument if the conclusion does follow from the premises. In other words, if an argument is valid and all its premises are true, then the conclusion must be true. There is no way for all the premises to be true and the conclusion to be false in a valid argument.

Here is an example of a valid argument:

Premise: If a shape is a square, then it is both a rectangle and a rhombus.

Premise: Central Park is not a rhombus.

Conclusion: Therefore, Central Park is not a square.

Here is another example of an argument:

Premise: If a shape is either a rhombus or a rectangle, then it is a square.

Premise: Central Park is a rectangle.

Conclusion: Therefore, Central Park is a square.

This is a valid argument, since the conclusion follows from the premises. However, one of the premises (the first one) is false. If any of the premises of an argument is false, then the argument is called an unsound argument.

Logic can be used to determine whether an argument is valid; however, logic alone cannot determine whether the premises are true or false. Once an argument has been shown to be valid, then all other arguments of the same general form will also be valid, even if their premises are different.

Arguments are composed of sentences. Sentences are said to have the truth value T (corresponding to what we normally think of as "true") or the truth value F (corresponding to "false"). In studying the general logical properties of sentences, it is customary to represent a sentence by a lower-case letter, such as p, q, or r, called a sentence variable or a Boolean variable. Sentences either can be simple sentences or can consist of simple sentences joined by connectives and called *compound sentences*. For example, "Spot is a dog" is a simple sentence. "Spot is a dog and Spot likes to bury bones" is a compound sentence. The connectives used in logic include AND, OR, and NOT. To learn how these are used, see **Boolean algebra**.

M

MACLAURIN SERIES The Maclaurin series for a function f at a point h is

$$f(h) = f(0) + hf'(0) + \frac{h^2 f''(0)}{2!} + \frac{h^3 f'''(0)}{3!} + \cdots.$$

In this expression, $f'(0)$ stands for the first derivative of f evaluated at the point $x = 0$, $f''(0)$ stands for the second derivative, and so on.

MAGNITUDE The magnitude of a vector $\mathbf{a}$ is its length:

$$\|\mathbf{a}\| = \sqrt{\mathbf{a} \cdot \mathbf{a}}.$$

For example, the magnitude of the vector $(1, 2)$ is

$$\sqrt{(1, 2) \cdot (1, 2)} = \sqrt{1 + 4} = \sqrt{5}.$$

MAJOR ARC A major arc of a circle is an arc with a measure greater than 180°. (See **arc**.)

MAJOR AXIS The major axis of an ellipse is the segment joining two points on the ellipse that passes through the two foci. It is the longest possible distance across the ellipse. (See **ellipse**.)

MAJOR PREMISE The major premise is the sentence in a syllogism that asserts a general relationship between classes of objects. (See **syllogism**.)

MANTISSA The mantissa is the part of a common logarithm to the right of the decimal point. For example, in the expression $\log 115 = 2.0607$, the quantity 0.0607 is the mantissa.

MAPPING A mapping is a rule that, to each member of one set, assigns a unique member of another set.

MATHEMATICAL INDUCTION Mathematical induction is a method for proving that a proposition is true for all whole numbers. First, show that the proposition is true for a few small numbers, such as 1, 2, or 3. Then show that, if the proposition is true for an arbitrary number j, then it must be true for the next number: $j + 1$. Once you have done these two steps, the proposition has been proved, since, if it is true for 1, then it must also be true for 2, which means it must be true for 3, which means it must be true for 4, and so on.

For example, we can prove that

$$\sum_{i=1}^{n} i = 1 + 2 + 3 + 4 + \cdots + n = \tfrac{1}{2}n(n+1)$$

is true for all natural numbers n. (See **summation notation**.) The proposition is true for $n = 1$, $n = 2$, and $n = 3$:

$$\sum_{i=1}^{1} i = 1 = \frac{1(1+1)}{2},$$

$$\sum_{i=1}^{2} i = 1 + 2 = 3 = \frac{2(2+1)}{2},$$

$$\sum_{i=1}^{3} i = 1 + 2 + 3 = 6 = \frac{3(3+1)}{2}.$$

Now assume that this formula is true for any arbitrary natural number j. Then:

$$\sum_{i=1}^{j+1} i = \sum_{i=1}^{j} i + (j+1) = \frac{j(j+1)}{2} + (j+1)$$

$$= \frac{j^2 + j + 2j + 2}{2} = \frac{(j+2)(j+1)}{2}.$$

Therefore the formula must work for $j + 1$ if it works for j, so it must be true for all j.

MATHEMATICS Mathematics is the orderly study of the structures and patterns of abstract entities. Normally the objects that mathematicians talk about correspond to objects about which we have an intuitive understanding. For example, we have an intuitive notion of what a number is, what a line in three-dimensional space is, and what the concept of probability is.

Applied mathematics is the field in which mathematical concepts are applied to practical problems. For example, the lines and points that pure mathematics deals with are abstractions that we can't see or touch. However, these abstract ideas correspond closely to the concrete objects that we think of as lines or points. Mathematics was originally developed for its applied value. The ancient Egyptians and Babylonians developed numerous properties of numbers and geometric figures that they used to solve practical problems.

The formal procedure of mathematics is this: Start with some concepts that will be left undefined, such as "number" or "line." Then make some postulates that will be assumed to be true, such as "Every natural number has a successor." Next make definitions using undefined terms and previously defined terms, such as "A circle is the set of all points in a plane that are a fixed distance from a given point." Then use the postulates to prove theorems, such as the Pythagorean theorem. Once a theorem has been proved, it can then be used in the proof of other theorems.

MATRIX A matrix is a table of numbers arranged in rows and columns. The plural of "matrix" is "matrices." The size of a matrix is characterized by two numbers: the number of rows and the number of columns. Matrix **A** is a 2×2 matrix, matrix **B** is 3×2, matrix **C** is 3×3, and matrix **D** is 2×3.

$$\mathbf{A} = \begin{pmatrix} 1 & 2 \\ 3 & 4 \end{pmatrix}, \quad \mathbf{B} = \begin{pmatrix} 0 & 6 \\ 10 & 5 \\ 4 & 2 \end{pmatrix}, \quad \mathbf{C} = \begin{pmatrix} 1 & 0 & 0 \\ 0 & 1 & 0 \\ 0 & 0 & 1 \end{pmatrix},$$
$$\mathbf{D} = \begin{pmatrix} 100 & 15 & 25 \\ 36 & 10 & 15 \end{pmatrix}.$$

(The number of rows is always listed first.) A baseball box score is an example of a 9×4 matrix.

	ab	*r*	*h*	*rbi*
shortstop	5	3	3	0
first baseman	4	1	2	1
right fielder	4	0	1	2
center fielder	4	0	1	1
left fielder	4	0	0	0
catcher	4	1	1	1
third baseman	4	0	1	0
pitcher	3	0	0	0
second baseman	3	0	1	0

The transpose of a matrix A (written as A^{tr} or A') is formed by turning all the rows into columns and all the columns into rows. For example:

$$\begin{pmatrix} a & b \\ c & d \end{pmatrix}^{tr} = \begin{pmatrix} a & c \\ b & d \end{pmatrix} \qquad \begin{pmatrix} 4 & 7 \\ 5 & 8 \\ 6 & 9 \end{pmatrix}^{tr} = \begin{pmatrix} 4 & 5 & 6 \\ 7 & 8 & 9 \end{pmatrix},$$

$$\begin{pmatrix} 1 & 0 & 0 \\ 0 & 1 & 0 \\ 0 & -1 & 1 \end{pmatrix}^{tr} = \begin{pmatrix} 1 & 0 & 0 \\ 0 & 1 & -1 \\ 0 & 0 & 1 \end{pmatrix}.$$

Matrices can be multiplied by the rules of matrix multiplication. If A is an $m \times n$ matrix, and B is an $n \times p$ matrix, then the product AB will be an $m \times p$ matrix. The product AB can be found only if the number of columns in matrix A is equal to the number of rows in matrix B. (See **matrix multiplication**.)

A square matrix is a matrix in which the numbers of rows and columns are equal. One important square matrix is the matrix with ones all along the diagonal from the upper left-hand corner to the lower right-hand corner, and zeros everywhere else. This type of matrix is called an identity matrix, written as I:

$$\begin{pmatrix} 1 & 0 & 0 \\ 0 & 1 & 0 \\ 0 & 0 & 1 \end{pmatrix}$$

3×3 identity matrix

An identity matrix has the important property that, whenever it multiplies another matrix, it leaves the other matrix unchanged: $IA = A$.

For many square matrices there exists a special matrix called the inverse matrix (written as A^{-1}), which satisfies the special property that $A^{-1}A = I$. (See **inverse matrix**.)

The determinant of a matrix (written as det A) is a number that characterizes some important properties of the matrix. If det $A = 0$, then A does not have an inverse matrix.

The trace of a matrix is the sum of the diagonal elements of the matrix. For example, the trace of a 3×3 identity matrix is 3.

The use of matrix multiplication makes it easier to express linear simultaneous equation systems. The system of equations can be written as $Ax = b$, where A is an $m \times m$ matrix of coefficients, x is an $m \times 1$ matrix of unknowns, and b is an $m \times 1$ matrix of known constants. If you know A^{-1}, you can find the solution for x:

$$Ax = b,$$
$$A^{-1}Ax = A^{-1}b,$$
$$Ix = A^{-1}b,$$
$$x = A^{-1}b.$$

MATRIX MULTIPLICATION The formal definition of matrix multiplication is as follows:

$$\begin{pmatrix} a_{11} & a_{12} & a_{13} & \cdots & a_{1n} \\ a_{21} & a_{22} & a_{23} & \cdots & a_{2n} \\ & & \vdots & & \\ a_{m1} & a_{m2} & a_{m3} & \cdots & a_{mn} \end{pmatrix} \times \begin{pmatrix} b_{11} & b_{12} & b_{13} & \cdots & b_{1p} \\ b_{21} & b_{22} & b_{23} & \cdots & b_{2p} \\ & & \vdots & & \\ b_{n1} & b_{n2} & b_{n3} & \cdots & b_{np} \end{pmatrix}$$

$$= \begin{pmatrix} \sum_{i=1}^{n} a_{1i}b_{i1} & \sum_{i=1}^{n} a_{1i}b_{i2} & \cdots & \sum_{i=1}^{n} a_{1i}b_{ip} \\ \sum_{i=1}^{n} a_{2i}b_{i1} & \sum_{i=1}^{n} a_{2i}b_{i2} & \cdots & \sum_{i=1}^{n} a_{2i}b_{ip} \\ & & \vdots & & \\ \sum_{i=1}^{n} a_{mi}b_{i1} & \sum_{i=1}^{n} a_{mi}b_{i2} & \cdots & \sum_{i=1}^{n} a_{mi}b_{ip} \end{pmatrix}.$$

Two matrices can be multiplied only if the number of columns in the left-hand matrix is equal to the number of rows in the right-hand matrix. If **A** is an $m \times n$ matrix (m rows and n columns) and **B** is an $n \times p$ matrix, then the product matrix **AB** exists and has m rows and p columns. Immediately we can see that matrix multiplication is not commutative, since it makes a difference which matrix is on the left and which is on the right.

The formula for matrix multiplication looks very complicated, but we can make more sense of it by using the dot product of two vectors. The dot product of two vectors is formed by multiplying together each pair of corresponding components and then adding the results of all these products. (See **dot product**.)

A matrix can be thought of either as a vertical stack of row vectors:

$$\begin{pmatrix} a_{11} & \cdots & a_{1n} \\ & \vdots & \\ a_{m1} & \cdots & a_{mn} \end{pmatrix} = \begin{pmatrix} \mathbf{a}_1 \\ \vdots \\ \mathbf{a}_m \end{pmatrix} \qquad \begin{aligned} \mathbf{a}_1 &= (a_{11}, a_{12}, \ldots, a_{1n}) \\ &\vdots \\ \mathbf{a}_m &= (a_{m1}, a_{m2}, \ldots, a_{mn}) \end{aligned}$$

or as a horizontal stack of column vectors:

$$\begin{pmatrix} b_{11} & \cdots & b_{1p} \\ & \vdots & \\ b_{n1} & \cdots & b_{np} \end{pmatrix} = (\mathbf{b}_1, \mathbf{b}_2, \ldots, \mathbf{b}_p) \qquad \mathbf{b}_1 = \begin{pmatrix} b_{11} \\ \vdots \\ b_{n1} \end{pmatrix} \cdots \mathbf{b}_p = \begin{pmatrix} b_{1p} \\ \vdots \\ b_{np} \end{pmatrix}.$$

For our purposes it is best to think of the left-hand matrix (**A**) as a collection of row vectors, and the right-hand matrix (**B**) as a collection of column vectors. Then each element in the matrix product **AB** can be found as a dot product of one row of **A** with one column of **B**:

$$\mathbf{AB} = \begin{pmatrix} \mathbf{a}_1 \cdot \mathbf{b}_1 & \mathbf{a}_1 \cdot \mathbf{b}_2 & \mathbf{a}_1 \cdot \mathbf{b}_3 & \cdots & \mathbf{a}_1 \cdot \mathbf{b}_p \\ \mathbf{a}_2 \cdot \mathbf{b}_1 & \mathbf{a}_2 \cdot \mathbf{b}_2 & \mathbf{a}_2 \cdot \mathbf{b}_3 & \cdots & \mathbf{a}_2 \cdot \mathbf{b}_p \\ & & \vdots & & \\ \mathbf{a}_m \cdot \mathbf{b}_1 & \mathbf{a}_m \cdot \mathbf{b}_2 & \mathbf{a}_m \cdot \mathbf{b}_3 & \cdots & \mathbf{a}_m \cdot \mathbf{b}_p \end{pmatrix}.$$

The element in position $(1, 1)$ of the product matrix is the dot product of the first row of **A** with the first column of **B**. In general, the element in position (i, j) is formed by the dot product of row i in **A** and column j in **B**.

Examples of matrix multiplication are

$$\begin{pmatrix} a & b \\ c & d \end{pmatrix}\begin{pmatrix} e & f \\ g & h \end{pmatrix} = \begin{pmatrix} ae+bg & af+bh \\ ce+dg & cf+dh \end{pmatrix},$$

$$\begin{pmatrix} 1 & 1 & 1 \\ 0 & 1 & 0 \\ 2 & 0 & 2 \end{pmatrix}\begin{pmatrix} 1 & 4 \\ 2 & 5 \\ 3 & 6 \end{pmatrix} = \begin{pmatrix} 6 & 15 \\ 2 & 5 \\ 8 & 20 \end{pmatrix}.$$

Matrix multiplication is a very valuable tool, making it much easier to write systems of linear simultaneous equations. The three-equation system

$$a_1 x + b_1 y + c_1 z = d_1,$$
$$a_2 x + b_2 y + c_2 z = d_2,$$
$$a_3 x + b_3 y + c_3 z = d_3,$$

can be rewritten using matrix multiplication as

$$\begin{pmatrix} a_1 & b_1 & c_1 \\ a_2 & b_2 & c_2 \\ a_3 & b_3 & c_3 \end{pmatrix}\begin{pmatrix} x \\ y \\ z \end{pmatrix} = \begin{pmatrix} d_1 \\ d_2 \\ d_3 \end{pmatrix}.$$

MAXIMA The maxima are the points where the value of a function is greater than it is at the surrounding points. For example, the function $y = -x^2 + 5$ has a maximum at the point $x = 0$, $y = 5$. A point will be a maximum point if the first derivative of the function is zero and the second derivative is negative at that point.

MAXIMUM LIKELIHOOD ESTIMATOR A maximum likelihood estimator has this property: if the true value of the unknown parameter is the same as the value of the maximum likelihood estimator, then the probability of obtaining the sample that was actually observed is maximized. (See **statistical inference**.)

MEAN The mean of a random variable is the same as its *expectation*. The mean of a group of numbers is the same as its *arithmetic mean*.

MEAN VALUE THEOREM If the derivative of a function f is defined everywhere between two points, $(a, f(a))$ and $(b, f(b))$, then the mean value theorem states that there will be at least one value of x between a and b such that the value of the derivative is equal to the slope of the line between $(a, f(a))$ and $(b, f(b))$. This means that there is at least one point in the interval where the tangent line to the curve is parallel to the secant line that passes through the curve at the two endpoints of the interval.

MEANS OF A PROPORTION In the proportion $a/b = c/d$, b and c are called the means of the proportion.

MEDIAN (1) The median of a group of n numbers is the number such that just as many numbers are greater than it as are less than it. For example, the median of the set of numbers $\{1, 2, 3\}$ is 2; the median of $\{1, 1, 1, 2, 10, 15, 16, 20, 100, 105, 110\}$ is 15.

(2) A median of a triangle is a line segment connecting one vertex to the midpoint of the opposite side. (See **triangle**.)

METALANGUAGE A metalanguage is a language that is used to describe other languages.

MIDPOINT Point B is the midpoint of the segment AC if it is between A and B and if $AB = BC$ (i.e., point B is halfway between points A and B).

MINIMA The minima are the points where the value of a function is less than it is at the surrounding points. For example, the function $y = x^2 - 5$ has a minimum at the point $x = 0$, $y = -5$. A point will be a minimum point if the first derivative of the function is zero and the second derivative is positive at that point.

MINOR The minor of an element in a matrix is the determinant of the matrix formed by crossing out the row and column containing that element. For example, the minor of the element d in

$$\begin{pmatrix} a & b & c \\ d & e & f \\ g & h & i \end{pmatrix}$$

is the determinant

$$\begin{vmatrix} b & c \\ h & i \end{vmatrix} = bi - ch.$$

MINOR ARC A minor arc of a circle is an arc with a measure less than $180°$. (See **arc**.)

MINOR PREMISE The minor premise is the sentence in a syllogism that asserts a property about a specific case. (See **syllogism**.)

MINUTE A minute is a unit of measure for angles equal to 1/60 of a degree.

MODE The mode of a group of numbers is the number that occurs most frequently in that group. For example, the mode of the set $\{0, 1, 1, 2, 2, 2, 3, 3, 3, 3, 5, 5, 6, 6, 6\}$ is 3, since 3 occurs four times.

MODULUS The modulus of a complex number is the same as its absolute value.

MONOMIAL A monomial is an algebraic expression that does not involve any additions or subtractions. For example, 4×3, a^2b^3, and $\frac{4}{3}\pi r^3$ are all monomials.

MULTINOMIAL A multinomial is the sum of two or more monomials. Each monomial is called a *term*. For example, $a^2b^3 + 6 + 4b^5$ is a multinomial with three terms.

MULTIPLE REGRESSION Suppose that a variable Y depends on a series of variables X_1, X_2, and X_3 according to the equation

$$Y = \beta_1 X_1 + \beta_2 X_2 + \beta_3 X_3 + \beta_4 + \varepsilon,$$

where β_1, β_2, β_3, and β_4 are unknown coefficients, and ε is a random variable called the error term. The problem in multiple regression is to use observed values of Y, X_1, X_2, and X_3 to estimate the values of the β's. For example, Y could be the amount of money spent on food, X_1 could be income, X_2 could be the price of food, and X_3 could be the average price of other goods. If we have t observations each for Y, X_1, X_2, and X_3, then we can arrange the observations of the X's into a matrix X of t rows and four columns (with the last column consisting only of ones). Y can be arranged into a matrix of t rows and one column. Then the ordinary least squares estimate for the coefficients β is

$$\beta = (X^{tr}X)^{-1}X^{tr}Y,$$

where $(X^{tr}X)^{-1}$ is the inverse of the matrix formed by multiplying X by X transpose. (See **matrix; matrix multiplication**.) The actual calculations of the regression coefficients are best left to a computer.

The R^2-statistic provides a way of determining how much of the variance in Y this equation is able to explain. The t-statistic for each coefficient provides an estimate of whether that coefficient really should be included in the regression (i.e., is it really different from zero?). Regression methods are used often in statistics and in the branch of economics known as econometrics.

MULTIPLICATION Multiplication is the operation of repeated addition. For example, $3 \times 5 = 5 + 5 + 5 = 15$. Multiplication is symbolized by a multiplication sign ("$\times$") or by a dot ("$\cdot$"). In algebra much writing can be saved by leaving out the multiplication sign when two letters are being multiplied, or when a number multiplies a letter. For example, the expressions ab, πr^2, and $\frac{1}{2}at^2$ mean $a \times b$, $\pi \times r^2$, and $\frac{1}{2} \times a \times t^2$, respectively.

Multiplication obeys the commutative property:

$$(a \times b) = (b \times a)$$

and the associative property:

$$(a \times b) \times c = a \times (b \times c).$$

Whenever an expression contains both additions and multiplications, the multiplications are done first (unless a set of parentheses indicates otherwise). For example:

$$3 \times 5 + 4 \times 5 = 15 + 20 = 35,$$
$$3 \times (5 + 5) \times 4 = 3 \times 10 \times 4 = 120,$$
$$ax^2 + bx + c = (a \cdot x^2) + (b \cdot x) + c.$$

The relation between addition and multiplication is given by the distributive property:

$$a(b + c) = ab + ac.$$

MULTIPLICATIVE IDENTITY The number 1 is the multiplicative identity, because $1 \times a = a$, for all a.

MULTIPLICATIVE INVERSE The multiplicative inverse of a number a (written as $1/a$ or a^{-1}) is the number that, when multiplied by a, gives a result of 1:

$$a\left(\frac{1}{a}\right) = 1.$$

The multiplicative inverse is also called the reciprocal. For example, $\frac{1}{2}$ is the reciprocal of 2. There exists a multiplicative inverse for every number except zero.

N

NATURAL LOGARITHM   The natural logarithm of a number x (written as $\ln x$) is the logarithm of x to the base e, where $e = 2.718\ldots$. The natural logarithm function can also be defined by the integral

$$\ln x = \int_1^x t^{-1}\, dt.$$

(See **logarithm; calculus**.)

Here is a table of some natural logarithms:

x	$\ln x$
0.2	-1.6094
0.5	-0.6931
0.8	-0.2231
1.0	0
2	0.6931
3	1.0986
4	1.3863
5	1.6094
6	1.7918
7	1.9459
8	2.0794
9	2.1972
10	2.3026
100	4.6052

NATURAL NUMBERS   The natural numbers are the set of numbers $\{1, 2, 3, 4, 5, 6, 7, 8, \ldots\}$. This set of numbers is also called the counting numbers, since they're the numbers used to count something. They can also be called the positive integers.

NECESSARY   In the statement $a \rightarrow b$, b is a necessary condition for a to be true. For example, having four $90°$ angles is a necessary condition for a quadrilateral to be a square (but it is not a sufficient condition).

NEGATION   The negation of a statement "p" is the statement "NOT p," symbolized by $\sim p$. If p is true, then $\sim p$ is false; if p is false, then $\sim p$ is true.

NEGATIVE A negative number is any number less than zero. The negative of any number a (written as $-a$) is defined by this equation: $a + (-a) = 0$.

NEWTON'S METHOD Newton's method (see Figure 1) provides a way to estimate the places where complicated functions cross the x-axis. First, make a guess, x_1, that seems reasonably close to the true value. Then approximate the curve by its tangent line to estimate a new value, x_2, from the equation

$$x_2 = x_1 - \frac{f(x_1)}{f'(x_1)},$$

where $f'(x_1)$ is the derivative of the function f at the point x_1. (See **calculus; derivative.**) You can repeat the procedure to find an even closer guess, x_3:

$$x_3 = x_2 - \frac{f(x_2)}{f'(x_2)}.$$

The process is iterative, that is, it can be repeated as often as you like. This means that you can get as close to the true value as you wish.

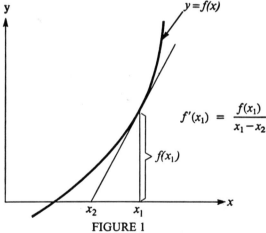

FIGURE 1

For example, Newton's method can be used to find the x-intercept of the function $y = x^3 - 2x^2 - 6x - 8$. Start with a guess, $x_1 = 10$:

x_i	$f(x_i)$	$f'(x_i)$	$-f(x)/f'(x)$
10	732	254	-2.88
7.118	209	117	-1.77
5.343	55.4	58.3	-0.95
4.393	11.8	34.3	-0.34
4.048	1.28	26.98	-0.047
4.00088	0.023		

In this case you can see that the true value of the intercept occurs at $x = 4$.

A brief word of warning: the method doesn't always work. The tangent line approximation will not always converge to the true value. The method will not work for the function shown in Figure 2.

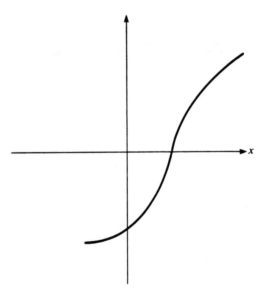

FIGURE 2

NON-EUCLIDIAN GEOMETRY Euclidian geometry describes the geometry of our everyday world. One postulate of Euclidian geometry describes the behavior of parallel lines. This postulate says that, if a straight line crosses two coplanar straight lines, and if the sum of the two interior angles formed on one side of the crossing line is less than 180°, then the two other lines will intersect at some point. In other words, they will not be parallel. If, on the other hand, the sum of the two interior angles is 180°, then the two lines will be parallel, meaning that they could be extended forever and never intersect. This postulate seems intuitively clear, but nobody has been able to prove it after several centuries of trying. Since we cannot travel to infinity to verify that two seemingly parallel lines never intersect, we cannot tell whether this postulate really is satisfied in our universe.

Some mathematicians decided to investigate what would happen to geometry if they changed the parallel postulate. They found that they were able to prove theorems in their new type of geometry. These theorems were consistent because no two theorems contradicted each other, but the geometry that resulted was different from the geometry developed by Euclid.

In one type of non-Euclidian geometry, called hyperbolic geometry, there is more than one line parallel to a given line through a given point. Janos Bolyai wrote one of the earliest descriptions of hyperbolic geometry in 1823.

In another type of non-Euclidian geometry, called elliptic geometry, there are no parallel lines. Elliptic geometry generalizes the situation in which you would find yourself if you were a two-dimensional being confined to the surface of a sphere. In that case any two "lines" would always intersect on the other side of the sphere. Ludwig Schlafli and Bernhard Riemann described elliptic geometry in the late 1800s.

Non-Euclidean geometries play an important role in the development of relativity theory. They also are important because they shed light on the nature of logical systems.

NORMAL In mathematics the word "normal" means "perpendicular." A line is normal to a curve if it is perpendicular to a tangent line to that curve at the point where it intersects the curve. Two vectors are normal to each other if their dot product is zero.

NORMAL DISTRIBUTION A random variable X has a normal distribution if its density function is

$$f(x) = \frac{1}{\sigma\sqrt{2\pi}} e^{-(x-\mu)^2/2\sigma^2}.$$

The mean (or expectation) of X is μ, and its variance is σ^2. If $\mu = 0$ and $\sigma = 1$, then X is said to have the standard normal distribution, which has the density function

$$f(x) = \frac{1}{\sqrt{2\pi}} e^{-(1/2)x^2}$$

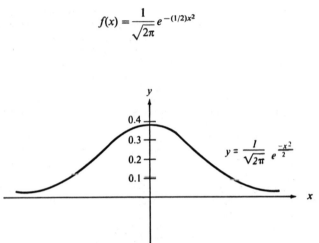

The figure shows a graph of the standard normal density function. The integral of this function cannot be found analytically, but Tables 3 and 4 list some values.

The central limit theorem is one important application of the normal distribution. The central limit theorem states that, if $X_1, X_2, \ldots, X_n$ are independent, identically distributed random variables, with mean μ and variance σ^2, then, in the limit that n goes to infinity,

$$S_n = X_1 + X_2 + X_3 + \cdots + X_n$$

will have a normal distribution with mean $n\mu$ and variance $n\sigma^2$. The reason that this theorem is so remarkable is that it is completely general. It says that, no matter how X is distributed, if you add up enough measurements, the sum of the X's will have a normal distribution.

NOT The word "NOT" is used in logic to indicate the negation of a statement. The statement "NOT p" is false if p is true, and it is true if p is false. The operation of NOT can be described by this truth table:

p	NOT p
T	F
F	T

The symbol " $\sim$ " is usually used to represent NOT. Some books use the symbol " $\neg$ " for NOT; others put a bar over a sentence variable to indicate NOT. (See logic; Boolean algebra.)

NULL HYPOTHESIS The null hypothesis is the hypothesis that is being tested in a hypothesis-testing situation. (See hypothesis testing.) Often the null hypothesis is of the form "There is no relation between two quantities." For example, if you were testing the effect of a new medicine, you would want to test the null hypothesis "This medicine has no effect on the patients who take it." If the medicine did work, then you would obtain statistical evidence that would cause you to reject the null hypothesis.

NULL SET The null set is the set that contains no elements. The term "null set" means the same as the term "empty set."

NUMBER Everyone first learns the basic set of numbers: 1, 2, 3, 4, 5, 6, ... These are known as the natural numbers, or counting numbers. The natural numbers are used to count discrete objects, such as two books, five trees, or five thousand people. There is an infinite number of natural numbers. Natural numbers obey an important property known as closure under addition. This means that, whenever you add two natural numbers together, the result will still be a natural number. The natural numbers also obey closure under multiplication.

One important number not included in the set of natural numbers is zero. It would be very difficult to measure the snowfall in the Sahara Desert without knowing the number zero. The union of the set of natural numbers and the set containing zero is the set of whole numbers.

The set of whole numbers does not obey closure under subtraction. If you subtract one whole number from another, there is no guarantee that you will get another whole number. This suggests the need for another kind of number: negative numbers. Also, there are times when the natural numbers do not do an adequate job of measuring certain quantities. If you are measuring the government surplus (equal to tax revenue minus government expenditures), you need negative numbers to represent the years when the government runs a deficit. If you are measuring the yardage gained by a football team, you need to use negative numbers to represent the yardage on the plays whereby the team loses yardage.

Every natural number has its own negative, or additive inverse. If a represents a natural number and $-a$ is its negative, then $a + -a = 0$. The union of the set of natural numbers and the set of the negatives of all the natural numbers and zero is the set of integers. The set of integers looks like this:

$$\ldots, -5, -4, -3, -2, -1, 0, 1, 2, 3, 4, 5, 6, 7, 8, \ldots.$$

Integers do not obey closure under division. A rational number is any number that can be obtained as the result of a division problem containing two integers. All fractions, such as $\frac{1}{2}$, 0.6, 3.4, and $5\frac{2}{3}$, are rational numbers. Also, all the integers are rational numbers, since any integer a can be written as $a/1$. You cannot make a list of the rational numbers, as you can for the integers, because the set of rational numbers is infinitely dense. That means that there is always an infinite number of other rational numbers between any two rational numbers.

Nevertheless, there are many numbers that aren't rational. The square roots of most integers are not rational. For example, $\sqrt{4} = 2$, but $\sqrt{5}$ is approximately equal to 2.236067977. . . , which cannot be expressed as the ratio of two integers. There are important geometric reasons for needing these irrational numbers. (See **Pythagorean theorem**.) Irrational numbers are also needed to express most of the values for trigonometric functions, and two special numbers, $\pi = 3.14159\ldots$ and $e = 2.71828\ldots$, are both irrational. For practical purposes you can always find a rational number that is a close approximation to any irrational number.

The set of all rational numbers and all irrational numbers is known as the set of real numbers. Each real number can be represented by a unique point on a straight line that extends off to infinity in both directions. Real numbers have a definite order, that is, for any two distinct real numbers you can always tell which one is bigger. The result of a measurement of a physical quantity, such as energy, distance, or momentum, will be a real number.

However, there are some numbers that are not real. There is no real number x that satisfies the equation $x^2 + 1 = 0$. Imaginary numbers are needed to describe the square roots of negative numbers. The basis of the imaginary numbers is the imaginary unit, i, which is defined so that $i^2 = -1$. Pure imaginary numbers are formed by multiplying a real number by i. For example:

$$\sqrt{(-64)} = \sqrt{64}\sqrt{-1} = 8i.$$

If a pure imaginary number is added to a real number, the result is known as a complex number. The real numbers and the imaginary numbers are both subsets of the set of complex numbers. The general form of a complex number is $a + bi$, where a and b are both real numbers. Complex numbers are important in some areas of physics, as when they are used to represent wave functions in quantum mechanics.

NUMBER LINE   A number line is a line on which each point represents a real number.

NUMERAL   A numeral is a symbol that stands for a number. For example, "4" is the Arabic numeral for the number four. "IV" is the Roman numeral for the same number.

NUMERATOR   The numerator is the number above the bar in a fraction. In the fraction $\frac{8}{9}$, 8 is the numerator. (See **denominator; fraction.**)

NUMERICAL INTEGRATION   The numerical integration method is used when it is not possible to find a formula that can be evaluated to give the value of a definite integral. For example, there is no formula that gives the value of the definite integral

$$\int_0^a e^{-x^2}\, dx.$$

The procedure in numerical integration is to divide the area under the curve into a series of tiny rectangles and then add up the areas of the rectangles. (See figure.) The height of each rectangle is equal to the value of the function at that point. As the number of rectangles increases (and the width of each rectangle becomes smaller), the accuracy of the method improves. In practice, the calculations for a numerical integration are carried out by a computer.

There are also alternative methods that use trapezoids or strips bounded by parabolas.

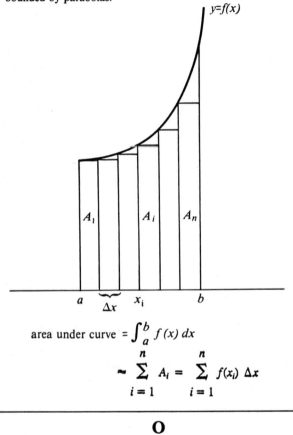

area under curve $= \int_a^b f(x)\,dx$

$$\sim \sum_{i=1}^{n} A_i = \sum_{i=1}^{n} f(x_i)\,\Delta x$$

O

OBJECTIVE FUNCTION   An objective function is a function whose value you are trying to maximize or minimize. The value of the objective function depends on the values of a set of choice variables, and the problem is to find the optimal values for those choice variables. For an example, see **linear programming**.

OBLIQUE ANGLE   An oblique angle is an angle that is not a right angle.

OBLIQUE TRIANGLE   An oblique triangle is a triangle that is not a right triangle.

OBTUSE ANGLE   An obtuse angle is an angle larger than a 90° angle and smaller than a 180° angle.

OBTUSE TRIANGLE   An obtuse triangle (see figure) is a triangle containing one obtuse angle. (Note that a triangle can never contain more than one obtuse angle.)

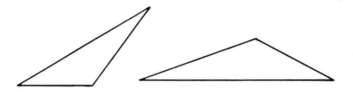

OCTAGON   An octagon is an eight-sided polygon. The best-known example of an octagon is a stop sign.

ODD FUNCTION   The function $f(x)$ is an odd function if it satisfies the property that $f(-x) = -f(x)$. For example, $f(x) = \sin x$ and $f(x) = x^3$ are both odd functions.

ODD NUMBER   An odd number is a whole number that is not divisible by 2, such as 1, 3, 5, 7, 9, 11, 13, 15, ...

ONE-TAILED TEST   In a one-tailed test the critical region consists of only one tail of a distribution. The null hypothesis is rejected only if the test statistic has an extreme value in one direction. (See **hypothesis testing**.)

OPEN INTERVAL   An open interval is an interval that does not contain both its endpoints. For example, the interval $0 < x < 1$ is an open interval because the endpoints 0 and 1 are not included. For contrast, see **closed interval**.

OPEN SENTENCE   An open sentence is a sentence containing one or more variables that can be either true or false, depending on the value of the variable(s). For example, $x = 7$ is an open sentence.

OPERAND   An operand is the number that is the subject of an operation. In the equation $5 + 3 = 8$, 5 and 3 are the operands.

OPERATION   An operation, such as addition or multiplication, is the process of carrying out a particular rule on a set of numbers. The four fundamental arithmetic operations are *addition*, *multiplication*, *division*, and *subtraction*.

OR   The word "OR" is a connective word used in logic. The sentence "p OR q" is false only if both p and q are false; it is true if either p or q or both are true. The operation of OR is illustrated by the truth table:

p	q	p OR q
T	T	T
T	F	T
F	T	T
F	F	F

The symbol " $\vee$ " is often used to represent OR. An OR sentence is also called a *disjunction*. (See **logic; Boolean algebra**.)

ORDERED PAIR   An ordered pair is a set of two numbers where the order in which the numbers are written has an agreed upon meaning. One common example of an ordered pair is the Cartesian coordinates (x, y), where it is agreed that the horizontal coordinate is always listed first and the vertical coordinate last.

ORDINATE   The ordinate of a point is another name for the y-coordinate. The ordinate of the point (a, b) is b. (See **Cartesian coordinates**.)

ORIGIN   The origin is the point $(0, 0)$ in Cartesian coordinates. It is the point where the x- and the y-axes intersect.

ORTHOCENTER   The orthocenter of a triangle is the point where the three altitudes of the triangle meet. (See **triangle**.)

P

PARABOLA   A parabola (see figure) is the set of all points that are

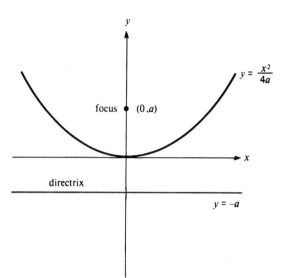

equally distant from a fixed point (called the *focus*) and a fixed line (called the *directrix*). If the focus is at $(0, a)$ and the directrix is the line $y = -a$, then the analytic equation can be found from the definition of the parabola:

$$y + a = \sqrt{x^2 + (y - a)^2},$$
$$y^2 + 2ay + a^2 = x^2 + y^2 - 2ay + a^2,$$
$$4ay = x^2,$$
$$y = \frac{1}{4a}x^2.$$

The final equation for a parabola is very simple. One example of a parabola is the graph of the equation $y = x^2$.

Parabolas have many practical uses. The course of any thrown object, such as a baseball, is a parabola (although it will be modified a bit by air resistance). The cross section of a telescopic mirror is a parabola. The telescopic mirror constitutes a surface known as a paraboloid, which is formed by rotating a parabola about its axis. When parallel light rays from a distant star strike the paraboloid, they are all reflected back to the focal point. For the same reason, the network microphones that pick up field noises at televised football games are shaped like paraboloids. Probably the largest parabola in practical use is the cross section of the 1000-foot-wide radio tele-scope carved out of the ground at Arecibo, Puerto Rico.

The parabola is an example of a more general class of curves known as *conic sections*.

PARABOLOID A paraboloid is a surface that is formed by rotating a parabola about its axis. (See **parabola**.)

PARALLEL Two lines are parallel if they are in the same plane but never intersect. In the figure lines *AB* and *CD* are parallel. A postu-

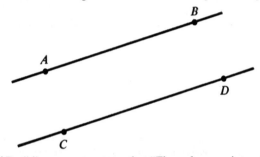

late of Euclidian geometry states that "Through any point not on a line there is one and only one line that is parallel to the first line." Two planes are parallel if they never intersect.

PARALLELEPIPED A parallelepiped is a solid figure with six faces such that the planes containing two opposite faces are parallel. (See figure.) Each face is a *parallelogram*.

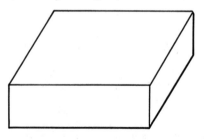

PARALLELOGRAM   A parallelogram is a quadrilateral with opposite sides parallel. (See **quadrilateral**.)

PARAMETER   In statistics a parameter is a quantity (often unknown) that characterizes a population. For example, the mean
height of all 6-year-olds in the United States is an unknown parameter. One of the goals of statistical inference is to estimate the values
of parameters.

PARAMETRIC EQUATION   A parametric equation in x and y is an
equation of the form $x = f(t)$, $y = g(t)$, where t is the parameter. For
example, the parametric equation $x = r \cos t$, $y = r \sin t$ defines the
circle centered at the origin with radius r. For another example of a
parametric equation, see **cycloid**.

PARENTHESIS   A set of parentheses ( ) indicates that the operation
in the parentheses is to be done first. For example, in the expression

$$y = 5 \times (2 + 10 + 30) = 5 \times 42 = 210,$$

the parentheses tell you to do the addition first.

PARTIAL   DERIVATIVE   The   partial   derivative   of
$y = f(x_1, x_2, \ldots, x_n)$ with respect to x_i is found by taking the derivative of y with respect to x_i while all the other independent variables
are held constant. For example, suppose that y is this function of two
variables: $y = f(x_1, x_2) = x_1^a x_2^b$. Then the partial derivative of y
with respect to x_1 (written as $\partial y / \partial x_1$) is $ax_1^{a-1} x_2^b$. Likewise,

$$\frac{\partial y}{\partial x_2} = bx_1^a x_2^{b-1}.$$

(See **derivative**.)

PARTIAL FRACTIONS   An algebraic expression of the form

$$\frac{b_m x^m + b_{m-1} x^{m-1} + \cdots + b_2 x^2 + b_1 x + b_0}{(x - a_1)(x - a_2)(x - a_3) \times \cdots \times (x - a_{n-1})(x - a_n)} \quad (m < n)$$

can be written as the sum of n partial fractions, like this:

$$\frac{C_1}{x - a_1} + \frac{C_2}{x - a_2} + \cdots + \frac{C_n}{x - a_n},$$

where $C_1, \ldots, C_n$ are constants for which we can solve.

For example, the expression

$$\frac{5x - 7}{(x - 1)(x - 2)}$$

can be split up into partial fractions as follows:

$$\frac{5x - 7}{(x - 1)(x - 2)} = \frac{A}{x - 1} + \frac{B}{x - 2}.$$

Now we need to solve for A and B, which we can do this way:

$$\frac{5x - 7}{(x - 1)(x - 2)} = \frac{A(x - 2) + B(x - 1)}{(x - 1)(x - 2)}.$$

For this equation to be true for all values of x, we must have A and B satisfy:

coefficients of x:

$$5 = A + B$$

constant terms:

$$-7 = -2A - B$$

This is a two-equation, two-unknown system, which has the solution $A = 2$, $B = 3$. Therefore:

$$\frac{5x - 7}{(x - 1)(x - 2)} = \frac{2}{x - 1} + \frac{3}{x - 2}.$$

PASCAL'S TRIANGLE Pascal's triangle is a triangular array of numbers in which each number is equal to the sum of the two numbers directly above it. The triangle looks like this:

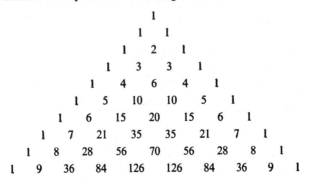

If you call the "1" in the top row zero, then the $(j + 1)$th element in row n (P_n^j) can be found from the formula

$$P_n^j = \binom{n}{j} = \frac{n!}{(n-j)!\,j!}.$$

(See **factorial; combinations**.)

An important use of Pascal's triangle is based on the fact that row n of the triangle gives the coefficients of the expansion of $(a + b)^n$. (See **binomial theorem**.)

PEARSON'S COEFFICIENT   See **correlation coefficient**.

PENTAGON   A pentagon is a five-sided polygon. The sum of the angles in a pentagon is 540°. A regular pentagon has all five sides equal, and each of the five angles equal to 108°. The most famous pentagon is the Pentagon building, near Washington, D.C., which has sides 921 feet long.

PERCENT   A percent is a fraction in which the denominator is assumed to be 100. The symbol "%" means "percent." For example, 50% means $50/100 = 0.50$, 2% means $2/100 = 0.02$ and 150% means $150/100 = 1.5$.

PERCENTILE   The pth percentile of a list is the number such that p percent of the elements in the list are less than that number. For example, if the height of a particular child is at the 55th percentile, then 55 percent of the children of the same age have heights less than this child.

PERIMETER   The perimeter of a polygon is the sum of the lengths of all the sides. If you had to walk all the way around the outer edge of a polygon, the total distance you would walk would be the perimeter.

PERIOD   The period of a periodic function is a measure of how often the function repeats the same values. For example, the function $f(x) = \cos x$ repeats its values every 2π units, so its period is 2π.

PERIODIC   A periodic function is a function that keeps repeating the same values. Formally, a function $f(x)$ is periodic if there exists a number p such that $f(x + p) = f(x)$, for all x. If p is the smallest number with this property, then p is called the period. For example, the function $y = \sin x$ is a periodic function with a period of 2π, because $\sin(x + 2\pi) = \sin x$, for all x.

PERMUTATIONS   The term "permutations" refers to the number of different ways of choosing *j* things from *n* objects, when you care about the order in which they are arranged. The number of permutations of *n* objects, taken *j* at a time, is $n!/(n-j)!$. (See **factorial; combinations**.) For example, in an eight-horse race there are $8!/5! = 8 \times 7 \times 6 = 336$ possible permutations for the top three winners. There are eight possibilities for the first horse, seven for the second horse, and six for the third horse.

PERPENDICULAR   Two lines are perpendicular if the angle between them is a 90° angle. Two vectors are perpendicular if their dot product is zero. (See **dot product**.)

If *AB* is the line where two planes intersect, then the two planes are perpendicular if the two lines, one in each plane, that are perpendicular to *AB* at point *A* are perpendicular to each other.

By definition, the two legs of a right triangle are perpendicular to each other. In a well-designed house the walls are perpendicular to the floor.

pi   The Greek letter π ("pi") is used to represent the ratio between the circumference of a circle and its diameter:

$$\pi = \frac{\text{(circumference of circle)}}{\text{(diameter)}}.$$

(This ratio is the same for any circle.) The number π is an irrational number with the decimal approximation $3.1415926536\ldots$; π can also be approximated by the fraction 22/7. For example, if a circle has a radius of 8 units, then it has a diameter of 16, a circumference of $16\pi \approx 16 \times 22/7 = 50.3$, and an area of $\pi r^2 = 64\pi \approx 201.1$.

There are several ways to find numerical approximations for pi. If we inscribe a regular polygon inside a circle (see figure), then the perimeter of the polygon is less than the circumference of the circle. However, if we double the number of sides in the polygon, keeping it inscribed in the same circle, then the perimeter of the polygon will be a closer approximation to the circumference of the circle. If we keep doubling the number of sides, we can come as close as we want to the true circumference. If s_n is the length of a side of a regular polygon inscribed in a circle of radius *r*, and s_{2n} is the length of the side of the inscribed polygon with twice as many sides, then

$$s_{2n}^2 = 2r^2 - r\sqrt{4r^2 - s_n^2}.$$

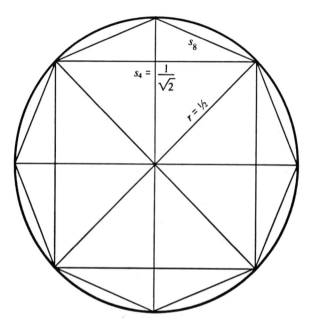

For $r = \frac{1}{2}$, the perimeter of the polygon will approach π as the number of sides is increased:

n	nS_n (approximation for π)
4	2.8284
8	3.0615
16	3.1214
32	3.1365
64	3.1403
128	3.1413
256	3.1415
512	3.14157
1024	3.14159

The arctangent function can be used to find a series approximation for π. We know that

$$\frac{1}{1-z} = 1 + z + z^2 + z^3 + z^4 + \cdots$$

(for $|z| < 1$). (See **geometric series**.) If $z = -x^2$, then

$$\frac{1}{1+x^2} = 1 - x^2 + x^4 - x^6 + x^8 - x^{10} + \cdots$$

($x < 1$).

From calculus we know that, if $y = \arctan x$, then $dy/dx = 1/(1+x^2)$. (See **integral**.) Then

$$\frac{dy}{dx} - 1 - x^2 + x^4 - x^6 + x^8 - x^{10} + \cdots$$

If we integrate this series term by term, then

$$y = \arctan x = x - \frac{x^3}{3} + \frac{x^5}{5} - \frac{x^7}{7} + \frac{x^9}{9} - \cdots.$$

Since $\tan(\pi/4) = 1$, then $\arctan 1 = \pi/4$. Therefore:

$$\frac{\pi}{4} = 1 - \tfrac{1}{3} + \tfrac{1}{5} - \tfrac{1}{7} + \tfrac{1}{9} - \tfrac{1}{11} + \cdots.$$

The table shows how this series converges to π as the number of terms increases.

n	Approximation for π
1	4
10	3.0418
50	3.1216
100	3.1316
500	3.1396
600	3.1399
601	3.1423
800	3.1403
801	3.1428
1000	3.1406
1001	3.1426

As you can see, this series takes a long time to converge to the true value of π.

Another way to find π is the infinite product:

$$\frac{\pi}{2} = \frac{2}{1} \times \frac{2}{3} \times \frac{4}{3} \times \frac{4}{5} \times \frac{6}{5} \times \frac{6}{7} \times \frac{8}{7} \times \frac{8}{9} \times \cdots.$$

After 200 factors this expression reaches the approximation $\pi \cong 3.1376$.

PLACEHOLDER Zero acts as a placeholder to indicate which power of 10 a digit is to be multiplied by. The importance of this role is indicated by considering the difference between the two numbers $300 = 3 \times 10^2$ and $3{,}000{,}000 = 3 \times 10^6$.

PLANE A plane is a flat surface (like a tabletop) that stretches off to infinity. A plane has zero thickness, but infinite length and width. "Plane" is one of the key undefined terms in Euclidian geometry. Any three noncollinear points will determine one and only one plane.

POISSON DISTRIBUTION The Poisson distribution is a discrete random variable distribution that often describes the frequency of occurrence of certain random events, such as the number of phone calls that arrive at an office in an hour. The Poisson distribution can also be used as an approximation for the binomial distribution in some cases. The Poisson distribution is characterized by a parameter usually written as λ (the Greek letter lambda).

If X has a Poisson distribution, then the density function is given by the formula

$$\Pr(X = k) = \frac{e^{-\lambda}\lambda^k}{k!},$$

where $e = 2.71828\ldots$, and the exclamation mark indicates factorial. The Poisson distribution has the unusual property that the expectation and the variance are equal (each is equal to λ).

POLAR COORDINATES Any point in a plane can be identified by its distance from the origin (r) and its angle of inclination (θ). This

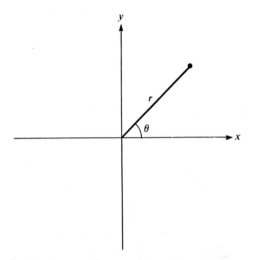

type of coordinate system is called a polar coordinate system (see figure). It is an alternative to rectangular (Cartesian) coordinates. Polar coordinates can be changed into Cartesian coordinates by the formulas

$$x = r \cos \theta, \qquad y = r \sin \theta.$$

Rectangular coordinates can be changed into polar coordinates by the formulas

$$r = \sqrt{x^2 + y^2}, \qquad \theta = \arctan \frac{y}{x}.$$

For example:

Cartesian Coordinates	Polar Coordinates
$(0, 0)$	$(0, 0°)$
$(3, 0)$	$(3, 0°)$
$(0, 4)$	$(4, 90°)$
$(\sqrt{3}, 1)$	$(2, 30°)$
$(3, 3)$	$(\sqrt{18}, 45°)$

The equation of a circle in polar coordinates is very simple: $r = R$, where R is the radius. The formula for the rotation of axes in polar coordinates is also very simple: $r' = r$, $\theta' = \theta - \phi$, where ϕ is the angle of rotation. (See **rotation**.)

POLYGON A polygon (see Figure 1) is the union of several line segments that are joined end to end so as to completely enclose an area. "Polygon" means "many-sided figure." Most useful polygons are convex polygons; in other words, the line segment connecting any two points inside the polygon will always stay completely inside the polygon. (A polygon that is not convex is concave, that is, it is caved in.)

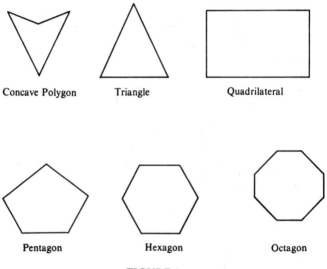

| Concave Polygon | Triangle | Quadrilateral |

| Pentagon | Hexagon | Octagon |

FIGURE 1

Polygons are classified by the number of sides they have. The most important ones are triangles (three sides), quadrilaterals (four sides), pentagons (five sides), hexagons (six sides), and octagons (eight sides). A polygon is a regular polygon if all its sides and angles are equal.

Two polygons are congruent (Figure 2) if they have exactly the same shape and size. Two polygons are similar if they have exactly the same shape but different sizes. Corresponding angles of similar polygons are equal, and corresponding sides have the same ratio.

The sum of all the angles in a polygon with n sides is $(n-2)180°$.

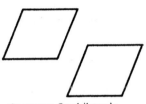

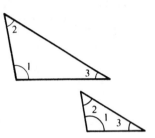

Congruent Quadrilaterals

Similar Triangles

FIGURE 2

POLYHEDRON A polyhedron is a solid that is bounded by plane polygons. The polygons are called the faces; the lines where the faces intersect are called the edges; and the points where three or more faces intersect are called the vertices. Some examples of polyhedrons are cubes (which have six sides), tetrahedrons (which have four sides), and prisms (see figure).

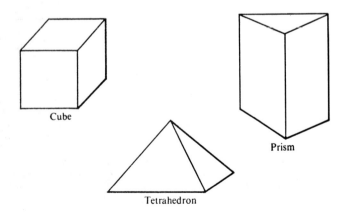

Cube

Prism

Tetrahedron

POLYNOMIAL A polynomial in x is an algebraic expression of the form

$$a_n x^n + a_{n-1} x^{n-1} + \cdots + a_3 x^3 + a_2 x^2 + a_1 x + a_0,$$

where $a_0, a_1, \ldots, a_n$ are constants that are the coefficients of the polynomial. The degree of the polynomial is the highest power of the variable that appears. The polynomial listed above has degree n, the polynomial $x^2 + 2x + 4$ has degree 2, and the polynomial $3y^3 + 2y$ has degree 3.

A polynomial equation is an equation with a polynomial on one side and zero on the other side:

$$a_n x^n + a_{n-1} x^{n-1} + \cdots + a_2 x^2 + a_1 x + a_0 = 0.$$

A polynomial of degree n can be written as the product of n first-degree (or linear) factors:

$$(x - r_1)(x - r_2) \times \cdots \times (x - r_n) = 0.$$

The equation will be true if either $x = r_1$ or $x = r_2$, and so on, so the equation will have n solutions. In general, a polynomial of degree n will have n solutions. For example, the figure shows that the third-degree polynomial $x^3 + 3x^2 - 9x + 3$ crosses the x-axis at three

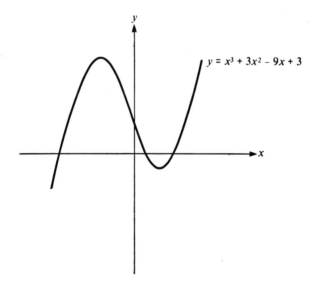

$y = x^3 + 3x^2 - 9x + 3$

places. However, there are two complications. First, not all of the solutions may be distinct. For example, the equation

$$x^2 - 4x + 4 = (x - 2)(x - 2) = 0$$

has two solutions, but they are both equal to 2. An extreme example is the equation $(x - a)^n = 0$, which has n solutions, but they are all equal to a.

Second, not all of the solutions will always be real numbers. For example, the equation

$$x^2 + 2x + 2 = 0$$

has two solutions: $x = -1 + i$, and $x = -1 - i$. (The letter i satisfies $i^2 = -1$. See **imaginary number**.) It is quite possible that a polynomial equation will have no real solutions at all. The complex solutions to a polynomial equation have the interesting property that they come in pairs: if $a + bi$ is a solution to a polynomial equation, then $a - bi$ will also be a solution.

If the degree of the polynomial equation is two, then the equation is called a quadratic equation. These equations can be solved fairly easily. (See **quadratic equation**.) It can be difficult to solve polynomial equations if the degree is higher than two. The *rational root theorem* can sometimes help to identify rational roots. *Newton's method* is a way to find numerical approximations to the roots of some polynomials.

If you can factor the polynomial into a product of linear and quadratic factors, it is easy to find the solution. However, the job of factoring can be very difficult. If you have found one solution (or root) of the equation, you can make the equation simpler. If you know that $x = r$ is a root of

$$a_n x^n + a_{n-1} x^{n-1} + \cdots + a_2 x^2 + a_1 x + a_0 = 0,$$

you can use *synthetic division* to rewrite the equation:

$$(x - r)(a'_{n-1} x^{n-1} + a'_{n-2} x^{n-2} + \cdots + a'_1 x + a'_0) = 0.$$

Now, to find more roots, you only have to solve an equation of degree $n - 1$, which should be a simpler task.

POPULATION A population consists of the set of all items of interest. The population may consist of a group of people or some other kind of object. In many practical situations the parameters that characterize the population are unknown. A sample of items is selected from the population, and the characteristics of that sample are used to estimate the characteristics of the population. (See **statistical inference**.)

POSITIVE NUMBER A positive number is any number greater than zero.

POSTULATE A postulate is a fundamental statement that is assumed to be true without proof. For example, the statement "Two distinct points are contained by one and only one line" is a postulate of Euclidian geometry.

POWER A power of a number indicates repeated multiplication. For example, "x to the third power" means "x multiplied by itself three times" ($x^3 = x \times x \times x$). Powers are written with little raised numbers known as exponents. (See **exponent**.)

POWER SERIES A series of the form

$$c_0 + c_1 x + c_2 x^2 + c_3 x^3 + \cdots,$$

where the c's are constants, is said to be a power series in x.

PRECEDENCE The rules of precedence determine the order in which operations are performed in an expression. For example, in ordinary algebraic notation and many computer programming languages, exponentiations are done first; then multiplications and divisions; and finally additions and subtractions. For example, in the expression $3 + 4 \times 5^2$ the exponentiation is done first, giving the result $3 + 4 \times 25$. Then the multiplication is done, resulting in $3 + 100$. Finally the addition is performed, yielding the final result, 103.

   An operation enclosed in parentheses is always performed before an operation that is outside the parentheses. For example, in the expression $3 \times (4 + 5)$, the addition is done first, giving 3×9. Then the multiplication is performed, yielding the final result, 27.

PREMISE A premise is one of the sentences in an argument; the conclusion of the argument follows as a result of the premises. (See **logic**.)

PRIME FACTORS Any natural number can be expressed as the product of several prime numbers, which are called the prime factors of that number. Here are some examples of prime factors:

$$4 = 2 \times 2,$$
$$6 = 2 \times 3,$$
$$8 = 2 \times 2 \times 2,$$
$$9 = 3 \times 3,$$
$$10 = 5 \times 2,$$
$$12 = 2 \times 2 \times 3,$$
$$14 = 2 \times 7,$$
$$15 = 5 \times 3,$$

$$16 = 2 \times 2 \times 2 \times 2,$$
$$18 = 2 \times 3 \times 3,$$
$$27 = 3 \times 3 \times 3,$$
$$32 = 2 \times 2 \times 2 \times 2 \times 2,$$
$$48 = 2 \times 2 \times 2 \times 2 \times 3,$$
$$60 = 2 \times 2 \times 3 \times 5,$$
$$72 = 2 \times 2 \times 2 \times 3 \times 3.$$

PRIME NUMBER A prime number is a natural number that has no integer factors other than itself and 1. The smallest prime numbers are 2, 3, 5, 7, 11, 13, 17, 19, 23, 29, 31, 37, 41.

PRINCIPAL VALUES The principal values of the arcsin and arctan functions lie between $-\pi/2$ and $\pi/2$. The principal values of the arccos function are between 0 and π.

There are many values of x that satisfy the equation $y = \sin x$ for a given value of y, provided that $-1 \le y \le 1$. For example, $\pi/4$, $3\pi/4$, $9\pi/4$, and $11\pi/4$ each has a sine equal to $1/\sqrt{2}$. Therefore, the equation $x = \arcsin y$ does not define a unique value of x unless it is assumed that the value of x is to be taken from the range of principal values. Sometimes the name of the function is capitalized (for example, Arcsin y) to indicate that the principal value is to be taken. The principal values of an inverse trigonometric function have been defined as the values that are most convenient.

PRISM A prism is a solid that is formed by the union of all the line segments that connect corresponding points on two congruent polygons that are located in parallel planes. The regions enclosed by the polygons are called the bases. A line segment that connects two corresponding vertices of the polygons is called a lateral edge. If the lateral edges are perpendicular to the planes containing the bases, then the prism is a right prism. The distance between the planes containing the bases is called the altitude. Prisms can be classified by the shape of their bases. A prism with triangular bases is a triangular prism (see figure). A cube is an example of a right square prism.

Triangular prisms made of glass have an important application. If sunlight is passed through the prism, it is split up into all the colors of the rainbow (because light of different wavelengths is refracted in different amounts by the glass).

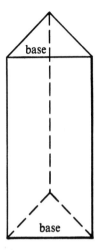

base

base

PROBABILITY Probability is the study of chance occurrences. Intuitively, we know that an event with a 50% probability is equally likely to occur or not occur.

Mathematically, probability is defined in terms of a probability space (called Ω—omega), which is the set of all possible outcomes of an experiment. Let s be the number of outcomes. For example, if you flip three coins, Ω contains eight outcomes: {(HHH), (HHT), (HTH), (HTT), (THH), (THT), (TTH), (TTT)}, where H stands for heads and T stands for tails. An event is a subset of Ω. For example, if A is the event that two heads appear, then $A = \{(HHT), (HTH), (THH)\}$. Let $N(A)$ be the number of points in A. Then the probability that the event A will occur (written as $\Pr(A)$) is defined as $\Pr(A) = N(A)/s$. In this case $N(A) = 3$ and $s = 8$, so the probability that two heads will appear if you flip three coins is 3/8. An important part of probability involves counting the number of possible outcomes in the probability space. (See **combinations; permutations; sampling**.)

A random variable is a variable that takes on different values when different random events occur. For example, if X is the number that appears on a set of two dice, then X is a random variable that can take on any value from 2 to 12. A discrete random variable has only a discrete number of possible values, and it is characterized by a density function, $f(x_i)$, such that

$$f(x_i) = \Pr(X = x_i).$$

For example, for the set of two dice,

$$f(2) = \Pr(X = 2) = \frac{1}{36}, \quad f(3) = \Pr(X = 3) = \frac{2}{36},$$

$$f(4) = \frac{3}{36}, \quad f(5) = \frac{4}{36}, \quad f(6) = \frac{5}{36}, \quad f(7) = \frac{6}{36},$$

$$f(8) = \frac{5}{36}, \quad f(9) = \frac{4}{36}, \quad f(10) = \frac{3}{36}, \quad f(11) = \frac{2}{36},$$

$$\text{and } f(12) = \frac{1}{36}.$$

A continuous random variable can have any value over a continuous range. It is characterized by a density function $f(x)$ such that

$$\int_a^b f(x)\, dx = \Pr(a < X < b).$$

PRODUCT The product is the result obtained when two numbers are multiplied. In the equation $4 \times 5 = 20$, the number 20 is the product of 4 and 5.

PROJECTION The projection of a point P on a line L is the point on L that is cut by the line that passes through P and is perpendicu-

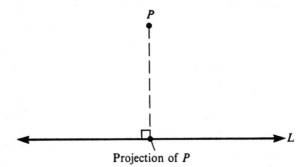

Projection of P

lar to L (see figure). In other words, the projection of point P is the point on line L that is the closest to point P. The projection of a set of points is the set of projections of all these points. Some shadows are examples of projections. Vectors can be projected on other vectors. (See **dot product**.)

PROOF   A proof is a sequence of statements that show a particular theorem to be true. In the course of a proof it is permissible to use only axioms (postulates) or theorems that have been previously proved.

PROPER FRACTION   A proper fraction is a fraction with a numerator that is smaller than the denominator, for example, $\frac{3}{4}$. For contrast, see **improper fraction**.

PROPORTION   A fractional equation of the form $a/b = c/d$ is called a proportion.

PROPOSITION   A proposition is a theorem that has yet to be proved.

PROTRACTOR   A protractor is a device for measuring the size of angles. Put the point marked with a star (see figure) at the vertex of

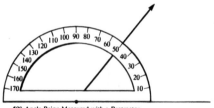

50° Angle Being Measured with a Protractor

the angle, and place the side of the protractor even with one side of the angle. Then the size of the angle can be read on the scale at the place where the other side of the angle crosses the protractor.

PYRAMID   A pyramid (see figure) is formed by the union of all line segments that connect a given point (called the vertex) and points that lie on a given polygon. (The vertex must not be in the same plane as the polygon.) The region enclosed by the plane is called the base, and the distance from the vertex to the plane containing the base is called the altitude. The volume of a pyramid is given by (volume) $= \frac{1}{3} \times$ (base area) $\times$ (altitude).

Pyramids are classified by the number of sides on their bases. (Note that all the faces other than the base are triangles.) A triangular pyramid, which contains four faces, is also known as a *tetrahedron*.

The most famous pyramids are the pyramids in Egypt. The largest of these pyramids originally had a base 756 feet square and an altitude of 481 feet.

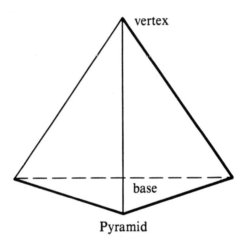

Pyramid

PYTHAGOREAN THEOREM The Pythagorean theorem relates the three sides of a right triangle: $c^2 = a^2 + b^2$, where c is the side opposite the right angle (the *hypotenuse*), and a and b are the sides adjacent to the right angle. The theorem is named after Pythagoras, a philosopher in the sixth century B.C.

For example, if one leg of a right triangle is 6 and the other leg is 8, then the hypotenuse has length $\sqrt{6^2 + 8^2} = 10$. The White House, the Washington Monument, and the Capitol in Washington, D.C., form a right triangle. The White House is 0.54 mile from the Washington Monument, and the Capitol is 1.4 miles from the monument. From this information we can determine that the distance from the White House to the Capitol is

$$\sqrt{(0.54)^2 + (1.4)^2} = 1.5 \text{ miles.}$$

Another application of the theorem is the distance formula, which says that the distance between two points in a plane, (x_1, y_1) and (x_2, y_2), is given by

$$\text{(distance)} = \sqrt{(x_1 - x_2)^2 + (y_1 - y_2)^2}.$$

There are many ways to prove the theorem. One way involves similar triangles. In the figure, triangles ABC and ACD have exactly

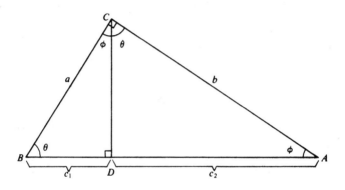

the same angles, so they are similar. Since corresponding sides of similar triangles are in proportion, we know that $c/b = b/c_2$. Likewise, triangles ABC and CBD are similar, so $c/a = a/c_1$. Therefore:

$$a^2 = cc_1 \qquad \text{and} \qquad b^2 = cc_2.$$

Add these together:

$$a^2 + b^2 = c(c_1 + c_2) = c^2,$$

and the theorem is demonstrated.

PYTHAGOREAN TRIPLE   If three integers a, b, and c satisfy $a^2 + b^2 = c^2$, then these three numbers are called a Pythagorean triple. For example, 3, 4, 5 and 5, 12, 13 are both Pythagorean triples, because $3^2 + 4^2 = 5^2$ and $5^2 + 12^2 = 13^2$.

Q

QUADRANT The x- and y-axes divide a plane into four regions, each of which is called a quadrant. The four quadrants are labeled the first quadrant, the second quadrant, and so on, as shown in the figure.

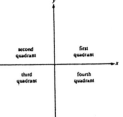

QUADRANTAL ANGLE The angles that measure $0°$, $90°$, $180°$, and $270°$, and all angles coterminal with these, are called quadrantal angles.

QUADRATIC EQUATION A quadratic equation is an equation involving the second power, but no higher power, of an unknown. The general form is

$$ax^2 + bx + c = 0$$

(a, b, and c are known; x is unknown; $a \neq 0$).

There are three ways to solve this kind of equation for x. One method is to factor the left-hand side into two linear factors. For example, to solve the equation $x^2 - 7x + 12 = 0$ we need to think of two numbers that multiply to give 12 and add to give -7. The two numbers that work are -4 and -3, which means that

$$(x - 4)(x - 3) = 0,$$

so

$$x = 4 \quad \text{or} \quad x = 3.$$

Often the factors are too complicated to determine by guessing, so we need another method. One possibility is *completing the square*. We write the equation like this:

$$x^2 + \frac{bx}{a} = -\frac{c}{a}.$$

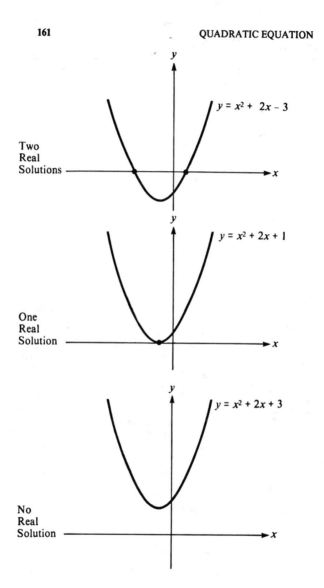

We can simplify the equation if we can add something to the left-hand side to make it a perfect square. We try adding $b^2/4a^2$ to both sides:

$$x^2 + \frac{bx}{a} + \frac{b^2}{4a^2} = \frac{b^2}{4a^2} - \frac{c}{a}.$$

The equation can now be rewritten as

$$\left(x + \frac{b}{2a}\right)^2 = \frac{b^2 - 4ac}{4a^2},$$

$$x + \frac{b}{2a} = \pm\sqrt{\frac{b^2 - 4ac}{4a^2}},$$

$$x = -\frac{b}{2a} \pm \frac{\sqrt{b^2 - 4ac}}{2a}$$

$$= \frac{-b \pm \sqrt{b^2 - 4ac}}{2a}.$$

The last equation is known as the quadratic formula. It allows us to solve for x, given any values for a, b, and c. The third way to solve a quadratic equation is simply to remember this formula.

The formula also reveals some properties of the solutions. The key quantity is $b^2 - 4ac$, which is known as the *discriminant*. If $b^2 - 4ac$ is positive, there will be two real values for x. If $b^2 - 4ac$ has a rational square root, then x will have two rational values; otherwise x will have two irrational values. If $b^2 - 4ac$ is zero, then x will have one real value. If $b^2 - 4ac$ is negative, then x will have two complex solutions. (See **complex number**.)

The real solutions to a quadratic equation can be illustrated on a graph of Cartesian coordinates. The graph of $ax^2 + bx + c$ is a parabola. The real solutions for x will occur at the places where the parabola intersects the x-axis. Three possibilities are shown in the figure.

QUADRATIC EQUATION, TWO UNKNOWNS   The general form of a quadratic equation in two unknowns is

(1) $$Ax^2 + Bxy + Cy^2 + Dx + Ey + F = 0,$$

where at least one of A, B, and C is nonzero. The graph of this equation will be one of the conic sections. To determine which one, you need to write the equation in a transformed set of coordinates so you can identify the standard form of the equation. First, rotate the coordinate axes by an angle θ, where

$$\tan 2\theta = \frac{B}{A - C}.$$

This procedure will get rid of the cross term Bxy. (See **rotation**.) In the new coordinates, x' and y', the equation becomes

(2) $$A'x'^2 + C'y'^2 + D'x' + E'y' + F' = 0.$$

If either A' or C' is zero, then the graph of this equation will be a parabola. For example, suppose that there is no y'^2 term, so $C' = 0$. If you perform this translation of coordinates:

$$x'' = x' + \frac{D'}{2A'} \qquad \text{and} \qquad y'' = y' + \frac{4A'F' - D'^2}{4A'E'},$$

the equation becomes

$$A'x''^2 + E'y'' = 0,$$

which can be graphed as a parabola.

If neither A' nor C' is zero in equation (2), then perform the translation

$$x'' = x' + \frac{D'}{2A'} \qquad \text{and} \qquad y'' = y' + \frac{E'}{2C'}.$$

Then the equation can be written in the form

$$A'x''^2 + C'y''^2 + F'' = 0.$$

If $A' = C'$, then this is the equation of a circle. If A' and C' have the same sign (i.e., they are both positive or both negative), the equation will be the equation of an ellipse. If A' and C' have opposite signs, the equation will be the equation of a hyperbola.

You can tell immediately what the graph of equation (1) will look like by examining the quantity $B^2 - 4AC$. It turns out that this quantity is invariant when you rotate the coordinate system. This means that $B'^2 - 4A'C'$ in equation (2) will equal $B^2 - 4AC$ in equation (1). If $B^2 - 4AC < 0$, the graph is an ellipse or a circle. If $B^2 - 4AC = 0$, the graph is a parabola. If $B^2 - 4AC > 0$, the graph is a hyperbola.

It is also possible for the solution to equation (1) to be either a pair of intersecting lines or a single point, or even for there to be no solution at all. In these cases the solution is said to be a degenerate conic section.

QUADRATIC FORMULA The quadratic formula says that the solution for x in the equation $ax^2 + bx + c = 0$ is

$$x = \frac{-b \pm \sqrt{b^2 - 4ac}}{2a}.$$

(See **quadratic equation**.)

QUADRILATERAL A quadrilateral (see Figure 1) is a four-sided polygon. A quadrilateral with two sides parallel is called a *trapezoid*, with area $\frac{1}{2}h(a + b)$. A *parallelogram* has its opposite sides parallel and equal. The area of a parallelogram is bh. A quadrilateral with all

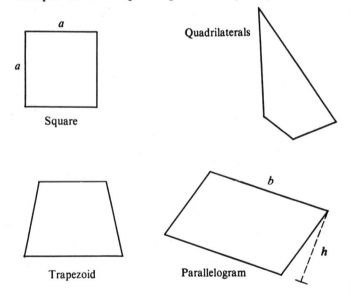

Quadrilaterals

Square

Trapezoid

Parallelogram

FIGURE 1

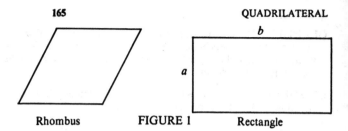

Rhombus   FIGURE 1   Rectangle

four sides equal is called a *rhombus*. A quadrilateral with all four angles equal is called a *rectangle*. The sum of the four angles in a quadrilateral is always 360°, so each angle in a rectangle is 90°. The area of a rectangle is ab. A regular quadrilateral has all four sides and all four angles equal, and is called a *square*. The area of a square is a^2.

A Venn diagram (see Figure 2) can be used to illustrate the relationship between different types of quadrilaterals.

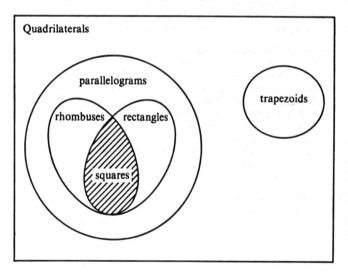

FIGURE 2

QUARTILE The first quartile of a list is the number such that one quarter of the numbers in the list are below it; the third quartile is the number such that three quarters of the numbers are below it; and the second quartile is the same as the median.

QUOTIENT The quotient is the answer to a division problem. In the equation $33/3 = 11$, the number 11 is the quotient.

R

R^2 The R^2 value for a regression is a number that indicates how well the regression explains the variance in the dependent variable. R^2 is always between 0 and 1. If it is close to 1, the regression has explained a lot of the variance; if it is close to 0, the regression has not explained very much. (See **multiple regression**.)

RADIAN MEASURE Radian measure is a way to measure angles that is often the most convenient for mathematical purposes. The radian measure of an angle is found by measuring the length of the intercepted arc and dividing it by the radius of the circle. For example, the circumference of a circle is $2\pi r$, so a full circle $(360°) = 2\pi r/r = 2\pi$ in radians. Also, 180 degrees equals π radians, and a right angle $(90°)$ has a measure of $\pi/2$ radians. The radian measure of an angle is unit-free (i.e., it does not matter whether the radius of the circle is measured in inches, meters, or miles). Radian measure is required when trigonometric functions are used in calculus applications.

RADICAL The radical symbol ("$\sqrt{}$") is used to indicate the taking of a root of a number. Thus $\sqrt[q]{x}$ means the qth root of x, which is the number that, when used as a factor q times, equals x: $(\sqrt[q]{x})^q = x$. Here q is called the *index* of the radical. If no index is specified, then the square root is meant. A radical always means to take the positive value. For example, both $y = 5$ and $y = -5$ satisfy $y^2 = 25$, but $\sqrt{25} = 5$. (See **root**.)

RADICAND The radicand is the part of an expression that is inside the radical sign. For example, in the expression $\sqrt{1 - x^2}$ the expression $(1 - x^2)$ is the radicand.

RADIUS The radius of a circle is the distance from the center of the circle to a point on the circle. The radius of a sphere is the distance from the center of the sphere to a point on the sphere. A line segment drawn from the center of a circle to any point on the circumference is also called a radius. The plural of "radius" is "radii."

RANDOM VARIABLE A random variable is a variable that takes on a particular value when a specified random event occurs. For example, if you flip a coin three times and X is the number of heads you toss, then X is a random variable with the possible values 0, 1, 2, and 3. In this case $\Pr(X = 0) = 1/8$, $\Pr(X = 1) = 3/8$, $\Pr(X = 2) = 3/8$, and $\Pr(X = 3) = 1/8$.

If a random variable has only a discrete number of possible values, it is called a discrete random variable. The density function for a discrete random variable is a function such that, for each possible value x_i, the value of the function is $f(x_i) = \Pr(X = x_i)$. In the three-coin example, $f(0) = 1/8$, $f(1) = 3/8$, $f(2) = 3/8$, and $f(3) = 1/8$. An important example of a discrete random variable is the binomial distribution.

A continuous random variable is a random variable that can have many possible values over a continuous range. The density function of a continuous random variable is a function such that

$$\Pr(a < x < b) = \int_a^b f(x)\, dx.$$

(See **integral**.) The density function for a continuous random variable must satisfy

$$\int_{-\infty}^{\infty} f(x)\, dx = 1.$$

Some important examples of distributions for continuous random variables are the *normal distribution*, the *chi-square distribution*, and the *t-distribution*.

RANGE (1) The range of a function is the set of all possible values for the output of the function. (See **function**.)

(2) The range of a list of numbers is equal to the largest value minus the smallest value. It is a measure of the dispersion of the list—in other words, how spread out the list is.

RANK The rank of a matrix is the number of linearly independent rows it contains. The $m \times m$ matrix **A** will have rank m if all of its rows are linearly independent, as will be the case if det $\mathbf{A} \neq 0$. (See **determinant**.) Otherwise, its rank will be less than m. In the matrix

$$\begin{pmatrix} 0 & 2 & 3 \\ 1 & 4 & 5 \\ 6 & 7 & 8 \end{pmatrix}$$

all the rows are linearly independent. In this matrix:

$$\begin{pmatrix} 1 & 2 & 3 \\ 1 & 0 & 0 \\ 2 & 4 & 6 \end{pmatrix}$$

the third row is a multiple of the first row, so the matrix has a rank of 2. In this matrix:

$$\begin{pmatrix} 1 & 2 & 3 \\ 2 & 4 & 6 \\ 3 & 6 & 9 \end{pmatrix}$$

all three rows are linearly dependent, so the rank is 1. The number of linearly independent columns in a matrix is the same as the number of linearly independent rows.

RATIO The ratio of two real numbers a and b is $a \div b$, or a/b. The ratio of a to b is sometimes written as $a : b$. For example, the ratio of the number of sides in a hexagon to the number of sides in a triangle is $6 : 3$, which is equal to $2 : 1$.

RATIONALIZING THE DENOMINATOR The process of rationalizing the denominator involves rewriting a fraction into an equivalent form that does not have an irrational number in the denominator. For example, the fraction $1/\sqrt{2}$ can be rationalized by multiplying the numerator and denominator by $\sqrt{2}$: $1/\sqrt{2} = \sqrt{2}/2$. The fraction $1/(a + \sqrt{2})$ can be rationalized by multiplying both the numerator and the denominator of the fraction by $a - \sqrt{2}$:

$$\frac{1}{a + \sqrt{2}} \times \frac{a - \sqrt{2}}{a - \sqrt{2}} = \frac{a - \sqrt{2}}{a^2 + a\sqrt{2} - a\sqrt{2} - 2} = \frac{a - \sqrt{2}}{a^2 - 2}.$$

RATIONAL NUMBER A rational number is any number that can be expressed as the ratio of two integers. The set of rational numbers includes all integers and all fractions. A rational number can be expressed either as a fraction, such as $\frac{1}{5}$, or as a decimal number, such as 0.2. A fraction written in decimal form will be either a terminating decimal, such as $\frac{5}{8} = 0.625$ or $\frac{1}{4} = 0.25$, or a decimal that endlessly repeats a particular pattern, such as $\frac{1}{3} = 0.333333\ldots,$ $\frac{2}{9} = 0.222222222\ldots,$ $\frac{10}{11} = 0.909090909090\ldots,$ or $\frac{1}{7} = 0.142857\ 142857\ 142857\ldots.$ If the decimal representation of a number goes on forever without repeating any pattern, then that number is an *irrational number*.

RATIONAL ROOT THEOREM The rational root theorem says that, if the polynomial equation

$$a_n x^n + a_{n-1} x^{n-1} + a_{n-2} x^{n-2} + \cdots + a_2 x^2 + a_1 x + a_0 = 0,$$

where $a_0, a_1, \ldots, a_n$ are all integers, has any rational roots, then each rational root can be expressed as a fraction in which the numerator is a factor of a_0 and the denominator is a factor of a_n. This theorem sometimes makes it easier to find the roots of complicated polynomial equations, but it provides no help if there are no rational roots to begin with.

For example, suppose that we are looking for the rational roots of the equation

$$x^3 - 9x^2 + 26x - 24 = 0.$$

In this case $a_n = 1$ and $a_0 = 24$. Therefore the rational roots, if any, must have a factor of 24 in the numerator and 1 in the denominator. The factors of 24 are 1, 2, 3, 4, 6, 12, 24. If we test all the possibilities, it turns out that the three roots are 2, 3, and 4.

RAY A ray is like half of a line: it has one endpoint, and then goes off forever in a straight line. You can think of a light ray from a star as being a ray, with the endpoint located at the star.

REAL NUMBERS The set of real numbers is the set of all numbers that can be represented by points on a number line (see figure).

The set of real numbers includes all rational numbers and all irrational numbers. Any real number can be expressed as a decimal fraction, which will either terminate or endlessly repeat a pattern (if the number is rational), or continue endlessly with no pattern (if the number is irrational).

Whenever the term "number" is used by itself, it is often assumed that the real numbers are meant. The measurement of a physical quantity, such as length, time, or energy, will be a real number.

The set of real numbers is a subset of the set of complex numbers, which includes the pure imaginary numbers plus combinations of real numbers and imaginary numbers.

RECIPROCAL The reciprocal of a number a is equal to $1/a$. For example, the reciprocal of 2 is $\frac{1}{2}$, the reciprocal of 0.01 is 100, and the reciprocal of 1 is 1. The reciprocal is the same as the multiplicative inverse.

RECTANGLE A rectangle is a quadrilateral with four 90° angles. The opposite sides of a rectangle are parallel, so the set of rectangles is a subset of the set of parallelograms. A square has four 90° angles, so the set of squares is a subset of the set of rectangles. The area of a rectangle is the product of the lengths of any two adjacent sides.

RECTANGULAR COORDINATES See **Cartesian coordinates**.

RECURSION "Recursion" is the term for a definition that refers to the object being defined. The use of a recursive definition requires care to make sure that an endless loop is not created.

Here is an example of a recursive definition for the factorial function $n!$:

$$n! = n(n-1)!$$

This definition leads to an endless loop.

Here is a better recursive definition that avoids the endless loop problem:

$$\text{If } n > 0, \text{ then } n! = n(n-1)!$$
$$\text{If } n = 0, \text{ then } n! = 1$$

Here are the steps to use this definition to find 3!:

$$3! = 3 \times 2!$$
> Look up 2!
> $$2! = 2 \times 1!$$
>> Look up 1!
>> $$1! = 1 \times 0!$$
>>> Look up 0!
>>> $$0! = 1$$
>> Then:
>> $$1! = 1 \times 1 = 1$$
> Then:
> $$2! = 2 \times 1 = 2$$

Then:
$$3! = 3 \times 2 = 6$$

REFLECTION   A reflection is a transformation in which the transformed figure is the mirror image of the original figure. The reflection is centered on a line called the *axis of symmetry.*

Here is how to find the reflection of a particular point. Draw, from the point to the axis, the line perpendicular to the axis. Then the point on that line that is the same distance from the axis as the original point, but on the opposite side of the axis, is the reflection of the original point. In other words, the axis of symmetry is the perpendicular bisector of the line segment joining a point and its reflection. (See figure.)

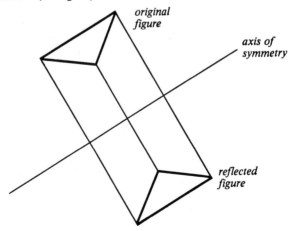

original figure

axis of symmetry

reflected figure

REFLEXIVE PROPERTY   The reflexive property of equality is an axiom that states an obvious but useful fact: $x = x$, for all x. That means that any number is equal to itself.

REGRESSION   Regression is a statistical technique for determining the relationship between quantities. In simple regression, there is one independent variable that is assumed to have an effect on one other variable (the dependent variable). It is necessary to have several observations, with each observation containing a pair of values (one for each of the two variables). The observations can be plotted on a two-dimensional diagram (see figure), where the independent variable, x, is measured along the horizontal axis and the dependent variable, y, is measured along the vertical axis.

The regression procedure determines the line that best fits the observations. The best-fit line is the line such that the sum of the squares of the deviations of all of the points from the line is at its minimum. The slope (m) of the best-fit line is given by the equation

$$m = \frac{\overline{xy} - \bar{x}\bar{y}}{\overline{x^2} - \bar{x}^2}.$$

A bar over a quantity represents the average value of the quantity.

After the slope has been found, the vertical intercept (b) of the line can be determined from the equation

$$b = \bar{y} - m\bar{x}.$$

The r^2 value for the regression is a number between 0 and 1 that indicates how well the line summarizes the pattern of the observations. In some cases the line will fit the data points very well, and then the r^2 value will be close to 1. In other cases the data points cannot be well summarized by a line, and the r^2 value will be close to 0.

For situations where there are several independent variables, each having an effect on the dependent variable, see **multiple regression**.

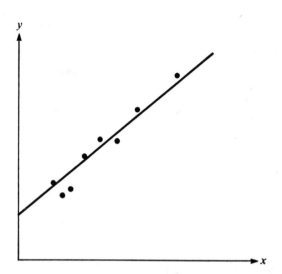

REGULAR POLYGON   A regular polygon is a polygon in which all the angles and all the sides are equal. For example, a regular triangle is an equilateral triangle with three 60° angles. A regular quadrilateral is a square. A regular hexagon has six 120° angles.

RELATION   A relation is a set of ordered pairs. The first entry in the ordered pair can be called x, and the second entry can be called y. For example, $\{(1, 0), (1, 1), (1, -1), (-1, 0)\}$ is an example of a relation. A function is also an example of a relation. A function has the special property that, for each value of x, there is a unique value of y. This property does not have to hold true for a relation. The equation of a circle $x^2 + y^2 = r^2$ defines a relation between x and y, but this relation is not a function because for every value of x there are two values of y: $\sqrt{r^2 - x^2}$ and $-\sqrt{r^2 - x^2}$.

REMAINDER   In the division problem $9 \div 4$ the quotient is 2 with a remainder of 1. In general, if $m = nq + r$ (where m, n, q, and r are integers and $r < n$), then the division problem m/n has the quotient q and the remainder r. The term "remainder" can also be used as a synonym for "difference" (i.e., the answer to a subtraction problem).

REPEATING DECIMAL   A repeating decimal is a decimal fraction in which the digits endlessly repeat a pattern, such as $\frac{2}{9} = 0.2222222\ldots$ or $\frac{2}{7} = 0.285714\,285714\,285714\ldots$. For contrast, see **terminating decimal**.

RESOLUTION OF FORCES   A force is something that pushes or pulls on an object, such as gravity. Forces can be represented by vectors, since forces have both magnitude and direction. If two forces are acting on an object, then the resulting force will be the sum of the two vectors representing these forces. For example, consider a

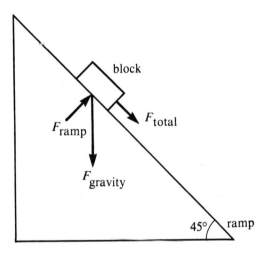

block that is sliding down a ramp inclined at a $45°$ angle (see figure). There are two forces acting on the block: the force of gravity, pulling it down, which can be represented by the vector $(0, -\sqrt{2})$, and the force of the ramp, which can be represented by the vector $(1/\sqrt{2}, 1/\sqrt{2})$. Then the total force acting on the block will be

$$\left(\frac{1}{\sqrt{2}}, \frac{1}{\sqrt{2}} - \sqrt{2} \right) = \left(\frac{1}{\sqrt{2}}, -\frac{1}{\sqrt{2}} \right),$$

which means that the block will slide down the ramp (unless another force, such as friction, acts to slow the block).

RESULTANT   The resultant is the vector that results from the addition of two other vectors.

RHOMBUS   A rhombus is a quadrilateral with four equal sides. A square is a rhombus, but in general a rhombus will look like a square that has been bent out of shape (see figure).

RIGHT ANGLE   A right angle is an angle that measures 90°. It is the type of angle that makes up a square corner, such as the corners on the pages of this book.

RIGHT CIRCULAR CONE   A right circular cone is a cone whose base is a circle located so that the line connecting the center of the circle to the vertex of the cone is perpendicular to the plane containing the circle. (See **cone**.)

RIGHT CIRCULAR CYLINDER   A right circular cylinder is a cylinder whose bases are circles and whose axis is perpendicular to the planes containing the two bases. (See **cylinder**.)

RIGHT TRIANGLE   A right triangle is a triangle that contains one right angle. The side opposite the right angle is called the hypotenuse; the other two sides are called the legs. Since the sum of the three angles of a triangle is 180°, no triangle can contain more than one right angle. The *Pythagorean theorem* expresses a relationship between the three sides of a right triangle:

$$(\text{hypotenuse})^2 = (\text{leg } 1)^2 + (\text{leg } 2)^2.$$

ROOT   (1) The root of an equation is the same as a solution to that equation. For example, the statement that a quadratic equation has two roots means that it has two solutions.

(2) The process of taking a root of a number is the opposite of raising the number to a power. The square root of a number x (written as $\sqrt{x}$) is the number that, when raised to the second power, gives x: $(\sqrt{x})^2 = x$. The symbol "$\sqrt{}$" is called the radical symbol.

Some examples of square roots are

$$\sqrt{1} = 1, \quad \sqrt{4} = 2, \quad \sqrt{9} = 3, \quad \sqrt{16} = 4, \quad \sqrt{25} = 5, \quad \sqrt{36} = 6.$$

The square roots of most integers are irrational numbers. For example, the square root of 2 can be approximated by $\sqrt{2} = 1.414\ldots$.

Square roots obey the property that $\sqrt{ab} = \sqrt{a}\sqrt{b}$. For example:

$$\sqrt{225} = \sqrt{9 \times 25} = \sqrt{9} \times \sqrt{25} = 3 \times 5 = 15.$$

A small number in front of the radical (called the *index* of the radical) is used to indicate that a root other than the square root is to be taken. For example $\sqrt[3]{x}$ is the cube root of x, defined so that $(\sqrt[3]{x})^3 = x$. Examples of other roots are

$$\sqrt[3]{8} = 2, \quad \sqrt[3]{27} = 3, \quad \sqrt[5]{32} = 2, \quad \sqrt[4]{10,000} = 10.$$

Roots can also be expressed as fractional exponents:

$$\sqrt[q]{x} = x^{1/q}.$$

(See **exponent**.)

ROTATION A rotation of a Cartesian coordinate system occurs when the orientation of the axes is changed, but the origin is kept fixed. In Figure 1 the coordinate axes x' and y' (x-prime and y-prime) are formed by rotating the original axes, x and y, by an angle θ. The main reason for doing this is that sometimes the equation for a particular figure will be much simpler in the new coordinate system than it was in the old one.

We need to find an expression for the new coordinates in terms of the old coordinates. Let α and ϕ be as shown in the figure. Then $\alpha = \phi - \theta$. From the definition of the trigonometric functions:

$$y' = r \sin \alpha, \qquad x' = r \cos \alpha.$$

Using the formula for the sine and cosine of a difference:

$$\sin \alpha = \sin \phi \cos \theta - \cos \phi \sin \theta,$$

$$\cos \alpha = \cos \phi \cos \theta + \sin \phi \sin \theta.$$

Substituting:

$$y' = r \sin \phi \cos \theta - r \cos \phi \sin \theta,$$
$$x' = r \cos \phi \cos \theta + r \sin \phi \sin \theta.$$

Since $y = r \sin \phi$ and $x = r \cos \phi$, we can write

$$y' = y \cos \theta - x \sin \theta,$$
$$x' = x \cos \theta + y \sin \theta.$$

The last two equations tell us how to transform any (x, y) pair into a new (x', y') pair. We can also derive the opposite transformation:

$$y = y' \cos \theta + x' \sin \theta,$$
$$x = x' \cos \theta - y' \sin \theta.$$

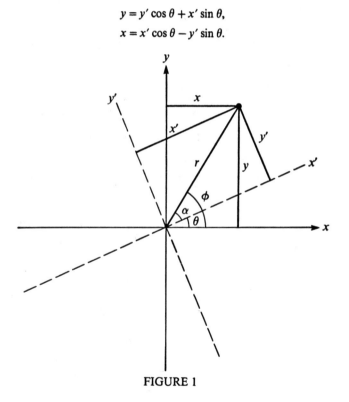

FIGURE 1

Coordinate rotation helps considerably when we try to make a graph of the two-unknown quadratic equation

$$Ax^2 + Bxy + Cy^2 + Dx + Ey + F = 0.$$

The problem is caused by the Bxy term. If that term weren't present, the equation could be graphed as a standard conic section. Therefore what we would like to do is to choose some angle of rotation θ so that the equation written in the new coordinates will not have any $x'y'$ term. We can use the rotation transformation to find out what the equation will be in the new coordinate system:

$$x = x' \cos \theta - y' \sin \theta,$$
$$y = y' \cos \theta + x' \sin \theta,$$
$$xy = x'y' \cos^2 \theta + x'^2 \sin \theta \cos \theta - y'^2 \sin \theta \cos \theta - y'x' \sin^2 \theta,$$
$$x^2 = x'^2 \cos^2 \theta - 2x'y' \cos \theta \sin \theta + y'^2 \sin^2 \theta,$$
$$y^2 = y'^2 \cos^2 \theta + 2x'y' \cos \theta \sin \theta + x'^2 \sin^2 \theta.$$

After we have combined all these terms, the equation becomes

$$x'^2[A \cos^2 \theta + C \sin^2 \theta + B \sin \theta \cos \theta] + x'[D \cos \theta + E \sin \theta]$$
$$+ y'^2[A \sin^2 \theta + C \cos^2 \theta - B \sin \theta \cos \theta] + y'[-D \sin \theta + E \cos \theta]$$
$$+ x'y'[-2A \cos \theta \sin \theta + 2C \cos \theta \sin \theta + B \cos^2 \theta - B \sin^2 \theta]$$
$$+ F = 0.$$

To get rid of the cross term (the $x'y'$ term) we need to choose θ so that

$$2 \cos \theta \sin \theta (C - A) + B(\cos^2 \theta - \sin^2 \theta) = 0,$$
$$(C - A) \sin 2\theta + B \cos 2\theta = 0,$$
$$\frac{\sin 2\theta}{\cos 2\theta} = \frac{B}{A - C},$$
$$\tan 2\theta = \frac{B}{A - C},$$
$$\theta = \tfrac{1}{2} \arctan \frac{B}{A - C}.$$

For an example of a rotation, consider the equation $xy = 1$. Here, we have $B = 1$, $F = -1$, and $A = C = D = E = 0$. To choose θ so as to eliminate the cross term, we must have $\theta = \frac{1}{2} \arctan (1/0)$, or $\theta = \pi/4$ (45°). To find the equation in terms of x' and y', we use the rotation transformation:

$$x = 2^{-1/2}(x' - y'), \qquad y = 2^{-1/2}(y' + x').$$

(Remember that $\sin \pi/4 = \cos \pi/4 = 2^{-1/2}$.) The rotated equation becomes

$$1 = \frac{1}{2}x'^2 - \frac{1}{2}y'^2,$$

which is the standard form for the equation of a hyperbola. (See Figure 2.)

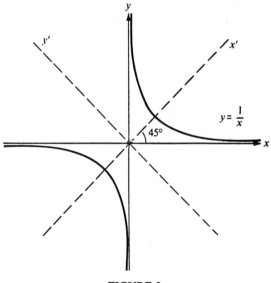

FIGURE 2

ROUNDING Rounding provides a way of approximating a number in a form with fewer digits. A number can be rounded to the nearest integer, or it can be rounded to a specified number of decimal places, or it can be rounded to the nearest number that is a multiple of a power of 10. For example, 3.52 rounded to the nearest integer is 4; 6.37 rounded to the nearest integer is 6. If 3.52 is rounded to one decimal place, the result is 3.5; if 6.37 is rounded to one decimal place, the result is 6.4. The number 343,619 becomes 344,000 when it is rounded to the nearest thousand. It is often helpful to present the final result of a calculation in rounded form, but the results of intermediate calculations should not be rounded because rounding could lead to an accumulation of errors.

S

SAMPLE A sample is a group of items chosen from a population. The characteristics of the sample are used to estimate the characteristics of the population. (See **statistical inference**.)

SAMPLING To sample j items from a population of n objects with replacement means to choose an item, then replace the item, and repeat the process j times. Flipping a coin j times is equivalent to sampling with replacement from a population of size 2. The fact that you've flipped heads once does not mean that you cannot flip heads the next time. There are n^j possible ways of selecting a sample of size j from a population of size n with replacement.

To sample j items from a population of n objects without replacement means to select an item, and then select another item from the remaining $n - 1$ objects, and repeat the process j times. Dealing a poker hand is an example of sampling without replacement from a population of 52 objects. After you've dealt the first card, you can't deal that card again, so there are 51 possibilities for the second card. There are $n!/(n - j)!$ ways of selecting j items from a population of size n without replacement.

The concept of the two different kinds of sampling provides the answer to the birthday problem in probability. Suppose that you have a group of s people. What is the probability that no two people in the group will have the same birthday? The number of possible ways of distributing the birthdays among the s people is 365^s. (That is the same as sampling s times from a population of size 365 with replacement.) To find the number of ways of distributing the birthdays so that nobody has the same birthday, you have to find out how many ways there are of sampling s items from a population of 365 without replacement, which is $365!/(365 - s)!$. The probability that no two people will have the same birthday is therefore

$$\frac{365!/(365 - s)!}{365^s}$$

The table gives the value of this probability for different values of s.

s	p
2	.997
3	.992
5	.973
10	.883
15	.747
20	.589
30	.294
50	.030

This result says that in a group of 50 people there is a 97% chance that at least two of them will have the same birthday.

SCALAR A scalar is a quantity that has size but not direction. For example, real numbers are scalars. By contrast, a vector is a quantity that has both size and direction.

SCALAR PRODUCT The scalar product (or dot product) of two vectors (x_1, y_1, z_1) and (x_2, y_2, z_2) is defined to be $(x_1 x_2 + y_1 y_2 + z_1 z_2)$. Note that this quantity is a regular number (a scalar) rather than a vector. (See **dot product**.)

SCALENE TRIANGLE A scalene triangle is a triangle in which no two sides are equal.

SCIENTIFIC NOTATION Scientific notation is a short-hand way of writing very large or very small numbers. A number expressed in scientific notation is expressed as a number between 1 and 10 multiplied by a power of 10. For example, the number of meters in a light year is 9,460,000,000,000,000. It is much easier to write this number as 9.46×10^{15}. The wavelength of red light is 0.0000007 meter, which can be written in scientific notation as 7×10^{-7} meter. Computers use a form of scientific notation for big numbers, as do some pocket calculators.

SECANT (1) A secant line is a line that intersects a circle, or some other curve, in two places. Lines *AB* and *CD* in the figure are both secant lines.

(2) The secant function is defined as the reciprocal of the cosine function: $\sec \theta = 1/\cos \theta$. (See **trigonometry**.)

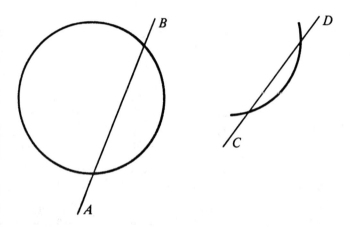

SECOND A second is a unit of measure of an angle equal to 1/60 of a minute (or 1/360 of a degree).

SECTOR A sector of a circle is a region bounded by two radii of the circle and by the arc of the circle whose endpoints lie on those radii. In other words, a sector is shaped like a pie slice (see figure). If *r* is

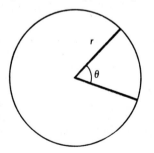

the radius of the circle and θ is the angle between the two radii (measured in radians), then the area of the sector is $\frac{1}{2}\theta r^2$.

SEGMENT (1) The segment AB is the union of point A and point B and all points between them. (See **between**.) A segment is like a piece of a straight line. A segment has two endpoints, whereas a line goes off to infinity in two directions.

(2) A segment of a circle is an area bounded by an arc and the chord that connects the two endpoints of the arc.

SEMILOG GRAPH PAPER Semilog graph paper has a logarithmic scale on one axis, and a uniform scale on the other axis. It is useful for graphing equations like $y = ck^x$.

SEMIMAJOR AXIS The semimajor axis of an ellipse is equal to one half of the longest distance across the ellipse. The semimajor axis of the orbit of the earth is 93.000 million miles.

SEMIMINOR AXIS The semiminor axis of an ellipse is equal to one half of the shortest distance across the ellipse. The semiminor axis of the orbit of the earth is 92.987 million miles.

SENTENCE See **logic**.

SEQUENCE A sequence is a set of numbers in which the numbers have a prescribed order. Some common examples of sequences are arithmetic sequences (where the difference between successive terms is constant) and geometric series (where the ratio between successive terms is constant). If all the terms in a sequence are to be added, it is called a series.

SERIES A series is the indicated sum of a sequence of numbers. Examples of series are as follows:

$1 + 3 + 5 + 7 + 9 + 11 + 13,$

$a + (a + b) + (a + 2b) + (a + 3b) + \cdots + [a + (n - 1)b],$

$2 + 4 + 8 + 16 + 32 + 64,$

$a + ar + ar^2 + ar^3 + \cdots + ar^{n - 1}.$

The first two series are examples of *arithmetic series*. The last two series are examples of *geometric series*. For another important type of series, see **Taylor series**.

SET A set is a well-defined group of objects. A set is described by some rule that makes it possible to tell whether or not a particular object is in the set. For example, the set of Presidents of the United States consists of {George Washington, John Adams, Thomas Jefferson, James Madison, James Monroe}. The set of all natural numbers less than 11 consists of {1, 2, 3, 4, 5, 6, 7, 8, 9, 10}. Sets can be defined by listing all their elements within braces, such as {10.5, 4.6, 3.3}, or by giving a description that determines what is in the set and what is not: "An ellipse is the set of all points in a plane such that the sum of the distances to two fixed points in the plane is a constant."

The relationship between sets can be indicated on a type of diagram known as a *Venn diagram* (see figure).

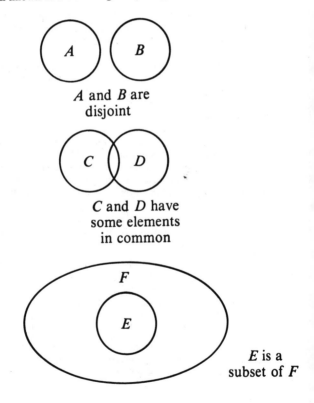

A and B are
disjoint

C and D have
some elements
in common

E is a
subset of F

SEXAGESIMAL SYSTEM   The basic unit in the sexagesimal system for measuring angles is the degree. If you place a 1° angle in the center of a circle, the angle will cut across 1/360 of the circumference of the circle.

SIGMA NOTATION   The Greek capital letter sigma (Σ) is used to indicate summation. (See **summation notation**.)

SIGN   The sign of a number is the symbol that tells whether the number is positive (+) or negative (−).

SIGNIFICANT DIGITS   The number of significant digits expressed in a measurement indicates how precise that measurement is. A nonzero digit is always a significant digit.

Trailing zeros to the left of the decimal point are not significant if there are no digits to the right of the decimal point. For example, the number 243,000,000 contains three significant digits; this means that the true value of the measurement is between 242,500,000 and 243,500,000.

Trailing zeros to the right of the decimal point are significant. For example, the number 2.1300 has five significant digits; this means that the true value is between 2.12995 and 2.13005.

Do not include more significant digits in the result of a calculation than were present in the original measurement. For example, if you calculate 243,000,000/7, do not express the result as 34,714,286, since you do not have eight significant digits to work from. Instead, express the result as 34,700,000, which, like the original measurement, has three significant digits. (However, if a calculation involves several steps, you should retain more digits during the intermediate stages.)

SIMILAR   Two polygons are similar (see figure) if they have exactly the same shape, but different sizes. For example, suppose that you look at a color slide showing a picture of a house shaped like a rectangle. If you put the slide into a projector, you will then see on the screen a much bigger image of the same rectangle. These two rectangles are similar. Each angle in the little polygon will be equal to one of the angles in the big polygon. Each pair of equal angles is called a pair of corresponding angles. Each side on the little polygon will have a corresponding side on the big polygon. If one side of the

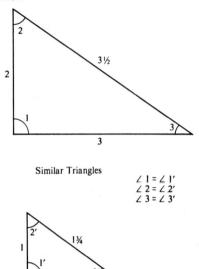

Similar Triangles

$\angle 1 = \angle 1'$
$\angle 2 = \angle 2'$
$\angle 3 = \angle 3'$

little polygon is half as big as its corresponding side on the big polygon, then all the sides on the little polygon will be half as big as the corresponding sides on the big polygon.

SIMPLEX METHOD The simplex method, developed by mathematician George Dantzig, is a procedure for solving linear programming problems. (See **linear programming**.) The method starts by identifying a point that is one of the basic feasible solutions to the problem. (See **basic feasible solution**.) Then it provides a procedure to test whether that point is the optimal solution. If it is not, then it provides a procedure for moving to a new basic feasible solution that will have a better value for the objective function. (If you are trying to maximize the objective function, then you want to move to a point with a larger objective function value.) The procedure described above is repeated until the optimal solution has been found. In practice the calculations are usually performed by a computer.

SIMULTANEOUS EQUATIONS A system of simultaneous equations is a group of equations that must all be true at the same time. If there are more unknowns then there are equations, there will usually be many possible solutions. For example, in the two-unknown, one-equation system $x_1 + x_2 = 5$, there will be an infinite number of solutions, all lying along a line. If there are more equations than there are unknowns, there will often be contradictory equations, which mean that no solution is possible. For example, the two-equation, one-unknown system

$$2x_1 = 10$$
$$3x_1 = 10$$

clearly has no solution that will satisfy both equations simultaneously. For there to be a unique solution to a system, there must be exactly as many distinct equations as there are unknowns. For example, the two-equation, two-unknown system

$$3x_1 + 2x_2 = 33,$$
$$-x_1 + x_2 = 4$$

has the unique solution $x_1 = 5$, $x_2 = 9$.

When counting equations, though, you have to be careful to

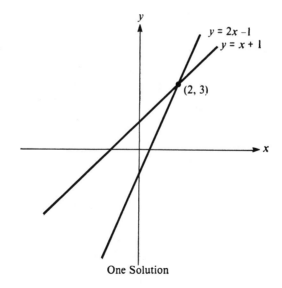

One Solution

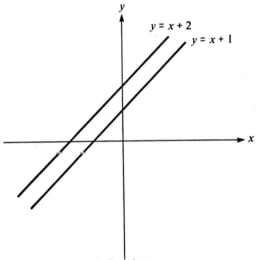

y = x + 2

y = x + 1

No Solutions

avoid counting equations that are redundant. For example, if you look closely at the three-equation, three-unknown system

$$2x_1 + x_2 + 3x_3 = 9,$$
$$4x_1 + 9x_2 + \tfrac{1}{2}x_3 = 1,$$
$$2x_1 + x_2 + 3x_3 = 9,$$

you will see that the first equation and the last equation are exactly the same. This means that there really are only two distinct equations. Equations can be redundant even if they are not exactly the same. If one equation can be written as a multiple of another equation (or if it can be written as a linear combination of some of the other equations in the system), then that equation is redundant. For example, the two equations:

$$x_1 + x_2 + x_3 = 1,$$
$$2x_1 + 2x_2 + 2x_3 = 2$$

say exactly the same thing.

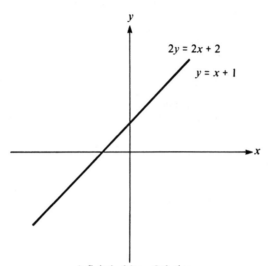

Infinitely Many Solutions

A linear equation is an equation that does not have any unknowns raised to any power (other than 1). Systems of simultaneous nonlinear equations can be very difficult to solve, but there are standard ways for solving simultaneous equations if all the equations are linear.

Simple systems can be solved by the method of substitution. For example, to solve the system

$$2x_1 + x_2 = 9,$$
$$x_1 + 3x_2 = 17,$$

first solve the second equation for x_1: $x_1 = 17 - 3x_2$. Now, substitute this expression for x_1 back into the first equation, and the result is a one-unknown equation. That equation can be solved for x_2: $x_2 = 5$. The value of x_1 can be found by substituting this value for x_2 into the second equation: $x_1 = 2$. The substitution method is often the simplest for two-equation systems, but it can be very cumbersome for longer systems.

If the simultaneous equation is written in matrix form: $\mathbf{Ax} = \mathbf{b}$, where $\mathbf{A}$ is an $n \times n$ matrix of known coefficients, $\mathbf{x}$ is an $n \times 1$ matrix of unknowns, and $\mathbf{b}$ is an $n \times 1$ matrix of known constants, then the solution can be found by finding the inverse matrix $\mathbf{A}^{-1}$:

$$\mathbf{x} = \mathbf{A}^{-1}\mathbf{b}.$$

(See **matrix; matrix multiplication**. See also **Cramer's rule; Gauss-Jordan elimination**.)

A two-equation system can also be solved by graphing (see figure). A linear equation in two unknowns defines a line. The solution to a two-equation system occurs at the point of intersection between the two lines. If the two equations are redundant, then they define the same line, so there is an infinite number of solutions. If the two equations are contradictory, then their graphs will be parallel lines, meaning that there will be no intersection and no solution.

SINE   The sine of angle θ that occurs in a right triangle (see Figure 1) is defined to be the length of the opposite side divided by the length

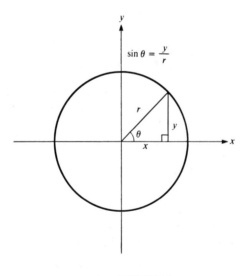

FIGURE 1

of the hypotenuse. For a general angle in standard position, pick any point on the terminal side of the angle, and then $\sin \theta = y/r$.

If $\theta = 0°$, then y is zero, so $\sin 0° = 0$ (see Figure 2). If $\theta = 90°$, $y = r$, so $\sin 90° = \sin(\pi/2) = 1$. For $\theta = 45°$ we can tell from the Pythagorean theorem that $\sin 45° = \sin(\pi/4) = 1/\sqrt{2}$. From the special properties of a 30-60-90 right triangle we can tell that $\sin 30° = \frac{1}{2}$, and $\sin 60° = \sqrt{3}/2$. For most other values of θ, though, there is no

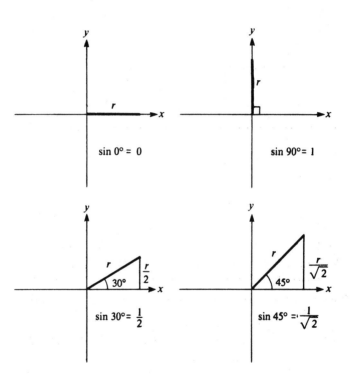

FIGURE 2

simple algebraic expression for $\sin \theta$. If x is measured in radians, then we can find the value for $\sin x$ from the series

$$\sin x = x - \frac{x^3}{3!} + \frac{x^5}{5!} - \frac{x^7}{7!} + \cdots$$

Figure 3 shows a graph of the sine function (x is measured in radians). The value of $\sin x$ is always between -1 and 1, and the function is periodic because

$$\sin x = \sin(x + 2\pi) = \sin(x + 4\pi) = \sin(x + 6\pi), \text{ and so on.}$$

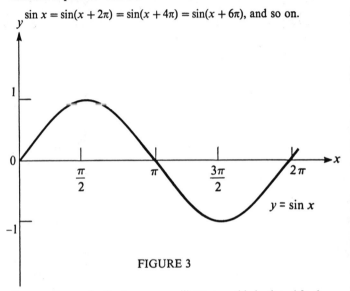

FIGURE 3

Because the graph of a sine wave oscillates smoothly back and forth, the sine function describes wave patterns, harmonic motion, and voltage in alternating-current circuits.

To learn how the sine function relates to the other trigonometric functions, see **trigonometry.**

SKEW Two lines are skew if they are not in the same plane. Any pair of lines will either intersect, be parallel, or be skew.

SLACK VARIABLE A slack variable is a variable that is added to a linear programming problem that measures the excess capacity associated with a constraint. (See **linear programming.**)

SLIDE RULE A slide rule is a calculating device consisting of two sliding logarithmic scales.

SLOPE The slope of a line is a number that measures how steep the line is. A horizontal line has a slope of zero. A vertical line has an infinite slope. The slope of a line is defined to be $\Delta y/\Delta x$, where Δy is the change in the vertical coordinate and Δx is the change in the horizontal coordinate between any two points on the line. The slope of the line $y = mx + b$ is m. To find the slope of a curve, see **calculus**.

SOLID A solid is a three-dimensional geometric figure that completely encloses a volume of space. Examples of solids are prisms, spheres, cylinders, pyramids, and polyhedrons. A cereal box is an example of a solid, but a cereal bowl is not.

SOLUTION If an ordered pair (x_1, y_1) makes an equation involving x and y true, then the point (x_1, y_1) is called a solution of that equation. For example, the point $(1, 5)$ is a solution of the equation $y = x^2 + 4$. The set of all solutions to an equation is called the solution set.

SOLUTION SET The solution set for an equation consists of all of the values of the unknowns that make the equation true.

SOLVE To solve an equation means to find the solutions for the equation (i.e., to find the values of the unknowns that make the equation true).

SPEED The speed of an object is the magnitude of its velocity. (See **velocity**.)

SPHERES A sphere is the set of all points in three-dimensional space that are a fixed distance from a given point (called the center). Some obvious examples of spheres include basketballs, baseballs, tennis balls, and (almost) the earth. The distance from the center to any point on the sphere is called the radius. The distance across the sphere through the center is called the diameter. The intersection between the sphere and a plane is a circle. The intersection between a sphere and a plane passing through the center is called a great circle. A great circle is larger than any other possible circle formed by intersecting the sphere by a plane. The shortest distance along the sphere between two points on the sphere is the path formed by the great circle that connects those two points.

The circumference of a great circle is also known as the circumference of the sphere. The circumference of the earth is about 24,000 miles. The volume of a sphere is $\frac{4}{3}\pi r^3$, where r is the radius. The surface area of a sphere is $4\pi r^2$.

SQUARE   (1) A square is a quadrilateral with four 90° angles and four equal sides. Chessboards are made up of 64 squares. (See **quadrilateral**.)

(2) The square of a number is found by multiplying that number by itself. For example, 4 squared equals 4 times 4, which is 16. If a square is formed with sides a units long, then the area of that square is a squared.

SQUARE ROOT   The square root of a number x (written as $\sqrt{x}$) is the number that, when multiplied by itself, gives x:

$$(\sqrt{x}) \times (\sqrt{x}) = x.$$

For example, $\sqrt{36} = 6$, because $6 \times 6 = 36$. Any number (except 0) has two square roots: one positive and one negative. The square root symbol always means to take the positive value of the square root. (See **root**.)

STANDARD DEVIATION   The standard deviation of a random variable (usually symbolized by the Greek lower-case letter sigma: σ) is the square root of the variance. (See **variance**.)

STANDARD POSITION   An angle is in standard position if its vertex is at the origin and its initial side is along the x-axis.

STATISTIC   A statistic is a quantity calculated from the items in a sample. For example, the average of a list of numbers is a statistic. In statistical inference, the value of a statistic is often used as an estimator of the unknown value of a population parameter.

STATISTICAL INFERENCE   The term "statistical inference" refers to the process of estimating unobservable characteristics on the basis of information that can be observed. The complete set of all items of interest is called the *population*. The characteristics of the population are usually not known. In most cases it is too expensive to survey the entire population. However, it is possible to obtain information on a group randomly selected from the population. This group is called a *sample*. For example, a pollster trying to predict the results of an election will interview a randomly selected sample of voters.

An unknown characteristic of the population is called a *parameter*. Here are two examples of parameters:

the fraction of voters in the state who support candidate **X**,

the mean height of all 9-year-olds in the country.

A quantity that is calculated from a sample is called a *statistic*.

Here are two examples of statistics:

the fraction of voters in a 200-person poll who support candidate X,

the mean height in a randomly selected group of 90 9-year-olds.

In many cases the value of a statistic is used as an indicator of the value of a parameter. This type of statistic is called an *estimator*. In some cases it is fairly obvious which estimator should be used. For example, we would use the fraction of voters in the sample who support candidate X as an estimator for the fraction of voters in the population supporting that candidate, and we would use the mean height of 9-year-olds in the sample as an estimator for the mean height of 9-year-olds in the population. In the formal theory of statistics, certain properties have been found to be characteristic of good estimators. (See **consistent estimator; maximum likelihood estimator; unbiased estimator**.) In some cases, as in both of the examples given above, an estimator has all of these desirable properties; in other cases it is not possible to find a single estimator that has all of them. Then it is more difficult to select the best estimator to use.

After calculating the value of an estimator, it is also necessary to determine whether that estimator is very reliable. If the fraction of voters in our sample who support candidate X is much different from the fraction of voters in the population, then our estimator will give us a very misleading result. There is no way to know with certainty whether an estimator is reliable, since the true value of the population parameter is unknown. However, the use of statistical inference provides some indication as to the reliability of an estimate. First, it is very important that the sample be selected randomly. For example, if we select the first 200 adults that we meet on the street, but it turns out that the street we chose is around the corner from candidate X's campaign headquarters, our sample will be highly unrepresentative. The best way to choose the sample would be to list the names of everyone in the population on little balls, put the balls in a big drum, mix them very thoroughly, and then select 200 balls to represent the people in the sample. That method is not very practical, but modern pollsters use methods that are based on similar concepts of random selection.

If the sample has been selected randomly, then the methods of *probability* can be used to determine the likely composition of the sample. Statistical inference is based on probability. Suppose a poll found that 45 percent of the people in the sample support candidate X. If the poll is a good one, the announced result will include a statement similar to this: "There is a 95 percent chance that, if the entire population had been interviewed, the fraction of people supporting candidate X would be between 42 percent and 48 percent." Note that there is always some uncertainty in the results of a poll, which means that a poll cannot predict the winner of a very close election. Also note that there is no guarantee that the fraction of candidate-X supporters in the population is between 42 percent and 48 percent; there is a 5 percent chance that the true figure is outside that range. For an example of how to calculate the range of uncertainty, see **confidence interval**.

For another important topic in statistical inference, see **hypothesis testing**.

For contrast, see **descriptive statistics**.

STATISTICS Statistics is the study of ways to analyze data. It consists of *descriptive statistics* and *statistical inference*. (Note that the word "statistics" is singular when it denotes the academic subject of statistics.)

STOCHASTIC A stochastic variable is the same as a random variable.

SUBSCRIPT A subscript is a little number or letter set slightly below a letter or another number or letter. In the expression x_1, the "1" is a subscript.

SUBSET Set B is a subset of set A if every element contained in B is also contained in A. For example, the set of high school seniors is a subset of the set of all high school students. The set of squares is a subset of the set of rectangles, which in turn is a subset of the set of parallelograms.

SUBSTITUTION PROPERTY The substitution property states that, if $a = b$, we can replace the expression a anywhere it appears by the expression b if we wish. For example, in solving the simultaneous equation system $2x + 3y = 24$, $2y = 8$, we can substitute 4 in place of y in the first equation:

$$2x + 3 \cdot 4 = 24.$$

Therefore $x = 6$.

SUBTRACTION Subtraction is the opposite of addition. If $a + b = c$, then $c - b = a$. For example, $8 - 3 = 5$. Subtraction does not satisfy the commutative property:

$$a - b \neq b - a$$

nor the associative property:

$$(a - b) - c \neq a - (b - c).$$

SUFFICIENT In the statement $a \rightarrow b$, a is said to be a sufficient condition for b to be true. For example, being born in the United States is sufficient to become a United States citizen. (It is not necessary, though, because a person can become a naturalized citizen.) Showing that a number x is prime is sufficient to show that x is odd (if $x > 2$), but it is not necessary (e.g., 9 is odd, but it is not prime).

SUM The sum is the result obtained when two numbers are added. In the equation $5 + 6 = 11$, 11 is the sum of 5 and 6.

SUMMATION NOTATION Summation notation provides a concise way of expressing long sums that follow a pattern. The Greek capital letter sigma (Σ) is used to represent summation. Put where to start at the bottom:

$$\sum_{i=1},$$

and where to stop at the top:

$$\sum_{i=1}^{5},$$

and put what you want to add up along the sides:

$$\sum_{i=1}^{5} i.$$

For example:

$$\sum_{i=1}^{5} i = 1 + 2 + 3 + 4 + 5 = 15,$$

$$\sum_{j=1}^{10} j^2 = 1 + 4 + 9 + 16 + 25 + 36 + 49 + 64 + 81 + 100 = 385,$$

$$\sum_{k=1}^{n} k = 1 + 2 + 3 + 4 + \cdots + (n-1) + n = \tfrac{1}{2}n(n+1),$$

SUPERPOSITION The principle of superposition in geometry refers to moving a figure without changing its size or shape in order to place it on top of another figure.

SUPPLEMENTARY   Two angles are supplementary if the sum of their measures is 180°. For example, two angles measuring 135° and 45° form a pair of supplementary angles.

SURFACE AREA   The surface area of a solid is a measure of how much area the solid would have if you could somehow break it apart and flatten it out. For example, a cube with edge a units long has six faces, each with area a^2. The surface area of the cube is the sum of the areas of these six faces, or $6a^2$. The surface area of any polyhedron can be found by adding together the areas of all the faces. The surface areas of curved solids are harder to find, but they can often be found with calculus. For example, the surface area of a sphere with radius r is $4\pi r^2$. Surface areas are important if you need to paint something. The amount of paint you need to completely paint an object depends on its surface area.

SYLLOGISM   In logic, a syllogism is a particular type of argument with three sentences: the major premise, which often asserts a general relationship between classes of objects; the minor premise, which asserts something about a specific case; and the conclusion, which follows from the two premises. Here is an example of a syllogism:

Major premise: All books about logic are interesting.

Minor premise: The *Dictionary of Mathematics Terms* is a book about logic.

Conclusion: Therefore, the *Dictionary of Mathematics Terms* is interesting.

The syllogism is said to have three terms: the minor term, which is the subject of the conclusion (the *Dictionary of Mathematics Terms* in our example); the major term, which is the other part of the conclusion (called the predicate, which is "is interesting" in our example); and the middle term, which does not occur in the conclusion ("books about logic" in our example.)

Syllogisms were investigated by Aristotle about 350 B.C. in one of the earliest works on the formal structure of logic. (See **logic**.)

SYMMETRIC   (1) Two points A and B are symmetric with respect to a third point (called the center of symmetry) (see figure) if the third point is the midpoint of the segment connecting the first two points.

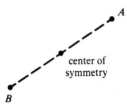

center of
symmetry

axis of
symmetry

(2) Two points A and B are symmetric with respect to a line (called the axis of symmetry) (see figure) if the line is the perpendicular bisector of the segment AB.

SYMMETRIC PROPERTY OF EQUALITY The symmetric property of equality states that, if $a = b$, then $b = a$. That means that you can reverse the two sides of an equation whenever you want to.

SYNTHETIC DIVISION Synthetic division is a short way of dividing a polynomial by a binomial of the form $x - b$. For example, to find

$$\frac{2x^3 - x^2 - 2x - 8}{x - 2}$$

by algebraic division, we would have to write

$$
\require{enclose}
\begin{array}{r}
2x^2 + 3x + 4 \\
x - 2 \enclose{longdiv}{2x^3 - x^2 - 2x - 8} \\
\underline{2x^3 - 4x^2} \\
3x^2 - 2x \\
\underline{3x^2 - 6x} \\
4x - 8 \\
\underline{4x - 8} \\
0
\end{array}
$$

To make synthetic division shorter, we leave out all the x's and just write the coefficients. Also, we reverse the sign of the divisor ($x - 2$ in this case) so as to make every intermediate subtraction become an addition. Finally, we condense everything onto three lines:

First, we write the coefficients on a line:

$$2 \quad -1 \quad -2 \quad -8 \quad) \; 2.$$

Second, we bring down the first coefficient into the answer line:

$$
\begin{array}{cccccc}
2 & -1 & -2 & -8 &) & 2 \\
\hline
2 & & & & &
\end{array}.
$$

Third, we multiply the 2 in the answer by the 2 in the divisor, and then add:

$$
\begin{array}{cccccc}
2 & -1 & -2 & -8 &) & 2 \\
 & 4 & & & & \\
\hline
2 & 3 & & & &
\end{array}.
$$

Fourth, we repeat the multiplication and addition procedure for the next two places:

$$
\begin{array}{cccccc}
2 & -1 & -2 & -8 &) & 2 \\
 & 4 & 6 & 8 & & \\
\hline
2 & 3 & 4 & 0 & &
\end{array}.
$$

The farthest right entry in the answer line is the remainder (in this case 0). Then the remaining elements in the answer line are (from right to left) the coefficients of x^0, x^1, and x^2, so in this case the answer is $2x^2 + 3x + 4$.

The general procedure for synthetic division is

$$\frac{a_3 x^3 + a_2 x^2 + a_1 x + a_0}{x - b} = c_2 x^2 + c_1 x + c_0 + \frac{R}{x - b},$$

where the answer is found from:

$$
\begin{array}{cccccc}
a_3 & a_2 & a_1 & a_0 &) & b \\
 & c_2 b & c_1 b & c_0 b & & \\
\hline
c_2 & c_1 & c_0 & R & &
\end{array},
$$

$$c_2 = a_3,$$
$$c_1 = c_2 b + a_2,$$
$$c_0 = c_1 b + a_1,$$
$$R = c_0 b + a_0.$$

SYSTEM OF EQUATIONS   See **simultaneous equations.**

SYSTEM OF INEQUALITIES   A system of inequalities is a group of inequalities that are all to be true simultaneously. For example, this system of three inequalities:

$$x > 2$$

$$y > 3$$

$$x + y < 10$$

defines a set of values for x and y that will make all of the inequalities true. The graph of these points is shown in the figure.

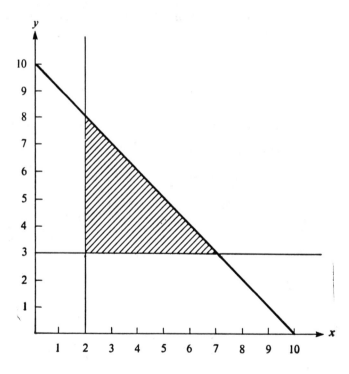

T

_t_-DISTRIBUTION   If Z is a random variable with a standard normal distribution, and Y is a χ^2 distribution with n degrees of freedom, then the random variable

$$X = \frac{Z}{(Y/n)^{1/2}}$$

has a *t*-distribution with n degrees of freedom. (See **chi square; normal distribution**.) As n approaches infinity, the density function for the *t*-distribution approaches the density function of a standard normal random variable. When X has the *t*-distribution with n degrees of freedom, then

$$E(X) = 0 \quad \text{if } n > 1,$$

and

$$\text{Var}(X) = \frac{n}{n-2} \quad \text{if } n > 2.$$

The *t*-distribution plays an important part in statistical estimation theory.

Tables 6 and 7 list some values for the *t*-distribution.

TANGENT   (1) A tangent line is a line that intersects a circle at one point. Line AB in Figure 1 is a tangent line. For example, the tires of a car are always tangent to the road. A tangent line to a curve is a line that just touches the curve, although it may intersect the curve at more than one point. For example, line CD in Figure 1 is tangent to the curve at point E. The slope of a curve at any point is defined to be equal to the slope of the tangent line to the curve at that point. (See **calculus**.)

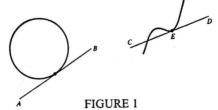

FIGURE 1

(2) If θ is an angle in a right triangle, then the tangent function in trigonometry is defined to be (opposite side)/(adjacent side).

For an example of an application, suppose that you need to measure the height of a tall tree. It would be difficult to climb the tree with a tape measure, but you can walk 50 feet away from the tree and measure the angle of elevation of the top of the tree (see Figure 2). If the angle is 55°, then you known that

$$\tan 55° = \frac{\text{(height of tree)}}{50}.$$

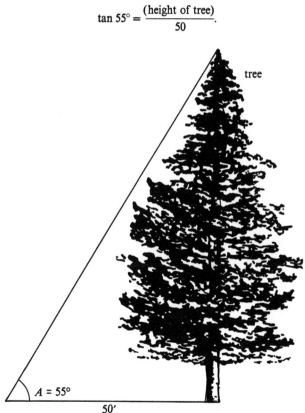

FIGURE 2

Tan 55° ≈ 1.43, which you can look up in a table. This means that the height of the tree is 1.43 × 50 = 71.5 feet. This type of method is often used by surveyors when they need to measure the distance to faraway objects, and a similar type of method is used by astronomers to measure the distance to stars.

A table of trigonometric functions will list values for the tangent function. (See **trigonometry**.) For $\theta = 0°$, the opposite side becomes zero, so tan 0° = 0. For $\theta = 45°$, the opposite side and the adjacent side are equal, so tan 45° = 1. When θ approaches 90°, the adjacent side goes to zero, so tan 90° is infinite. For most values of θ, tan θ will be an irrational number.

TAUTOLOGY   A tautology is a sentence that is necessarily true because of its logical structure, regardless of the facts. For example, the sentence "The earth is flat or else it is not flat" is a tautology. A tautology does not give you any information about the world, but studying the logical structure of tautologies is interesting. For example, the following truth table shows that the sentence

$$[(p \text{ AND } q) \text{ OR } (\sim p \text{ OR } \sim q)]$$

is a tautology:

p	q	p AND q	~p	~q	~p OR ~q	[(p AND q) OR (~p OR ~q)]
T	T	T	F	F	F	T
T	F	F	F	T	T	T
F	T	F	T	F	T	T
F	F	F	T	T	T	T

All of the values in the last column are true. Therefore, the sentence

$$[(p \text{ AND } q) \text{ OR } (\sim p \text{ OR } \sim q)]$$

will necessarily be true, whether or not p or q is true.

The negation of a tautology is necessarily false; it is called a *contradiction*.

TAYLOR SERIES   The Taylor series expansion of a function $f(x)$ states that

$$f(x + h) = f(x) + hf'(x) + \frac{h^2 f''(x)}{2!} + \frac{h^3 f'''(x)}{3!} + \frac{h^4 f''''(x)}{4!} + \cdots.$$

In this expression $f'(x)$ means the first derivative of f, $f''(x)$ means the second derivative, etc.

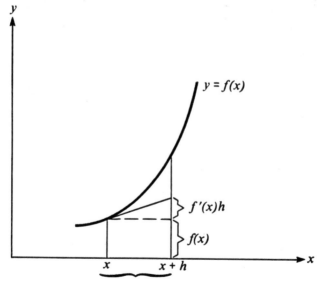

Taylor series are helpful when we know $f(x)$, but not $f(x + h)$. If the series goes on infinitely, we can approximate the value of $f(x + h)$ by taking the first few terms of the series. By adding more and more terms we can make the approximation as close to the true value as we wish.

The first two terms of the series can be reached by approximating the curve by its tangent line (see figure).

For an example of where the additional terms come from, consider the third-degree polynomial function

$$f(x) = a_0 + a_1 x + a_2 x^2 + a_3 x^3.$$

Then:

$$\begin{aligned}
f(x + h) &= a_0 + (a_1 x + a_1 h) + (a_2 x^2 + 2a_2 xh + a_2 h^2) \\
&\quad + (a_3 x^3 + 3a_3 x^2 h + 3a_3 xh^2 + a_3 h^3) \\
&= f(x) + (a_1 h + 2a_2 xh + 3a_3 x^2 h) \\
&\quad + (a_2 h^2 + 3a_3 xh^2) + a_3 h^3 \\
&= f(x) + h[a_1 + 2a_2 x + 3a_3 x^2] + \frac{h^2}{2}[2a_2 + 6a_3 x] \\
&\quad + \frac{h^3}{6}[6a_3].
\end{aligned}$$

By taking the values of the derivatives of f, we can see that

$$\begin{aligned}
f'(x) &= a_1 + 2a_2 x + 3a_3 x^2, \\
f''(x) &= 2a_2 + 6a_3 x, \\
f'''(x) &= 6a_3.
\end{aligned}$$

Therefore:

$$f(x + h) = f(x) + hf'(x) + \frac{h^2}{2!}f''(x) + \frac{h^3}{3!}f'''(x).$$

Taylor series make it possible to find expressions to calculate some functions, such as $\sin \theta$. Since $\sin \theta = \sin(0 + \theta)$, we can form the Taylor expansion:

$$\sin \theta = \sin 0 + \theta \cos 0 - \frac{\theta^2 \sin 0}{2} - \frac{\theta^3 \cos 0}{3!} + \frac{\theta^4 \sin 0}{4!} + \frac{\theta^5 \cos 0}{5!}$$

(using the fact that $d \sin \theta / d\theta = \cos \theta$, and $d \cos \theta / d\theta = -\sin \theta$). (Note that θ is in radians.)

Since $\sin 0 = 0$ and $\cos 0 = 1$, we have

$$\sin \theta = \theta - \frac{\theta^3}{3!} + \frac{\theta^5}{5!} - \frac{\theta^7}{7!} + \frac{\theta^9}{9!} - \cdots.$$

Other examples of Taylor series are as follows:

$$\cos x = 1 - \frac{x^2}{2!} + \frac{x^4}{4!} - \frac{x^6}{6!} + \cdots,$$

$$e^x = 1 + x + \frac{x^2}{2!} + \frac{x^3}{3!} + \frac{x^4}{4!} + \cdots.$$

TERM A term is a part of a sum. For example, in the polynomial $ax^2 + bx + c$, ax^2 is the first term, bx is the second term, and c is the third term. The different terms in an expression are separated by addition (or subtraction) signs.

TERMINAL SIDE When discussing general angles in trigonometry, it is convenient to place the vertex of the angle at the origin and to orient the angle in such a way that one side points along the positive x-axis. Then the other side of the angle is said to be the terminal side.

TERMINATING DECIMAL A terminating decimal is a fraction whose decimal representation contains a finite number of digits. For example, $\frac{1}{4} = 0.25$, and $\frac{5}{32} = 0.15625$. For contrast, see **repeating decimal**.

TEST STATISTIC A test statistic is a quantity calculated from observed sample values that is used to test a null hypothesis. The test statistic is constructed so that it will come from a known distribution if the null hypothesis is true. Therefore, the null hypothesis is rejected if it seems implausible that the observed value of the test statistic could have come from that distribution. (See **hypothesis testing**.)

TETRAHEDRON A tetrahedron is a polyhedron with four faces. Each face is in a triangle. A tetrahedron is an example of a pyramid. A regular tetrahedron has all four faces congruent.

THEN The word "THEN" is used as a connective word in logic sentences of the form "$p \rightarrow q$" ("IF p, THEN q.") Here is an example: "If a triangle has three equal sides, then it has three equal angles."

THEOREM A theorem is a statement that has been proved, such as the *Pythagorean theorem*.

TOROID A toroid is a solid figure shaped like a doughnut. In general, a toroid can be formed by rotating a closed curve for a full turn about a line that is in the same plane as the curve, but does not cross it. The set of all points that the curve crosses in the course of the rotation forms a toroid.

TRACE The trace of a matrix is the sum of the diagonal elements of the matrix. For example, the trace of

$$\begin{pmatrix} 1 & 2 & 3 \\ 2 & 3 & 4 \\ 4 & 5 & 6 \end{pmatrix}$$

is $1 + 3 + 6 = 10$.

TRANSCENDENTAL NUMBER A transcendental number is a number that cannot occur as the root of a polynomial equation with rational coefficients. The transcendental numbers are a subset of the irrational numbers. Most values for trigonometric functions are transcendental, as is the number e. The number π is transcendental, but this fact was not proved until 1882. The square roots of rational numbers are not transcendental, even though they are irrational. For example, $\sqrt{6}$ is a root of the equation $x^2 - 6 = 0$, so it is not transcendental.

TRANSITIVE PROPERTY The transitive property of equality states that, if $a = b$ and $b = c$, then $a = c$. All real and complex numbers obey this property.

The transitive property of inequality states that, if $a > b$ and $b > c$, then $a > c$. Real numbers obey this property, but complex numbers do not.

TRANSLATION A translation occurs when we shift the axes of a Cartesian coordinate system (see figure). (We keep the orientation of the axes the same; otherwise there would be a *rotation*.) If the new coordinates are called x' and y' (x-prime and y-prime), and the

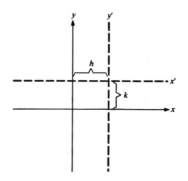

amount that the y-axis is shifted is h and the amount that the x-axis is shifted is k, then there is a simple relation between the new coordinates and the old coordinates:

$$x' = x - h,$$
$$y' = y - k.$$

TRANSPOSE The transpose of a matrix is formed by turning all the columns in the original matrix into rows in the transposed matrix. For example:

$$\begin{pmatrix} a & b \\ c & d \end{pmatrix}^{\text{tr}} = \begin{pmatrix} a & c \\ b & d \end{pmatrix},$$

$$\begin{pmatrix} 1 & 2 & 3 \\ 4 & 5 & 6 \end{pmatrix}^{\text{tr}} = \begin{pmatrix} 1 & 4 \\ 2 & 5 \\ 3 & 6 \end{pmatrix}.$$

If a matrix **A** has *m* rows and *n* columns, then $\mathbf{A}^{tr}$ will have *n* rows and *m* columns.

TRANSVERSAL A transversal is a line that intersects two lines. For examples, see **corresponding angles** and **alternate interior angles**.

TRAPEZOID A trapezoid is a quadrilateral that has exactly two sides parallel.

TREE DIAGRAM A tree diagram illustrates all of the possible results for a process with several stages. The figure illustrates a tree diagram that shows all of the possible results for tossing three coins.

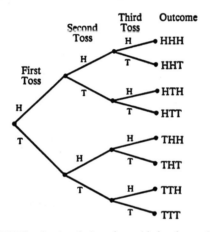

TRIANGLE A triangle is a three-sided polygon (see Figure 1). The three points where the sides intersect are called vertices. Triangles are sometimes identified by listing their vertices, as in triangle *ABC*.

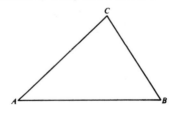

FIGURE 1

One reason that triangles are important is that they are rigid. If you imagine the three sides of a triangle as joined by hinges, you could not bend the triangle out of shape. However, you could easily bend a quadrilateral or any other polygon out of shape if its vertices were formed with hinges. Triangle-shaped supports are often used in bridge construction.

If you add together the three angles in any triangle, the result will be 180°. To prove this, draw line *DE* parallel to line *AC*, as in Figure 2. Then angle 1 = angle 2, and angle 4 = angle 5, since they are alternate interior angles between parallel lines. We can also see

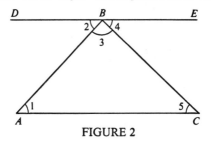

FIGURE 2

that angle 2 + angle 3 + angle 4 = 180°, since *DBE* is a straight line. Then, by substitution, angle 1 + angle 3 + angle 5 = 180°.

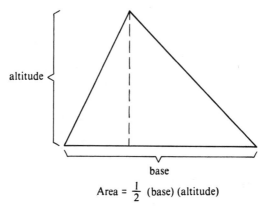

Area = $\frac{1}{2}$ (base) (altitude)

FIGURE 3

The area of a triangle is equal to $\frac{1}{2}$(base)(altitude), where (base) is the length of one of the sides, and (altitude) is the perpendicular distance from the base to the opposite vertex (see Figure 3).

If one of the three angles in a triangle is an obtuse angle, the triangle is called an obtuse triangle. If each of the three angles is less than 90°, it is called an acute triangle. If one angle equals 90°, it is called a right angle.

If the three sides of a triangle are equal, it is called an equilateral triangle. If two sides are equal, it is called an isosceles triangle. Otherwise, it is a scalene triangle.

Two triangles are congruent if they have the same shape and size. There are several ways to show that triangles are congruent:

1. Side-side-side: Two triangles are congruent if all three of their corresponding sides are equal.
2. Side-angle-side: Two triangles are congruent if two corresponding sides and the angle between them are equal.
3. Angle-side-angle: Two triangles are congruent if two corresponding angles and the side between them are equal.
4. Angle-angle-side: Two triangles are congruent if two corresponding angles and any corresponding side are equal.
5. Leg-hypotenuse: Two right triangles are congruent if the hypotenuse and two corresponding legs are equal.

If all three of the angles of the two triangles are equal, then the triangles have exactly the same shape. However, they may not have the same size. For example, the White House, the Capitol, and the Washington Monument form a triangle, and the marks representing these three buildings on a map also form a triangle. The two triangles have the same shape, so they are said to be similar, but the triangle formed by the real buildings is clearly much bigger than the triangle formed by the marks on the map. The corresponding sides of similar triangles are in proportion (meaning that, if one side of the big triangle is 10 times as large as the corresponding side on the little triangle, then the other two sides on the big triangle will also be 10 times as large as their corresponding sides on the little triangle).

A line segment that joins the vertex of a triangle to the midpoint of the opposite side is called a *median*. The point where the three medians intersect is called the *centroid*; it is the point where the triangle would balance if supported at a single point. The point where the three altitudes of the triangle join is called the *orthocenter*. The point where the perpendicular bisectors of the three sides cross is called the *circumcenter*; it is the center of the circle that can be circumscribed about that triangle. (See Figure 4.)

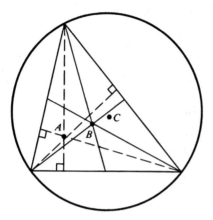

— — — —: altitudes
————————: medians
Point A: orthocenter
Point B: centroid
Point C: circumcenter

FIGURE 4

TRIGONOMETRIC FUNCTIONS OF A SUM Suppose that we
need to find $\sin(\theta + \phi)$, where θ and ϕ are two angles as shown in the
figure. We can see that

$$\sin(\theta + \phi) = \frac{s_1 + s_2}{h}.$$

We can find s_2 from the equation

$$s_2 = t_1 \sin \theta.$$

We can find t_1:

$$\frac{t_1 + t_2}{h} = \cos \phi \rightarrow t_1 = h \cos \phi - t_2.$$

Now we find t_2 from

$$t_2 = s_1 \sin \theta,$$

and put this value for t_2 back in the equation for t_1:

$$t_1 = h \cos \phi - s_1 \sin \theta.$$

Putting this expression back in the equation for s_2 gives

$$s_2 = h \cos \phi \sin \theta - s_1 \sin^2 \theta.$$

Putting this expression back in the equation for $\sin(\theta + \phi)$, we obtain

$$\sin(\theta + \phi) = \frac{1}{h}[s_1 + h \cos \phi \sin \theta - s_1 \sin^2 \theta]$$

$$= \frac{1}{h}[s_1(1 - \sin^2 \theta) + h \cos \phi \sin \theta]$$

$$= \frac{1}{h}[s_1 \cos^2 \theta + h \cos \phi \sin \theta]$$

$$= \frac{s_1 \cos^2 \theta}{h} + \cos \phi \sin \theta.$$

From the definitions of the trigonometric functions, we know that

$$h = \frac{d}{\sin \phi}, \qquad s_1 = \frac{d}{\cos \theta}, \qquad \frac{s_1}{h} = \frac{\sin \phi}{\cos \theta}.$$

The final formula becomes

$$\sin(\theta + \phi) = \sin \phi \cos \theta + \sin \theta \cos \phi.$$

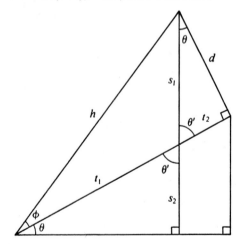

$$\theta' = 90° - \theta$$

From this formula we can derive a similar formula for cosine:

$$\cos(\theta + \phi) = \sin(90° - \theta - \phi)$$
$$= \sin(90° - \theta) \cos(-\phi) + \cos(90° - \theta) \sin(-\phi)$$
$$= \cos\theta \cos\phi - \sin\theta \sin\phi,$$

and a formula for tangent:

$$\tan(\theta + \phi) = \frac{\sin(\theta + \phi)}{\cos(\theta + \phi)}$$

$$= \frac{\sin\theta \cos\phi + \sin\phi \cos\theta}{\cos\theta \cos\phi - \sin\theta \sin\phi}$$

$$= \frac{\dfrac{\sin\theta \cos\phi}{\cos\theta \cos\phi} + \dfrac{\sin\phi \cos\theta}{\cos\theta \cos\phi}}{\dfrac{\cos\theta \cos\phi}{\cos\theta \cos\phi} - \dfrac{\sin\theta \sin\phi}{\cos\theta \cos\phi}}$$

$$= \frac{\tan\theta + \tan\phi}{1 - \tan\theta \tan\phi}.$$

We can find double-angle formulas by setting $\theta = \phi$:

$$\sin 2\theta = 2 \sin\theta \cos\theta,$$
$$\cos 2\theta = \cos^2\theta - \sin^2\theta = 1 - 2\sin^2\theta = 2\cos^2\theta - 1,$$
$$\tan 2\theta = \frac{2\tan\theta}{1 - \tan^2\theta}.$$

TRIGONOMETRY Trigonometry is the study of triangles. In particular, six functions are called the trigonometric functions: sine,

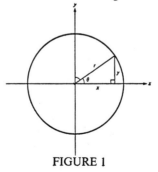

FIGURE 1

cosine, tangent, cotangent, secant, and cosecant. Although these functions were originally developed to help solve problems involving triangles, it turns out that they have many other applications.

Trigonometric functions can be illustrated by considering a circle of radius r centered at the origin. An angle θ can be characterized by two numbers x and y, as shown in Figure 1. The definitions of the trigonometric functions are:

$$\sin \theta = \frac{y}{r}, \qquad \csc \theta = \frac{r}{y},$$

$$\cos \theta = \frac{x}{r}, \qquad \sec \theta = \frac{r}{x},$$

$$\tan \theta - \frac{y}{x}, \qquad \text{ctn } \theta = \frac{x}{y}.$$

The value of $\sin \theta$ is positive when y is positive, as occurs when $0 < \theta < \pi$. Likewise, $\cos \theta$ is positive when x is positive, as occurs when $-\pi/2 < \theta < \pi/2$.

Some properties follow directly from the definitions:

$$\sec \theta = \frac{1}{\cos \theta},$$

$$\csc \theta = \frac{1}{\sin \theta},$$

$$\text{ctn } \theta = \frac{1}{\tan \theta},$$

$$\cos \theta = \sin \left(\frac{\pi}{2} - \theta \right),$$

$$\text{ctn } \theta = \tan \left(\frac{\pi}{2} - \theta \right),$$

$$\csc \theta = \sec \left(\frac{\pi}{2} - \theta \right),$$

$$\cos \theta = \cos \left(-\theta \right),$$

$$\sin \theta = \sin \left(\pi - \theta \right),$$

$$\sin(-\theta) = -\sin \theta,$$

$$\tan \theta = \frac{\sin \theta}{\cos \theta}.$$

(All of these equations are identities, meaning that they are true for all values of θ.)

From the Pythagorean theorem we can derive two more important identities:

$$\frac{x^2}{r^2} + \frac{y^2}{r^2} = \frac{r^2}{r^2} \rightarrow \sin^2 \theta + \cos^2 \theta = 1,$$

$$\frac{x^2}{x^2} + \frac{y^2}{x^2} = \frac{r^2}{x^2} \rightarrow \tan^2 \theta + 1 = \sec^2 \theta.$$

See **trigonometric functions of a sum** for some more identities involving the trigonometric functions.

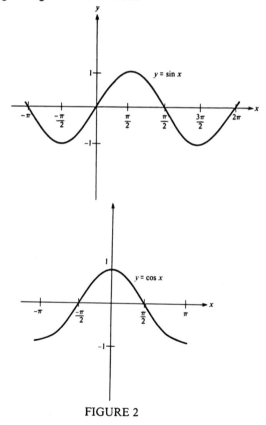

FIGURE 2

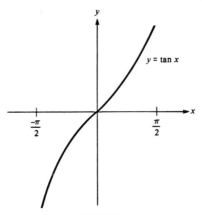

FIGURE 2

Another type of problem may occur if we know the sides of a triangle but we don't know the angles. The values of the angles can be found by using the *inverse trigonometric functions*.

An angle is completely unchanged if we add 2π radians to it. This means that

$$\sin \theta = \sin(\theta + 2\pi) = \sin(\theta + 4\pi) = \sin(\theta + 6\pi) = \cdots.$$

Therefore the trigonometric functions are periodic, or cyclic. For every 2π units, they will have the same value. Figure 2 shows the graphs of the sine, cosine, and tangent functions.

The sine function can be used to describe many types of periodic motion. The curve describes the motion of weight attached to a spring or a swinging pendulum. It describes the voltage change with time in an alternating-current circuit with a rotating generator. The movement of the tides is approximately sine-shaped, as is the variation of the length of the day throughout the year. The sine function is also used to describe light waves, water waves, and sound waves.

Table 2 lists some values for trigonometric functions.

TRINOMIAL A trinomial is the indicated sum of three monomials. For example, $10 + 13x^2 + 20a^3b^2$ is a trinomial.

TRUE "True" is one of the two truth values attached to sentences in logic. It corresponds to what we normally suppose: "true" means "accurate," "correct." (See **logic; Boolean algebra**.)

TRUNCATED CONE   A truncated cone consists of the section of a cone between the base and another plane that intersects the cone between the base and the vertex. It looks like a cone whose top has been chopped off.

TRUNCATED PYRAMID   A truncated pyramid consists of the section of a pyramid between the base and another plane that intersects the pyramid between the base and the vertex. It looks like a pyramid whose top has been chopped off.

TRUNCATION   The truncation of a number is found by dropping the fractional part of that number. It is equal to the largest integer that is less than or equal to the original number. For example, the truncation of 17.89 is equal to 17.

TRUTH TABLE   A truth table is a table showing whether a compound logic sentence will be true or false, based on whether the simple sentences contained in the compound sentence are true. Each row of the table corresponds to one set of possible truth values for the simple sentences. For example, if there are three simple sentences, then there will be $2^3 = 8$ rows in the truth table.

Here is a truth table that demonstrates De Morgan's law:

$\sim(p \text{ OR } q)$ is equivalent to $\sim p \text{ AND } \sim q$.

p	q	$p \text{ OR } q$	$\sim(p \text{ OR } q)$	$\sim p$	$\sim q$	$\sim p \text{ AND } \sim q$
T	T	T	F	F	F	F
T	F	T	F	F	T	F
F	T	T	F	T	F	F
F	F	F	T	T	T	T

The first two columns contain the simple sentences "p" and "q." Since there are four possible combinations of truth values for p and q, the table contains four rows. Each of the five remaining columns tells us whether the indicated expression will be true or false, given the possible values for p and q. Note that the column for $\sim(p \text{ OR } q)$ and the column for $\sim p \text{ AND } \sim q$ have exactly the same values, so these two sentences are equivalent.

TRUTH VALUE   In logic, a sentence is assigned one of two truth values. One of the truth values is labeled T, or 1; it corresponds to "true." The other truth value is labeled F, or 0; it corresponds to "false." The question "What does it mean for a sentence to be true?" is a very difficult philosophical question. In logic a sentence is said to have the truth value T or F, rather than to be "true" or "false"; this makes it possible to analyze the validity of arguments containing "true" or "false" sentences without having to answer the question as to what "truth" really means.

TURING MACHINE The Turing machine is an imaginary device conceived by A. M. Turing in the 1930s to help identify the kinds of problems that are potentially solvable by machines. The Turing machine is a kind of simple computer. It consists of a long string of paper tape and a machine through which the tape can be fed. The machine can do four things: it can move the tape one space, it can place a mark on a space, it can erase a mark, and it can halt. Turing's thesis states that this simple machine can solve any problem that can be expressed as an algorithm (if it has an unlimited supply of paper tape). As you might imagine, in practice it would be very difficult to give instructions to a Turing machine so that it could solve a particular problem. The Turing machine is important theoretically, however, because it provides an indication of what kinds of problems computers can solve, and what kinds they can never solve.

TWO-TAILED TEST In a two-tailed test the critical region consists of both tails of a distribution. The null hypothesis is rejected if the test-statistic value is either too large or too small. (See **hypothesis testing**.)

TYPE 1 ERROR A type 1 error occurs when the null hypothesis is rejected when it is actually true. (See **hypothesis testing**.)

TYPE 2 ERROR A type 2 error occurs when the null hypothesis is accepted when it is actually false. (See **hypothesis testing**.)

U

UNBIASED ESTIMATOR An unbiased estimator is an estimator whose expected value is equal to the true value of the parameter it is trying to estimate. (See **statistical inference**.)

UNDEFINED TERM An undefined term is a basic concept that is described, rather than given a rigorous definition. It would be impossible to rigorously define every term, because sooner or later the definitions would become circular. "Line" is an example of an undefined term from geometry.

UNION The union of two sets A and B (written as $A \cap B$) is the set of all elements that are either members of A or members of B, or both. For example, the union of the sets $A = \{0, 1, 2, 3, 4\}$

and $B = \{2, 2\frac{1}{2}, 3, 3\frac{1}{2}, 4, 4\frac{1}{2}, 5\}$ is the set $A \cap B = \{0, 1, 2, 2\frac{1}{2}, 3, 3\frac{1}{2}, 4, 4\frac{1}{2}, 5\}$. The union of the set of whole numbers and the set of negative integers is the set of all integers.

UNIVERSAL QUANTIFIER An upside-down letter A, "$\forall$," is used to represent the expression "For all. . . ," and is called the universal quantifier. For example, if x is allowed to take on real-number values, then the sentence "For all real numbers, the square of the number is nonnegative" can be written as

$$(1) \qquad \forall_x (x^2 \geq 0).$$

For another example, let L_x represent the sentence "x is a lawyer," and let R_x represent the sentence "x is rich." Then the expression

$$(2) \qquad \forall_x [(L_x) \rightarrow (R_x)]$$

represents the sentence "For all x, if x is a lawyer, then x is rich." In more informal terms, the sentence could be written as "All lawyers are rich."

Be careful when taking the negation of a sentence that uses the universal quantifier. The negation of sentence (2) is not the sentence "All lawyers are not rich," which would be written as

$$(3) \qquad \forall_x [(L_x) \rightarrow (\sim R_x)].$$

Instead, the negation of sentence (2) is the sentence "Not all lawyers are rich," which can be written as

$$(4) \qquad \sim \forall_x [(L_x) \rightarrow (R_x)].$$

Sentence (4) could also be written as

$$(5) \qquad \exists_x [(L_x) \text{ AND } (\sim R_x)].$$

(See **existential quantifier**.)

UNIVERSAL SET The universal set is the set of all objects in which you are interested during a particular discussion. For example, in talking about numbers the relevant universal set might be the set of all complex numbers.

V

VARIABLE A variable is a symbol that is used to represent a value from a particular set. For example, in algebra it is common to use letters to represent values from the set of real numbers. (See **algebra**.)

VARIANCE The variance of a random variable X is defined to be

$$\text{Var}(X) = E[(X - E(X)) \times (X - E(X))] = E[(X - E(X))^2],$$

where E stands for "expectation."

The variance is a measure of how widespread the realizations of X are likely to be. If you know for sure what the value of X will be, then $\text{Var}(X) = 0$. The variance is often written as σ^2. (The Greek lower-case letter sigma (σ), is used to represent the square root of the variance, known as the standard deviation.)

The variance can also be found from the formula:

$$\text{Var}(X) = E(X^2) - [E(X)]^2.$$

For example, if X is the number of heads that appear when a coin is tossed four times, then $\Pr(X = 0) = 1/16$, $\Pr(X = 1) = 1/4$, $\Pr(X = 2) = 3/8$, $\Pr(X = 3) = 1/4$, and $\Pr(X = 4) = 1/16$ (Pr stands for probability). From this information we can calculate that

$$E(X) = 2, \qquad E(X^2) = 5,$$

so

$$\text{Var}(X) = 5 - 4 = 1.$$

Some properties of the variance are as follows.
If a and b are constants:

$$\text{Var}(aX + b) = a^2 \text{Var}(X).$$

If X and Y are independent random variables:

$$\text{Var}(X + Y) = \text{Var}(X) + \text{Var}(Y).$$

In general:

$$\text{Var}(X + Y) = \text{Var}(X) + \text{Var}(Y) + 2\text{Cov}(X, Y),$$

where $\text{Cov}(X, Y)$ is the covariance.

VECTOR A vector is a quantity that has both magnitude and direction. The quantity "60 miles per hour" is a regular number, or scalar. The quantity "60 miles per hour to the northwest" is a vector, because it has both size and direction.

Vectors can be represented by drawing pictures of them. A vector is drawn as an arrow pointing in the direction of the vector, with length proportional to the size of the vector (see Figure 1).

Vectors can also be represented by an ordered list of numbers, such as $(60\sqrt{2}, 60\sqrt{2})$ or $(1, 0, 3)$. Each number in this list is called a component of the vector. A vector in a plane (two dimensions) can be represented as an ordered pair. A vector in space (three dimensions) can be represented as an ordered triple.

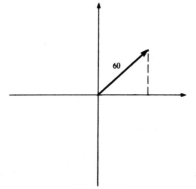

FIGURE 1

Vectors are symbolized in print by boldface type, as in "vector **a**." A vector can also be symbolized by placing an arrow over it: $\vec{a}$. The length of a vector **a** is written as $\|\mathbf{a}\|$.

Addition of vectors is defined as follows: Move the tail of the second vector so that it touches the head of the first vector, and then the sum vector (called the resultant) stretches from the tail of the first vector to the head of the second vector (see Figure 2). For vectors expressed by components, addition is easy: just add the components:

$$(3, 2) + (4, 1) = (7, 3),$$

$$(a, b) + (c, d) = (a + c, b + d).$$

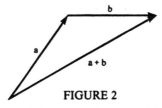

FIGURE 2

To find two different ways of multiplying vectors, see **dot product** and **cross product**.

VELOCITY   The velocity vector represents the rate of change of position of an object. To specify a velocity, it is necessary to specify both a speed and a direction (for example, 50 miles per hour to the northwest).

If the motion is in one dimension, then the velocity is the derivative of the function that gives the position of the object as a function of time. The derivative of the velocity is called the *acceleration*.

VENN DIAGRAM   A Venn diagram (see Figure 1) is a picture that

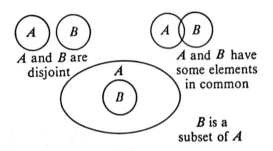

FIGURE 1

illustrates the relationships between sets. The universal set you are considering is represented by a rectangle, and sets are represented by circles. The possible relationships between two sets A and B are as follows:

set B is a subset of set A, or set A is a subset of set B,
set A and set B are disjoint (they have no elements in common),
set A and set B have some elements in common.

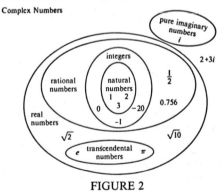

FIGURE 2

Figure 2 is a Venn diagram for the universal set of complex numbers.

VERTEX   The vertex of an angle is the point where the two sides of the angle intersect.

VERTICAL ANGLES   Two pairs of vertical angles are formed when two lines intersect. In the figure, angle 1 and angle 2 are a pair of vertical angles. Angle 3 and angle 4 are another pair of vertical angles. The two angles in a pair of vertical angles are always equal to each other.

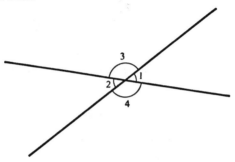

VINCULUM   A vinculum is a horizontal line placed over an operation to indicate that that operation is to be done first. For example, the expression $6 \div \overline{(5 + 4 \times 5)}$ means $6 \div (9 \times 5) = 6 \div 45$.

VOLUME   The volume of a solid is a measure of how much space it occupies. The volume of a cube with edge a units long is a^3. Volumes of other solids are measured in cubic units. For example, the volume of a sphere is $\frac{4}{3}\pi r^3$, where r is the radius of the sphere. The volumes of other figures of revolution can be found by calculus. The volume of a prism or cylinder is (base area) × (altitude), and the volume of a pyramid or cone is $\frac{1}{3}$ × (base area) × (altitude).

W

WELL-FORMED FORMULA   A well-formed formula (or *wff*) is a sequence of symbols that is an acceptable formula in logic. For example, the sequence

$$p \text{ AND } q$$

is a *wff*, but the sequence

$$\text{AND } p\,q$$

is not a *wff*.

Certain rules govern the formation of *wff*'s in a particular type of logic. Here is an example of such a rule: If *a* and *b* are *wff*'s, then (*a* AND *b*) is also a *wff*.

WHOLE NUMBERS   The set of whole numbers includes zero and all the natural numbers: 0, 1, 2, 3, 4, 5, 6, ...

X

X-AXIS   The *x*-axis is the horizontal axis in a Cartesian coordinate system.

X-INTERCEPT   The *x*-intercept of a curve is the value of *x* at the point where the curve crosses the *x*-axis.

Y

Y-AXIS   The *y*-axis is the vertical axis in a Cartesian coordinate system.

Y-INTERCEPT   The *y*-intercept of a curve is the value of *y* at the point where the curve crosses the *y*-axis.

Z

ZERO   Intuitively, zero means nothing—for example, the score that each team has at the beginning of a game is zero. Formally, zero is the identity element for addition, which means that, if you add zero to any number, the number remains unchanged.

In our number system the symbol "0" also serves as a place holder in the decimal representation of a number. Without zero we would have trouble telling the difference between 1000 and 10. Historically, the use of zero as a placeholder preceded the use of zero as a number in its own right.

APPENDIX

TABLE 1

Common Logarithm Table
The table gives log $(a + b)$.

a	b: .00	.01	.02	.03	.04	.05	.06	.07	.08	.09
1.0	.0000	.0043	.0086	.0128	.0170	.0212	.0253	.0294	.0334	.0374
1.1	.0414	.0453	.0492	.0531	.0569	.0607	.0645	.0682	.0719	.0755
1.2	.0792	.0828	.0864	.0899	.0934	.0969	.1004	.1038	.1072	.1106
1.3	.1139	.1173	.1206	.1239	.1271	.1303	.1335	.1367	.1399	.1430
1.4	.1461	.1492	.1523	.1553	.1584	.1614	.1644	.1673	.1703	.1732
1.5	.1761	.1790	.1818	.1847	.1875	.1903	.1931	.1959	.1987	.2014
1.6	.2041	.2068	.2095	.2122	.2148	.2175	.2201	.2227	.2253	.2279
1.7	.2304	.2330	.2355	.2380	.2405	.2430	.2455	.2480	.2504	.2529
1.8	.2553	.2577	.2601	.2625	.2648	.2672	.2695	.2718	.2742	.2765
1.9	.2788	.2810	.2833	.2856	.2878	.2900	.2923	.2945	.2967	.2989
2.0	.3010	.3032	.3054	.3075	.3096	.3118	.3139	.3160	.3181	.3201
2.1	.3222	.3243	.3263	.3284	.3304	.3324	.3345	.3365	.3385	.3404
2.2	.3424	.3444	.3464	.3483	.3502	.3522	.3541	.3560	.3579	.3598
2.3	.3617	.3636	.3655	.3674	.3692	.3711	.3729	.3747	.3766	.3784
2.4	.3802	.3820	.3838	.3856	.3874	.3892	.3909	.3927	.3945	.3962
2.5	.3979	.3997	.4014	.4031	.4048	.4065	.4082	.4099	.4116	.4133
2.6	.4150	.4166	.4183	.4200	.4216	.4232	.4249	.4265	.4281	.4298
2.7	.4314	.4330	.4346	.4362	.4378	.4393	.4409	.4425	.4440	.4456
2.8	.4472	.4487	.4502	.4518	.4533	.4548	.4564	.4579	.4594	.4609
2.9	.4624	.4639	.4654	.4669	.4683	.4698	.4713	.4728	.4742	.4757
3.0	.4771	.4786	.4800	.4814	.4829	.4843	.4857	.4871	.4886	.4900
3.1	.4914	.4928	.4942	.4955	.4969	.4983	.4997	.5011	.5024	.5038
3.2	.5052	.5065	.5079	.5092	.5105	.5119	.5132	.5145	.5159	.5172
3.3	.5185	.5198	.5211	.5224	.5237	.5250	.5263	.5276	.5289	.5302
3.4	.5315	.5328	.5340	.5353	.5366	.5378	.5391	.5403	.5416	.5428
3.5	.5441	.5453	.5465	.5478	.5490	.5502	.5515	.5527	.5539	.5551
3.6	.5563	.5575	.5587	.5599	.5611	.5623	.5635	.5647	.5658	.5670
3.7	.5682	.5694	.5705	.5717	.5729	.5740	.5752	.5763	.5775	.5786
3.8	.5798	.5809	.5821	.5832	.5843	.5855	.5866	.5877	.5888	.5899
3.9	.5911	.5922	.5933	.5944	.5955	.5966	.5977	.5988	.5999	.6010
4.0	.6021	.6031	.6042	.6053	.6064	.6075	.6085	.6096	.6107	.6117
4.1	.6128	.6138	.6149	.6160	.6170	.6180	.6191	.6201	.6212	.6222
4.2	.6232	.6243	.6253	.6263	.6274	.6284	.6294	.6304	.6314	.6325
4.3	.6335	.6345	.6355	.6365	.6375	.6385	.6395	.6405	.6415	.6425
4.4	.6435	.6444	.6454	.6464	.6474	.6484	.6493	.6503	.6513	.6522
4.5	.6532	.6542	.6551	.6561	.6571	.6580	.6590	.6599	.6609	.6618
4.6	.6628	.6637	.6646	.6656	.6665	.6675	.6684	.6693	.6702	.6712
4.7	.6721	.6730	.6739	.6749	.6758	.6767	.6776	.6785	.6794	.6803
4.8	.6812	.6821	.6830	.6839	.6848	.6857	.6866	.6875	.6884	.6893
4.9	.6902	.6911	.6920	.6928	.6937	.6946	.6955	.6964	.6972	.6981

a b:	.00	.01	.02	.03	.04	.05	.06	.07	.08	.09
5.0	.6990	.6998	.7007	.7016	.7024	.7033	.7042	.7050	.7059	.7067
5.1	.7076	.7084	.7093	.7101	.7110	.7118	.7126	.7135	.7143	.7152
5.2	.7160	.7168	.7177	.7185	.7193	.7202	.7210	.7218	.7226	.7235
5.3	.7243	.7251	.7259	.7267	.7275	.7284	.7292	.7300	.7308	.7316
5.4	.7324	.7332	.7340	.7348	.7356	.7364	.7372	.7380	.7388	.7396
5.5	.7404	.7412	.7419	.7427	.7435	.7443	.7451	.7459	.7466	.7474
5.6	.7482	.7490	.7497	.7505	.7513	.7520	.7528	.7536	.7543	.7551
5.7	.7559	.7566	.7574	.7582	.7589	.7597	.7604	.7612	.7619	.7627
5.8	.7634	.7642	.7649	.7657	.7664	.7672	.7679	.7686	.7694	.7701
5.9	.7709	.7716	.7723	.7731	.7738	.7745	.7752	.7760	.7767	.7774
6.0	.7782	.7789	.7796	.7803	.7810	.7818	.7825	.7832	.7839	.7846
6.1	.7853	.7860	.7868	.7875	.7882	.7889	.7896	.7903	.7910	.7917
6.2	.7924	.7931	.7938	.7945	.7952	.7959	.7966	.7973	.7980	.7987
6.3	.7993	.8000	.8007	.8014	.8021	.8028	.8035	.8041	.8048	.8055
6.4	.8062	.8069	.8075	.8082	.8089	.8096	.8102	.8109	.8116	.8122
6.5	.8129	.8136	.8142	.8149	.8156	.8162	.8169	.8176	.8182	.8189
6.6	.8195	.8202	.8209	.8215	.8222	.8228	.8235	.8241	.8248	.8254
6.7	.8261	.8267	.8274	.8280	.8287	.8293	.8299	.8306	.8312	.8319
6.8	.8325	.8331	.8338	.8344	.8351	.8357	.8363	.8370	.8376	.8382
6.9	.8388	.8395	.8401	.8407	.8414	.8420	.8426	.8432	.8439	.8445
7.0	.8451	.8457	.8463	.8470	.8476	.8482	.8488	.8494	.8500	.8506
7.1	.8513	.8519	.8525	.8531	.8537	.8543	.8549	.8555	.8561	.8567
7.2	.8573	.8579	.8585	.8591	.8597	.8603	.8609	.8615	.8621	.8627
7.3	.8633	.8639	.8645	.8651	.8657	.8663	.8669	.8675	.8681	.8686
7.4	.8692	.8698	.8704	.8710	.8716	.8722	.8727	.8733	.8739	.8745
7.5	.8751	.8756	.8762	.8768	.8774	.8779	.8785	.8791	.8797	.8802
7.6	.8808	.8814	.8820	.8825	.8831	.8837	.8842	.8848	.8854	.8859
7.7	.8865	.8871	.8876	.8882	.8887	.8893	.8899	.8904	.8910	.8915
7.8	.8921	.8927	.8932	.8938	.8943	.8949	.8954	.8960	.8965	.8971
7.9	.8976	.8982	.8987	.8993	.8998	.9004	.9009	.9015	.9020	.9025
8.0	.9031	.9036	.9042	.9047	.9053	.9058	.9063	.9069	.9074	.9079
8.1	.9085	.9090	.9096	.9101	.9106	.9112	.9117	.9122	.9128	.9133
8.2	.9138	.9143	.9149	.9154	.9159	.9165	.9170	.9175	.9180	.9186
8.3	.9191	.9196	.9201	.9206	.9212	.9217	.9222	.9227	.9232	.9238
8.4	.9243	.9248	.9253	.9258	.9263	.9269	.9274	.9279	.9284	.9289
8.5	.9294	.9299	.9304	.9309	.9315	.9320	.9325	.9330	.9335	.9340
8.6	.9345	.9350	.9355	.9360	.9365	.9370	.9375	.9380	.9385	.9390
8.7	.9395	.9400	.9405	.9410	.9415	.9420	.9425	.9430	.9435	.9440
8.8	.9445	.9450	.9455	.9460	.9465	.9469	.9474	.9479	.9484	.9489
8.9	.9494	.9499	.9504	.9509	.9513	.9518	.9523	.9528	.9533	.9538
9.0	.9542	.9547	.9552	.9557	.9562	.9566	.9571	.9576	.9581	.9586
9.1	.9590	.9595	.9600	.9605	.9609	.9614	.9619	.9624	.9628	.9633
9.2	.9638	.9643	.9647	.9652	.9657	.9661	.9666	.9671	.9675	.9680
9.3	.9685	.9689	.9694	.9699	.9703	.9708	.9713	.9717	.9722	.9727
9.4	.9731	.9736	.9741	.9745	.9750	.9754	.9759	.9764	.9768	.9773
9.5	.9777	.9782	.9786	.9791	.9795	.9800	.9805	.9809	.9814	.9818
9.6	.9823	.9827	.9832	.9836	.9841	.9845	.9850	.9854	.9859	.9863
9.7	.9868	.9872	.9877	.9881	.9886	.9890	.9894	.9899	.9903	.9908
9.8	.9912	.9917	.9921	.9926	.9930	.9934	.9939	.9943	.9948	.9952
9.9	.9956	.9961	.9965	.9969	.9974	.9978	.9983	.9987	.9991	.9996

TABLE 2

Trigonometric Function Table

Degrees	Sin	Cos	Tan	Radians
0.0	0.00000	1.00000	0.00000	0.00000
0.2	0.00349	0.99999	0.00349	0.00349
0.4	0.00698	0.99998	0.00698	0.00698
0.6	0.01047	0.99995	0.01047	0.01047
0.8	0.01396	0.99990	0.01396	0.01396
1.0	0.01745	0.99985	0.01746	0.01745
1.2	0.02094	0.99978	0.02095	0.02094
1.4	0.02443	0.99970	0.02444	0.02443
1.6	0.02792	0.99961	0.02793	0.02793
1.8	0.03141	0.99951	0.03143	0.03142
2.0	0.03490	0.99939	0.03492	0.03491
2.2	0.03839	0.99926	0.03842	0.03840
2.4	0.04188	0.99912	0.04191	0.04189
2.6	0.04536	0.99897	0.04541	0.04538
2.8	0.04885	0.99881	0.04891	0.04887
3.0	0.05234	0.99863	0.05241	0.05236
3.2	0.05582	0.99844	0.05591	0.05585
3.4	0.05931	0.99824	0.05941	0.05934
3.6	0.06279	0.99803	0.06291	0.06283
3.8	0.06627	0.99780	0.06642	0.06632
4.0	0.06976	0.99756	0.06993	0.06981
4.2	0.07324	0.99731	0.07344	0.07330
4.4	0.07672	0.99705	0.07695	0.07679
4.6	0.08020	0.99678	0.08046	0.08029
4.8	0.08368	0.99649	0.08397	0.08378
5.0	0.08716	0.99619	0.08749	0.08727
5.2	0.09063	0.99588	0.09101	0.09076
5.4	0.09411	0.99556	0.09453	0.09425
5.6	0.09758	0.99523	0.09805	0.09774
5.8	0.10106	0.99488	0.10158	0.10123
6.0	0.10453	0.99452	0.10510	0.10472
6.2	0.10800	0.99415	0.10863	0.10821
6.4	0.11147	0.99377	0.11217	0.11170
6.6	0.11494	0.99337	0.11570	0.11519
6.8	0.11840	0.99297	0.11924	0.11868
7.0	0.12187	0.99255	0.12278	0.12217
7.2	0.12533	0.99211	0.12633	0.12566
7.4	0.12880	0.99167	0.12988	0.12915
7.6	0.13226	0.99122	0.13343	0.13264
7.8	0.13572	0.99075	0.13698	0.13614
8.0	0.13917	0.99027	0.14054	0.13963
8.2	0.14263	0.98978	0.14410	0.14312
8.4	0.14608	0.98927	0.14767	0.14661
8.6	0.14954	0.98876	0.15124	0.15010
8.8	0.15299	0.98823	0.15481	0.15359
9.0	0.15643	0.98769	0.15838	0.15708
9.2	0.15988	0.98714	0.16196	0.16057
9.4	0.16333	0.98657	0.16555	0.16406
9.6	0.16677	0.98600	0.16914	0.16755
9.8	0.17021	0.98541	0.17273	0.17104

Degrees	Sin	Cos	Tan	Radians
10.0	0.17365	0.98481	0.17633	0.17453
10.2	0.17708	0.98420	0.17993	0.17802
10.4	0.18052	0.98357	0.18353	0.18151
10.6	0.18395	0.98294	0.18714	0.18500
10.8	0.18738	0.98229	0.19076	0.18850
11.0	0.19081	0.98163	0.19438	0.19199
11.2	0.19423	0.98096	0.19801	0.19548
11.4	0.19766	0.98027	0.20164	0.19897
11.6	0.20108	0.97958	0.20527	0.20246
11.8	0.20450	0.97887	0.20891	0.20595
12.0	0.20791	0.97815	0.21256	0.20944
12.2	0.21132	0.97742	0.21621	0.21293
12.4	0.21474	0.97667	0.21986	0.21642
12.6	0.21814	0.97592	0.22353	0.21991
12.8	0.22155	0.97515	0.22719	0.22340
13.0	0.22495	0.97437	0.23087	0.22689
13.2	0.22835	0.97358	0.23455	0.23038
13.4	0.23175	0.97278	0.23823	0.23387
13.6	0.23514	0.97196	0.24193	0.23736
13.8	0.23853	0.97113	0.24562	0.24086
14.0	0.24192	0.97030	0.24933	0.24435
14.2	0.24531	0.96945	0.25304	0.24784
14.4	0.24869	0.96858	0.25676	0.25133
14.6	0.25207	0.96771	0.26048	0.25482
14.8	0.25545	0.96682	0.26421	0.25831
15.0	0.25882	0.96593	0.26795	0.26180
15.2	0.26219	0.96502	0.27169	0.26529
15.4	0.26556	0.96410	0.27545	0.26878
15.6	0.26892	0.96316	0.27920	0.27227
15.8	0.27228	0.96222	0.28297	0.27576
16.0	0.27564	0.96126	0.28675	0.27925
16.2	0.27899	0.96029	0.29053	0.28274
16.4	0.28234	0.95931	0.29432	0.28623
16.6	0.28569	0.95832	0.29811	0.28972
16.8	0.28903	0.95732	0.30192	0.29322
17.0	0.29237	0.95631	0.30573	0.29671
17.2	0.29571	0.95528	0.30955	0.30020
17.4	0.29904	0.95424	0.31338	0.30369
17.6	0.30237	0.95319	0.31722	0.30718
17.8	0.30570	0.95213	0.32106	0.31067
18.0	0.30902	0.95106	0.32492	0.31416
18.2	0.31233	0.94997	0.32878	0.31765
18.4	0.31565	0.94888	0.33266	0.32114
18.6	0.31896	0.94777	0.33654	0.32463
18.8	0.32227	0.94665	0.34033	0.32812
19.0	0.32557	0.94552	0.34433	0.33161
19.2	0.32887	0.94438	0.34824	0.33510
19.4	0.33216	0.94322	0.35216	0.33859
19.6	0.33545	0.94206	0.35608	0.34208
19.8	0.33874	0.94088	0.36002	0.34557
20.0	0.34202	0.93969	0.36397	0.34907
20.2	0.34530	0.93849	0.36793	0.35256
20.4	0.34857	0.93728	0.37190	0.35605
20.6	0.35184	0.93606	0.37587	0.35954
20.8	0.35511	0.93483	0.37986	0.36303

Degrees	Sin	Cos	Tan	Radians
21.0	0.35837	0.93358	0.38386	0.36652
21.2	0.36162	0.93232	0.38787	0.37001
21.4	0.36488	0.93106	0.39190	0.37350
21.6	0.36812	0.92978	0.39593	0.37699
21.8	0.37137	0.92849	0.39997	0.38048
22.0	0.37461	0.92718	0.40403	0.38397
22.2	0.37784	0.92587	0.40809	0.38746
22.4	0.38107	0.92455	0.41217	0.39095
22.6	0.38430	0.92321	0.41626	0.39444
22.8	0.38752	0.92186	0.42036	0.39793
23.0	0.39073	0.92051	0.42447	0.40143
23.2	0.39394	0.91914	0.42860	0.40492
23.4	0.39715	0.91775	0.43274	0.40841
23.6	0.40035	0.91636	0.43689	0.41190
23.8	0.40354	0.91496	0.44105	0.41539
24.0	0.40674	0.91355	0.44523	0.41888
24.2	0.40992	0.91212	0.44942	0.42237
24.4	0.41310	0.91068	0.45362	0.42586
24.6	0.41628	0.90924	0.45784	0.42935
24.8	0.41945	0.90778	0.46206	0.43284
25.0	0.42262	0.90631	0.46631	0.43633
25.2	0.42578	0.90483	0.47056	0.43982
25.4	0.42893	0.90334	0.47483	0.44331
25.6	0.43209	0.90183	0.47912	0.44680
25.8	0.43523	0.90032	0.48342	0.45029
26.0	0.43837	0.89879	0.48773	0.45379
26.2	0.44151	0.89726	0.49206	0.45728
26.4	0.44463	0.89571	0.49640	0.46077
26.6	0.44776	0.89415	0.50076	0.46426
26.8	0.45088	0.89259	0.50514	0.46775
27.0	0.45399	0.89101	0.50952	0.47124
27.2	0.45710	0.88942	0.51393	0.47473
27.4	0.46020	0.88782	0.51835	0.47822
27.6	0.46330	0.88620	0.52279	0.48171
27.8	0.46639	0.88458	0.52724	0.48520
28.0	0.46947	0.88295	0.53171	0.48869
28.2	0.47255	0.88130	0.53619	0.49218
28.4	0.47562	0.87965	0.54070	0.49567
28.6	0.47869	0.87798	0.54522	0.49916
28.8	0.48175	0.87631	0.54975	0.50265
29.0	0.48481	0.87462	0.55431	0.50615
29.2	0.48786	0.87292	0.55888	0.50964
29.4	0.49090	0.87121	0.56347	0.51313
29.6	0.49394	0.86950	0.56808	0.51662
29.8	0.49697	0.86777	0.57270	0.52011
30.0	0.50000	0.86603	0.57735	0.52360
30.2	0.50302	0.86428	0.58201	0.52709
30.4	0.50603	0.86251	0.58670	0.53058
30.6	0.50904	0.86074	0.59140	0.53407
30.8	0.51204	0.85896	0.59612	0.53756
31.0	0.51504	0.85717	0.60086	0.54105
31.2	0.51803	0.85536	0.60562	0.54454
31.4	0.52101	0.85355	0.61040	0.54803
31.6	0.52399	0.85173	0.61520	0.55152
31.8	0.52696	0.84989	0.62003	0.55501

Degrees	Sin	Cos	Tan	Radians
32.0	0.52992	0.84805	0.62487	0.55850
32.2	0.53288	0.84619	0.62973	0.56200
32.4	0.53583	0.84433	0.63462	0.56549
32.6	0.53877	0.84245	0.63953	0.56898
32.8	0.54171	0.84057	0.64446	0.57247
33.0	0.54464	0.83867	0.64941	0.57596
33.2	0.54756	0.83676	0.65438	0.57945
33.4	0.55048	0.83485	0.65938	0.58294
33.6	0.55339	0.83292	0.66440	0.58643
33.8	0.55630	0.83098	0.66944	0.58992
34.0	0.55919	0.82904	0.67451	0.59341
34.2	0.56208	0.82708	0.67960	0.59690
34.4	0.56497	0.82511	0.68471	0.60039
34.6	0.56784	0.82314	0.68985	0.60388
34.8	0.57071	0.82115	0.69502	0.60737
35.0	0.57358	0.81915	0.70021	0.61086
35.2	0.57643	0.81715	0.70542	0.61436
35.4	0.57928	0.81513	0.71066	0.61785
35.6	0.58212	0.81310	0.71593	0.62134
35.8	0.58496	0.81106	0.72122	0.62483
36.0	0.58778	0.80902	0.72654	0.62832
36.2	0.59061	0.80696	0.73189	0.63181
36.4	0.59342	0.80489	0.73726	0.63530
36.6	0.59622	0.80282	0.74266	0.63879
36.8	0.59902	0.80073	0.74809	0.64228
37.0	0.60181	0.79864	0.75355	0.64577
37.2	0.60460	0.79653	0.75904	0.64926
37.4	0.60738	0.79442	0.76456	0.65275
37.6	0.61014	0.79229	0.77010	0.65624
37.8	0.61291	0.79016	0.77568	0.65973
38.0	0.61566	0.78801	0.78128	0.66322
38.2	0.61841	0.78586	0.78692	0.66672
38.4	0.62115	0.78369	0.79259	0.67021
38.6	0.62388	0.78152	0.79829	0.67370
38.8	0.62660	0.77934	0.80402	0.67719
39.0	0.62932	0.77715	0.80978	0.68068
39.2	0.63203	0.77495	0.81558	0.68417
39.4	0.63473	0.77273	0.82141	0.68766
39.6	0.63742	0.77051	0.82727	0.69115
39.8	0.64011	0.76828	0.83317	0.69464
40.0	0.64279	0.76604	0.83910	0.69813
40.2	0.64546	0.76380	0.84506	0.70162
40.4	0.64812	0.76154	0.85107	0.70511
40.6	0.65077	0.75927	0.85710	0.70860
40.8	0.65342	0.75700	0.86318	0.71209
41.0	0.65606	0.75471	0.86929	0.71558
41.2	0.65869	0.75242	0.87543	0.71908
41.4	0.66131	0.75011	0.88162	0.72257
41.6	0.66393	0.74780	0.88784	0.72606
41.8	0.66653	0.74548	0.89410	0.72955
42.0	0.66913	0.74315	0.90040	0.73304
42.2	0.67172	0.74081	0.90674	0.73653
42.4	0.67430	0.73846	0.91312	0.74002
42.6	0.67688	0.73610	0.91955	0.74351
42.8	0.67944	0.73373	0.92601	0.74700

Degrees	Sin	Cos	Tan	Radians
43.0	0.68200	0.73135	0.93251	0.75049
43.2	0.68455	0.72897	0.93906	0.75398
43.4	0.68709	0.72658	0.94565	0.75747
43.6	0.68962	0.72417	0.95229	0.76096
43.8	0.69214	0.72176	0.95896	0.76445
44.0	0.69466	0.71934	0.96569	0.76794
44.2	0.69716	0.71691	0.97246	0.77144
44.4	0.69966	0.71447	0.97927	0.77493
44.6	0.70215	0.71203	0.98613	0.77842
44.8	0.70463	0.70957	0.99304	0.78191
45.0	0.70711	0.70711	1.00000	0.78540
45.2	0.70957	0.70463	1.00700	0.78889
45.4	0.71203	0.70215	1.01406	0.79238
45.6	0.71447	0.69966	1.02116	0.79587
45.8	0.71691	0.69717	1.02832	0.79936
46.0	0.71934	0.69466	1.03553	0.80285
46.2	0.72176	0.69214	1.04279	0.80634
46.4	0.72417	0.68962	1.05010	0.80983
46.6	0.72657	0.68709	1.05747	0.81332
46.8	0.72897	0.68455	1.06489	0.81681
47.0	0.73135	0.68200	1.07237	0.82030
47.2	0.73373	0.67944	1.07990	0.82379
47.4	0.73610	0.67688	1.08749	0.82729
47.6	0.73845	0.67430	1.09514	0.83078
47.8	0.74080	0.67172	1.10284	0.83427
48.0	0.74314	0.66913	1.11061	0.83776
48.2	0.74548	0.66653	1.11844	0.84125
48.4	0.74780	0.66393	1.12633	0.84474
48.6	0.75011	0.66131	1.13428	0.84823
48.8	0.75241	0.65869	1.14229	0.85172
49.0	0.75471	0.65606	1.15037	0.85521
49.2	0.75699	0.65342	1.15851	0.85870
49.4	0.75927	0.65077	1.16672	0.86219
49.6	0.76154	0.64812	1.17499	0.86568
49.8	0.76380	0.64546	1.18334	0.86917
50.0	0.76604	0.64279	1.19175	0.87266
50.2	0.76828	0.64011	1.20024	0.87615
50.4	0.77051	0.63742	1.20879	0.87965
50.6	0.77273	0.63473	1.21742	0.88314
50.8	0.77494	0.63203	1.22612	0.88663
51.0	0.77715	0.62932	1.23490	0.89012
51.2	0.77934	0.62660	1.24375	0.89361
51.4	0.78152	0.62388	1.25268	0.89710
51.6	0.78369	0.62115	1.26168	0.90059
51.8	0.78586	0.61841	1.27077	0.90408
52.0	0.78801	0.61566	1.27994	0.90757
52.2	0.79015	0.61291	1.28919	0.91106
52.4	0.79229	0.61015	1.29852	0.91455
52.6	0.79441	0.60738	1.30794	0.91804
52.8	0.79653	0.60460	1.31745	0.92153
53.0	0.79864	0.60182	1.32074	0.92502
53.2	0.80073	0.59902	1.33673	0.92851
53.4	0.80282	0.59623	1.34650	0.93201
53.6	0.80489	0.59342	1.35636	0.93550
53.8	0.80696	0.59061	1.36632	0.93899

Degrees	Sin	Cos	Tan	Radians
54.0	0.80902	0.58779	1.37638	0.94248
54.2	0.81106	0.58496	1.38653	0.94597
54.4	0.81310	0.58212	1.39678	0.94946
54.6	0.81513	0.57928	1.40713	0.95295
54.8	0.81714	0.57643	1.41759	0.95644
55.0	0.81915	0.57358	1.42815	0.95993
55.2	0.82115	0.57071	1.43881	0.96342
55.4	0.82314	0.56784	1.44958	0.96691
55.6	0.82511	0.56497	1.46046	0.97040
55.8	0.82708	0.56208	1.47145	0.97389
56.0	0.82904	0.55919	1.48256	0.97738
56.2	0.83098	0.55630	1.49378	0.98087
56.4	0.83292	0.55339	1.50512	0.98436
56.6	0.83485	0.55048	1.51658	0.98786
56.8	0.83676	0.54756	1.52816	0.99135
57.0	0.83867	0.54464	1.53986	0.99484
57.2	0.84057	0.54171	1.55169	0.99833
57.4	0.84245	0.53877	1.56365	1.00182
57.6	0.84433	0.53583	1.57574	1.00531
57.8	0.84619	0.53288	1.58797	1.00880
58.0	0.84805	0.52992	1.60033	1.01229
58.2	0.84989	0.52696	1.61283	1.01578
58.4	0.85173	0.52399	1.62547	1.01927
58.6	0.85355	0.52101	1.63826	1.02276
58.8	0.85536	0.51803	1.65119	1.02625
59.0	0.85717	0.51504	1.66428	1.02974
59.2	0.85896	0.51204	1.67751	1.03323
59.4	0.86074	0.50904	1.69090	1.03672
59.6	0.86251	0.50603	1.70446	1.04022
59.8	0.86427	0.50302	1.71817	1.04371
60.0	0.86602	0.50000	1.73205	1.04720
60.2	0.86777	0.49697	1.74610	1.05069
60.4	0.86949	0.49394	1.76032	1.05418
60.6	0.87121	0.49090	1.77471	1.05767
60.8	0.87292	0.48786	1.78929	1.06116
61.0	0.87462	0.48481	1.80404	1.06465
61.2	0.87631	0.48175	1.81899	1.06814
61.4	0.87798	0.47869	1.83413	1.07163
61.6	0.87965	0.47563	1.84946	1.07512
61.8	0.88130	0.47255	1.86499	1.07861
62.0	0.88295	0.46947	1.88072	1.08210
62.2	0.88458	0.46639	1.89666	1.08559
62.4	0.88620	0.46330	1.91282	1.08908
62.6	0.88781	0.46020	1.92919	1.09258
62.8	0.88942	0.45710	1.94578	1.09607
63.0	0.89101	0.45399	1.96261	1.09956
63.2	0.89259	0.45088	1.97966	1.10305
63.4	0.89415	0.44776	1.99695	1.10654
63.6	0.89571	0.44464	2.01448	1.11003
63.8	0.89726	0.44151	2.03226	1.11352
64.0	0.89879	0.43837	2.05030	1.11701
64.2	0.90032	0.43523	2.06859	1.12050
64.4	0.90183	0.43209	2.08716	1.12399
64.6	0.90333	0.42894	2.10599	1.12748
64.8	0.90483	0.42578	2.12510	1.13097

Degrees	Sin	Cos	Tan	Radians
65.0	0.90631	0.42262	2.14450	1.13446
65.2	0.90778	0.41945	2.16419	1.13795
65.4	0.90924	0.41628	2.18418	1.14144
65.6	0.91068	0.41311	2.20448	1.14494
65.8	0.91212	0.40992	2.22510	1.14843
66.0	0.91355	0.40674	2.24603	1.15192
66.2	0.91496	0.40355	2.26730	1.15541
66.4	0.91636	0.40035	2.28890	1.15890
66.6	0.91775	0.39715	2.31086	1.16239
66.8	0.91914	0.39394	2.33317	1.16588
67.0	0.92050	0.39073	2.35585	1.16937
67.2	0.92186	0.38752	2.37890	1.17286
67.4	0.92321	0.38430	2.40234	1.17635
67.6	0.92455	0.38107	2.42617	1.17984
67.8	0.92587	0.37784	2.45042	1.18333
68.0	0.92718	0.37461	2.47508	1.18682
68.2	0.92849	0.37137	2.50017	1.19031
68.4	0.92978	0.36813	2.52570	1.19380
68.6	0.93106	0.36488	2.55169	1.19729
68.8	0.93232	0.36163	2.57815	1.20079
69.0	0.93358	0.35837	2.60508	1.20428
69.2	0.93483	0.35511	2.63251	1.20777
69.4	0.93606	0.35184	2.66045	1.21126
69.6	0.93728	0.34857	2.68891	1.21475
69.8	0.93849	0.34530	2.71791	1.21824
70.0	0.93969	0.34202	2.74747	1.22173
70.2	0.94088	0.33874	2.77760	1.22522
70.4	0.94206	0.33545	2.80832	1.22871
70.6	0.94322	0.33216	2.83964	1.23220
70.8	0.94438	0.32887	2.87160	1.23569
71.0	0.94552	0.32557	2.90420	1.23918
71.2	0.94665	0.32227	2.93747	1.24267
71.4	0.94777	0.31896	2.97143	1.24616
71.6	0.94888	0.31565	3.00610	1.24965
71.8	0.94997	0.31234	3.04151	1.25315
72.0	0.95106	0.30902	3.07767	1.25664
72.2	0.95213	0.30570	3.11462	1.26013
72.4	0.95319	0.30237	3.15239	1.26362
72.6	0.95424	0.29904	3.19099	1.26711
72.8	0.95528	0.29571	3.23047	1.27060
73.0	0.95630	0.29237	3.27084	1.27409
73.2	0.95732	0.28903	3.31215	1.27758
73.4	0.95832	0.28569	3.35442	1.28107
73.6	0.95931	0.28234	3.39769	1.28456
73.8	0.96029	0.27899	3.44201	1.28805
74.0	0.96126	0.27564	3.48740	1.29154
74.2	0.96222	0.27228	3.53391	1.29503
74.4	0.96316	0.26892	3.58158	1.29852
74.6	0.96410	0.26556	3.63046	1.30201
74.8	0.96502	0.26219	3.68059	1.30551
75.0	0.96593	0.25882	3.73203	1.30900
75.2	0.96682	0.25545	3.78483	1.31249
75.4	0.96771	0.25207	3.83904	1.31598
75.6	0.96858	0.24869	3.89473	1.31947
75.8	0.96945	0.24531	3.95194	1.32296

Degrees	Sin	Cos	Tan	Radians
76.0	0.97030	0.24192	4.01076	1.32645
76.2	0.97113	0.23853	4.07125	1.32994
76.4	0.97196	0.23514	4.13348	1.33343
76.6	0.97278	0.23175	4.19754	1.33692
76.8	0.97358	0.22835	4.26350	1.34041
77.0	0.97437	0.22495	4.33145	1.34390
77.2	0.97515	0.22155	4.40149	1.34739
77.4	0.97592	0.21814	4.47372	1.35088
77.6	0.97667	0.21474	4.54823	1.35437
77.8	0.97742	0.21133	4.62516	1.35787
78.0	0.97815	0.20791	4.70460	1.36136
78.2	0.97887	0.20450	4.78670	1.36485
78.4	0.97958	0.20108	4.87159	1.36834
78.6	0.98027	0.19766	4.95942	1.37183
78.8	0.98096	0.19424	5.05034	1.37532
79.0	0.98163	0.19081	5.14452	1.37881
79.2	0.98229	0.18738	5.24215	1.38230
79.4	0.98294	0.18395	5.34342	1.38579
79.6	0.98357	0.18052	5.44853	1.38928
79.8	0.98420	0.17709	5.55773	1.39277
80.0	0.98481	0.17365	5.67124	1.39626
80.2	0.98541	0.17021	5.78935	1.39975
80.4	0.98600	0.16677	5.91231	1.40324
80.6	0.98657	0.16333	6.04046	1.40673
80.8	0.98714	0.15988	6.17414	1.41023
81.0	0.98769	0.15644	6.31370	1.41372
81.2	0.98823	0.15299	6.45956	1.41721
81.4	0.98876	0.14954	6.61213	1.42070
81.6	0.98927	0.14608	6.77193	1.42419
81.8	0.98978	0.14263	6.93946	1.42768
82.0	0.99027	0.13917	7.11531	1.43117
82.2	0.99075	0.13572	7.30010	1.43466
82.4	0.99122	0.13226	7.49458	1.43815
82.6	0.99167	0.12880	7.69950	1.44164
82.8	0.99211	0.12533	7.91574	1.44513
83.0	0.99255	0.12187	8.14426	1.44862
83.2	0.99297	0.11841	8.38617	1.45211
83.4	0.99337	0.11494	8.64266	1.45560
83.6	0.99377	0.11147	8.91509	1.45909
83.8	0.99415	0.10800	9.20506	1.46258
84.0	0.99452	0.10453	9.51424	1.46608
84.2	0.99488	0.10106	9.84469	1.46957
84.4	0.99523	0.09758	10.19860	1.47306
84.6	0.99556	0.09411	10.57880	1.47655
84.8	0.99588	0.09063	10.98800	1.48004
85.0	0.99619	0.08716	11.42990	1.48353
85.2	0.99649	0.08368	11.90850	1.48702
85.4	0.99678	0.08020	12.42860	1.49051
85.6	0.99705	0.07672	12.99590	1.49400
85.8	0.99731	0.07324	13.61710	1.49749
86.0	0.99756	0.06976	14.30040	1.50098
86.2	0.99780	0.06628	15.05540	1.50447
86.4	0.99803	0.06279	15.89420	1.50796
86.6	0.99824	0.05931	16.83150	1.51145
86.8	0.99844	0.05582	17.88590	1.51494

Degrees	Sin	Cos	Tan	Radians
87.0	0.99863	0.05234	19.08060	1.51844
87.2	0.99881	0.04885	20.44590	1.52193
87.4	0.99897	0.04536	22.02100	1.52542
87.6	0.99912	0.04188	23.85860	1.52891
87.8	0.99926	0.03839	26.02980	1.53240
88.0	0.99939	0.03490	28.63530	1.53589
88.2	0.99951	0.03141	31.81900	1.53938
88.4	0.99961	0.02792	35.79910	1.54287
88.6	0.99970	0.02443	40.91510	1.54636
88.8	0.99978	0.02094	47.73610	1.54985
89.0	0.99985	0.01745	57.28550	1.55334
89.2	0.99990	0.01396	71.60780	1.55683
89.4	0.99995	0.01047	95.47760	1.56032
89.6	0.99998	0.00698	143.20900	1.56381
89.8	0.99999	0.00349	286.37600	1.56730

TABLE 3

The Standard Normal Distribution

If Z has a standard normal distribution, the table gives the value of $\Pr(Z < z)$.

z	$\Pr(Z < z)$	z	$\Pr(Z < z)$	z	$\Pr(Z < z)$	z	$\Pr(Z < z)$
0.01	.5040	0.29	.6141	0.57	.7157	0.85	.8023
0.02	.5080	0.30	.6179	0.58	.7190	0.86	.8051
0.03	.5120	0.31	.6217	0.59	.7224	0.87	.8079
0.04	.5160	0.32	.6255	0.60	.7257	0.88	.8106
0.05	.5199	0.33	.6293	0.61	.7291	0.89	.8133
0.06	.5239	0.34	.6331	0.62	.7324	0.90	.8159
0.07	.5279	0.35	.6368	0.63	.7357	0.91	.8186
0.08	.5319	0.36	.6406	0.64	.7389	0.92	.8212
0.09	.5359	0.37	.6443	0.65	.7422	0.93	.8238
0.10	.5398	0.38	.6480	0.66	.7454	0.94	.8264
0.11	.5438	0.39	.6517	0.67	.7486	0.95	.8289
0.12	.5478	0.40	.6554	0.68	.7517	0.96	.8315
0.13	.5517	0.41	.6591	0.69	.7549	0.97	.8340
0.14	.5557	0.42	.6628	0.70	.7580	0.98	.8365
0.15	.5596	0.43	.6664	0.71	.7611	0.99	.8389
0.16	.5636	0.44	.6700	0.72	.7642	1.00	.8413
0.17	.5675	0.45	.6736	0.73	.7673	1.01	.8438
0.18	.5714	0.46	.6772	0.74	.7704	1.02	.8461
0.19	.5753	0.47	.6808	0.75	.7734	1.03	.8485
0.20	.5793	0.48	.6844	0.76	.7764	1.04	.8508
0.21	.5832	0.49	.6879	0.77	.7794	1.05	.8531
0.22	.5871	0.50	.6915	0.78	.7823	1.06	.8554
0.23	.5910	0.51	.6950	0.79	.7852	1.07	.8577
0.24	.5948	0.52	.6985	0.80	.7881	1.08	.8599
0.25	.5987	0.53	.7019	0.81	.7910	1.09	.8621
0.26	.6026	0.54	.7054	0.82	.7939	1.10	.8643
0.27	.6064	0.55	.7088	0.83	.7967	1.11	.8665
0.28	.6103	0.56	.7123	0.84	.7995	1.12	.8686

z	Pr(Z < z)	z	Pr(Z < z)	z	Pr(Z < z)	z	Pr(Z < z)
1.13	.8708	1.44	.9251	1.75	.9599	2.06	.9803
1.14	.8729	1.45	.9265	1.76	.9608	2.07	.9808
1.15	.8749	1.46	.9279	1.77	.9616	2.08	.9812
1.16	.8770	1.47	.9292	1.78	.9625	2.09	.9817
1.17	.8790	1.48	.9306	1.79	.9633	2.10	.9821
1.18	.8810	1.49	.9319	1.80	.9641	2.11	.9826
1.19	.8830	1.50	.9332	1.81	.9649	2.12	.9830
1.20	.8849	1.51	.9345	1.82	.9656	2.13	.9834
1.21	.8869	1.52	.9357	1.83	.9664	2.14	.9838
1.22	.8888	1.53	.9370	1.84	.9671	2.15	.9842
1.23	.8907	1.54	.9382	1.85	.9678	2.16	.9846
1.24	.8925	1.55	.9394	1.86	.9686	2.17	.9850
1.25	.8944	1.56	.9406	1.87	.9693	2.18	.9854
1.26	.8962	1.57	.9418	1.88	.9699	2.19	.9857
1.27	.8980	1.58	.9429	1.89	.9706	2.20	.9861
1.28	.8997	1.59	.9441	1.90	.9713	2.25	.9878
1.29	.9015	1.60	.9452	1.91	.9719	2.30	.9893
1.30	.9032	1.61	.9463	1.92	.9726	2.35	.9906
1.31	.9049	1.62	.9474	1.93	.9732	2.40	.9918
1.32	.9066	1.63	.9484	1.94	.9738	2.50	.9938
1.33	.9082	1.64	.9495	1.95	.9744	2.60	.9953
1.34	.9099	1.65	.9505	1.96	.9750	2.70	.9965
1.35	.9115	1.66	.9515	1.97	.9756	2.80	.9974
1.36	.9131	1.67	.9525	1.98	.9761	2.90	.9981
1.37	.9147	1.68	.9535	1.99	.9767	3.00	.9987
1.38	.9162	1.69	.9545	2.00	.9773	3.10	.9990
1.39	.9177	1.70	.9554	2.01	.9778	3.20	.9993
1.40	.9192	1.71	.9564	2.02	.9783	3.30	.9995
1.41	.9207	1.72	.9573	2.03	.9788	3.40	.9997
1.42	.9222	1.73	.9582	2.04	.9793	3.50	.9998
1.43	.9236	1.74	.9591	2.05	.9798		

TABLE 4

The Standard Normal Distribution

z	Pr(−z < Z < z)	z	Pr(−z < Z < z)
0.10	.0796	1.30	.8064
0.20	.1586	1.40	.8384
0.30	.2358	1.50	.8664
0.40	.3108	1.60	.8904
0.50	.3830	1.70	.9108
0.60	.4514	1.80	.9282
0.70	.5160	1.90	.9426
0.80	.5762	1.96	.9500
0.90	.6318	2.00	.9546
1.00	.6826	2.50	.9876
1.10	.7286	3.00	.9974

TABLE 5

The Chi-square Cumulative Distribution Function

If X has a chi-square distribution with n degrees of freedom, the table gives the value x such that $\Pr(X < x) = p$. For example, if X has a chi-square distribution with 10 degrees of freedom, there is a probability of .95 that X will be less than 18.3.

n	$p = .005$	$p = .01$	$p = .05$	$p = .25$	$p = .50$	$p = .75$	$p = .90$	$p = .95$	$p = .975$	$p = .99$
2	0.01	.02	.10	.57	1.38	2.77	4.60	5.99	7.37	9.21
3	0.07	.11	.35	1.21	2.36	4.10	6.24	7.80	9.33	11.31
4	0.20	.29	.71	1.92	3.35	5.38	7.77	9.48	11.14	13.27
5	0.41	.55	1.14	2.67	4.35	6.62	9.23	11.07	12.83	15.08
6	0.67	.87	1.63	3.45	5.34	7.84	10.64	12.59	14.44	16.81
7	0.98	1.24	2.17	4.26	6.35	9.04	12.02	14.07	16.01	18.48
8	1.34	1.65	2.73	5.07	7.34	10.22	13.36	15.51	17.54	20.09
9	1.73	2.09	3.33	5.90	8.34	11.39	14.68	16.92	19.02	21.67
10	2.16	2.56	3.94	6.74	9.3	12.5	15.9	18.3	20.5	23.2
11	2.60	3.05	4.57	7.58	10.3	13.7	17.3	19.7	21.9	24.7
12	3.07	3.57	5.23	8.44	11.3	14.8	18.6	21.0	23.3	26.2
13	3.56	4.11	5.89	9.30	12.3	16.0	19.8	22.4	24.7	27.7
14	4.08	4.66	6.57	10.17	13.3	17.1	21.1	23.7	26.1	29.1
15	4.60	5.23	7.26	11.04	14.3	18.2	22.3	25.0	27.5	30.6
16	5.14	5.81	7.96	11.91	15.3	19.4	23.5	26.3	28.8	32.0
17	5.70	6.41	8.67	12.79	16.3	20.5	24.8	27.6	30.2	33.4
18	6.26	7.02	9.39	13.68	17.3	21.6	26.0	28.9	31.5	34.8
19	6.85	7.63	10.12	14.56	18.3	22.7	27.2	30.1	32.9	36.2
20	7.43	8.26	10.85	15.45	19.3	23.8	28.4	31.4	34.2	37.6
21	8.03	8.90	11.59	16.34	20.3	24.9	29.6	32.7	35.5	38.9
22	8.64	9.54	12.34	17.24	21.3	26.0	30.8	33.9	36.8	40.3
23	9.26	10.19	13.09	18.14	22.3	27.1	32.0	35.2	38.1	41.6
24	9.89	10.86	13.85	19.04	23.3	28.2	33.2	36.4	39.4	43.0
25	10.52	11.52	14.61	19.94	24.3	29.3	34.4	37.7	40.7	44.3
30	13.79	14.95	18.49	24.48	29.3	34.8	40.3	43.8	47.0	50.9
40	20.70	22.16	26.51	33.66	39.3	45.6	51.8	55.7	59.3	63.7
50	27.99	29.70	34.76	42.94	49.3	56.3	63.2	67.5	71.4	76.2
60	35.53	37.48	43.19	52.29	59.3	67.0	74.4	79.1	83.3	88.4
70	43.27	45.44	51.74	61.70	69.3	77.6	85.5	90.5	95.0	100.4
80	51.18	53.54	60.38	71.15	79.3	88.1	96.6	101.9	106.6	112.3
90	59.19	61.74	69.12	80.62	89.3	98.7	107.6	113.2	118.1	124.1

TABLE 6

The *t*-Distribution

If X has a t-distribution with n degrees of freedom, the table gives the value of x such that $Pr(X < x) = p$. For example, if X has a t-distribution with 15 degrees of freedom there is a 95 percent chance X will be less than 1.753.

n	p = .750	p = .900	p = .950	p = .975	p = .990	p = .995
1	1.000	3.078	6.314	12.706	31.821	63.657
2	0.817	1.886	2.920	4.303	6.965	9.925
3	0.765	1.638	2.353	3.182	4.541	5.841
4	0.741	1.533	2.132	2.776	3.747	4.604
5	0.727	1.476	2.015	2.571	3.365	4.032
6	0.718	1.440	1.943	2.447	3.143	3.707
7	0.711	1.415	1.895	2.365	3.000	3.499
8	0.706	1.397	1.860	2.306	2.896	3.355
9	0.703	1.383	1.833	2.262	2.821	3.250
10	0.700	1.372	1.812	2.228	2.764	3.169
11	0.697	1.363	1.796	2.201	2.718	3.106
12	0.695	1.356	1.782	2.179	2.681	3.055
13	0.694	1.350	1.771	2.160	2.650	3.012
14	0.692	1.345	1.761	2.145	2.600	2.977
15	0.691	1.341	1.753	2.131	2.600	2.947
16	0.690	1.337	1.746	2.120	2.584	2.921
17	0.689	1.333	1.740	2.110	2.567	2.898
18	0.688	1.330	1.734	2.101	2.552	2.878
19	0.688	1.328	1.729	2.093	2.539	2.861
20	0.687	1.325	1.725	2.086	2.528	2.845
21	0.686	1.323	1.721	2.080	2.518	2.831
22	0.686	1.321	1.717	2.074	2.508	2.819
23	0.685	1.319	1.714	2.069	2.500	2.807
24	0.685	1.318	1.711	2.064	2.492	2.797
25	0.684	1.316	1.708	2.060	2.485	2.787
26	0.684	1.315	1.706	2.056	2.479	2.779
27	0.684	1.314	1.703	2.052	2.473	2.771
28	0.683	1.313	1.701	2.048	2.467	2.763
29	0.683	1.311	1.699	2.045	2.462	2.756
30	0.683	1.310	1.697	2.042	2.457	2.750
35	0.682	1.306	1.690	2.030	2.438	2.724
40	0.681	1.303	1.684	2.021	2.423	2.704
50	0.679	1.299	1.676	2.009	2.400	2.678
60	0.679	1.296	1.671	2.000	2.400	2.660
100	0.677	1.290	1.660	1.984	2.364	2.626
120	0.677	1.289	1.658	1.980	2.358	2.617

TABLE 7

The *t*-distribution

If X has a t-distribution with n degrees of freedom, the table gives the value of x such that $\Pr(-x < X < x) = p$.

n	p = .95	p = .99	n	p = .95	p = .99
1	12.706	63.657	20	2.086	2.845
2	4.303	9.925	21	2.080	2.831
3	3.182	5.841	22	2.074	2.819
4	2.776	4.604	23	2.069	2.807
5	2.571	4.032	24	2.064	2.797
6	2.447	3.707	25	2.060	2.787
7	2.365	3.499	26	2.056	2.779
8	2.306	3.355	27	2.052	2.771
9	2.262	3.250	28	2.048	2.763
10	2.228	3.169	29	2.045	2.756
11	2.201	3.106	30	2.042	2.750
12	2.179	3.055	35	2.030	2.724
13	2.160	3.012	40	2.021	2.704
14	2.145	2.977	50	2.009	2.678
15	2.131	2.947	60	2.000	2.660
16	2.120	2.921	100	1.984	2.626
17	2.110	2.898	120	1.980	2.617
18	2.101	2.878			
19	2.093	2.861			

TABLE 8

The *F*-distribution

If F has an F-distribution with m and n degrees of freedom, then the table gives the value of x such that $\Pr(F < x) = .95$.

n	m = 2	m = 3	m = 4	m = 5	m = 10	m = 15	m = 20	m = 30	m = 60	m = 120
2	19.00	19.16	19.25	19.30	19.40	19.43	19.45	19.46	19.48	19.49
3	9.55	9.28	9.12	9.01	8.79	8.70	8.66	8.62	8.57	8.55
4	6.94	6.59	6.39	6.26	5.96	5.86	5.80	5.75	5.69	5.66
5	5.79	5.41	5.19	5.05	4.74	4.62	4.56	4.50	4.43	4.40
6	5.14	4.76	4.53	4.39	4.06	3.94	3.87	3.81	3.74	3.70
7	4.74	4.35	4.12	3.97	3.64	3.51	3.44	3.38	3.30	3.27
8	4.46	4.07	3.84	3.69	3.35	3.22	3.15	3.08	3.01	2.97
9	4.26	3.86	3.63	3.48	3.14	3.01	2.94	2.86	2.79	2.75
10	4.10	3.71	3.48	3.33	2.98	2.85	2.77	2.70	2.62	2.58
15	3.68	3.29	3.06	2.90	2.54	2.40	2.33	2.25	2.16	2.11
20	3.49	3.10	2.87	2.71	2.35	2.20	2.12	2.04	1.95	1.90
30	3.32	2.92	2.69	2.53	2.16	2.01	1.93	1.84	1.74	1.68
60	3.15	2.76	2.53	2.37	1.99	1.84	1.75	1.65	1.53	1.47
120	3.07	2.68	2.45	2.29	1.91	1.75	1.66	1.55	1.43	1.35

More selected BARRON'S titles:

DICTIONARY OF ACCOUNTING TERMS
Siegel and Shim
Nearly 2500 terms related to accounting are defined.
Paperback, $9.95, Can. $13.95 (3766-9)

DICTIONARY OF ADVERTISING AND DIRECT MAIL TERMS
Imber and Toffler
Nearly 3000 terms used in the ad industry are defined.
Paperback, $9.95, Can. $13.95 (3765-0)

DICTIONARY OF BANKING TERMS
Fitch
Nearly 3000 terms related to banking, finance and money
management.
Paperback, $10.95, Can. $14.95 (3946-7)

DICTIONARY OF BUSINESS TERMS
Friedman, general editor
Over 6000 entries define business terms.
Paperback, $9.95, Can. $13.95 (3775-8)

BARRON'S BUSINESS REVIEW SERIES
These guides explain topics covered in a college-level business
course.
Each book: paperback
ACCOUNTING, 2nd EDITION. *Eisen.* $11.95, Can. $15.95 (4375-8)
BUSINESS LAW, *Hardwicke and Emerson.* $11.95, Can. $15.95 (3495-3)
BUSINESS STATISTICS, *Downing and Clark.* $11.95, Can. $15.95 (3576-3)
ECONOMICS, *Wessels.* $10.95, Can. $14.95 (3560-7)
FINANCE, 2nd EDITION. *Groppelli and Nikbakht.* $11.95,
Can. $15.95 (4373-1)
MANAGEMENT, *Montana and Charnov.* $10.95, Can. $14.95 (3559-3)
MARKETING, *Sandhusen.* $11.95, Can. $15.95 (3494-5)
QUANTITATIVE METHODS, *Downing and Clark.* $10.95,
Can. $14.95 (3947-5)

TALKING BUSINESS SERIES: BILINGUAL DICTIONARIES
Five bilingual dictionaries translate about 3000 terms not found in
most foreign phrasebooks.
Each book: paperback
TALKING BUSINESS IN FRENCH, *Le Gal.* $9.95, Can. $13.95
(3745-6)
TALKING BUSINESS IN GERMAN, *Strutz.* $8.95, Can. $11.95
(3747-2)
TALKING BUSINESS IN ITALIAN, *Rakus.* $6.95, Can. $9.95
(3754-5)
TALKING BUSINESS IN JAPANESE, *C. Akiyama and N. Akiyama.*
$8.95, Can. $11.95 (3848-7)
TALKING BUSINESS IN KOREAN, *Cheong.* $8.95, Can. $11.95
(3992-0)
TALKING BUSINESS IN SPANISH, *Fryer and Faria.* $9.95,
Can. $13.95 (3769-3)

Barron's Educational Series, Inc.
250 Wireless Boulevard, Hauppauge, NY 11788
Call toll-free: 1-800-645-3476, in NY 1-800-257-5729
In Canada: Georgetown Book Warehouse
34 Armstrong Ave., Georgetown, Ontario L7G 4R9
Call toll-free: 1-800-247-7160